AFGHANISTAN

AFGHANISTAN
HOW THE WEST LOST ITS WAY

Tim Bird and Alex Marshall

YALE UNIVERSITY PRESS
NEW HAVEN AND LONDON

To

Louise, Emily and Jessica Bird
and
John and Dorothy Marshall

For information about this and other Yale University Press publications, please
contact:
U.S. Office: sales.press@yale.edu   yalebooks.com
Europe Office: sales@yaleup.co.uk   www.yalebooks.co.uk

Library of Congress Cataloging-in-Publication Data

Bird, Tim, 1962-
    Afghanistan: how the West lost its way / Tim Bird & Alex Marshall.
      p. cm.
    ISBN 978-0-300-15457-3 (cl: alk. paper)
    1. Afghan War, 2001-2. North Atlantic Treaty Organization—Afghanistan. 3.
United States. Army—History—Afghan War, 2001-4. Strategy. I. Marshall, Alex,
1976 Feb 11-II. Title.
    DS371.412.B53 2011
    958.104′7—dc22   2010051043

Set in Janson Text by IDSUK (DataConnection Ltd)
Printed in Great Britain by TJ International Ltd, Padstow, Cornwall

A catalogue record for this book is available from the British Library.

2015 2014 2013 2012 2011
10 9 8 7 6 5 4 3 2 1

CONTENTS

Introduction		1
CHAPTER 1	The great enigma: Afghanistan in historical context	9
CHAPTER 2	9/11 and the response, 11–25 September 2001	47
CHAPTER 3	'Boots on the ground': From the arrival of the CIA to the emergency Loya Jirga, 26 September 2001–June 2002	73
CHAPTER 4	'Taking the eye off the ball?' The roots of Taliban revival in Afghanistan, 2002–05	111
CHAPTER 5	Return to the 'forgotten war', 2006–08	153
CHAPTER 6	The Pakistan problem	185
CHAPTER 7	Silver bullets and the search for an exit, 2009–11	217
Conclusion		249
Notes		263
Bibliography		289
Index		299

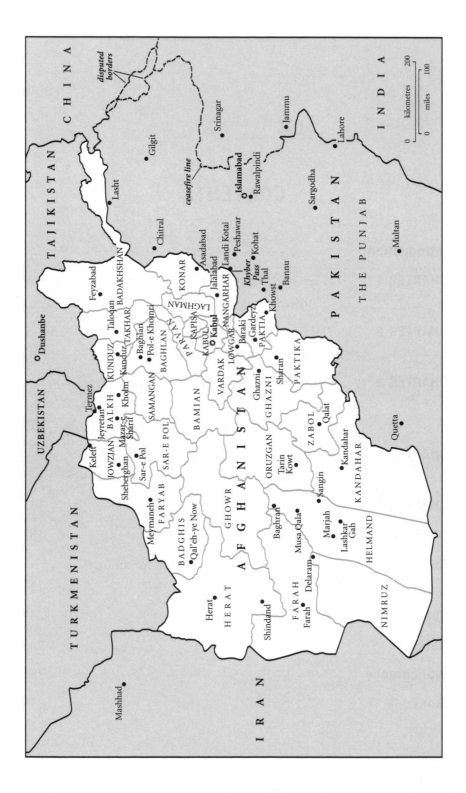

INTRODUCTION

IT ALL BEGAN so well. As the Northern Alliance, heavily supported by US Special Forces and massive airpower, swept through Afghanistan in October and November of 2001, Al Qaeda and its Taliban allies fled to the mountains and havens of the south and east, or over the border into the Pakistani tribal areas, in seeming disarray. While a number of questions remained about the whereabouts of Osama bin Laden, and about the nature of the post-conflict configuration of Afghanistan, the overall impression was still one of stunning victory. The remaining few thousand, mostly American, troops were left to conduct what were termed 'mopping-up' operations, while their political and military leaders, with a certain degree of smugness and hubris about a job well done, began to turn their attention to the inexorable march of events in Iraq.

However, as the intervening powers pondered what they had wrought in Afghanistan, and as declarations of 'victory' began to seem increasingly premature, a series of basic, nagging, yet profoundly important questions circulated around policymaking communities. What was considered to be at stake in Afghanistan? What were realistically achievable goals? How much blood and treasure was the West willing to expend to bring about its preferred outcomes? In a disturbing preview of the incoherence that was to come, the answers provided to these questions in the immediate wake of the overthrow of the Taliban lacked both clarity and consistency.

As we approach the tenth anniversary of this initial intervention, answers to these original, fundamental questions (as well as to a bewildering array of subordinate ones) remain frustratingly elusive. In addition, severe doubts are being expressed about some traditionally unquestioned policy assumptions. The future of Afghanistan and that of its near neighbour Pakistan are so suffused with doubt – and yet are seen as so inextricably linked – that commentators routinely refer to the 'AfPak theatre' with despair. NATO, arguably the most successful military alliance in history, appears to view success in Afghanistan as the engineering of any kind of withdrawal that will maintain some semblance of Alliance credibility. The phrase 'Global War on Terror', such a powerful rhetorical construct in 2001, is now rarely heard in polite company and viewed as an embarrassment. Deeply held policy prescriptions based on Western models of development are being fundamentally questioned because of their perceived total failure in the country. The American 'rediscovery' of counterinsurgency doctrine, lauded as the means by which anarchy was averted in Iraq, also seems to be foundering in the crucible of Afghanistan. Even the utility and viability of 'state-building', a shibboleth of Western-dominated international organizations, is under scrutiny and attack as never before.

This is a book about an intervention. Its focus is the ten-year journey from the perceived triumph of 2001 to the complex and Byzantine conflict that characterizes contemporary Afghanistan.

2

The aim of the work is straightforward. It is to provide an understanding of why a large swathe of the international community, with the leading members of NATO in the vanguard, has found it so difficult to achieve its goals in this decade-long conflict – or even to answer the basic questions noted above.

The explanations can be grouped under two broad themes. The main theme examines the manner with which the intervention has been conceptualized and conducted. In particular, the focus will be on the way in which the intervening coalition has thought about, and sought to execute, strategy. As has usually been the case in Afghanistan's history, most of the drivers that have shaped the politics of intervention in this unluckiest of countries are regional or international, rather than local, in nature. Therefore, many of the defining and consequential decisions and events that have shaped the intervention have occurred in national capitals such as Washington, Islamabad, London, Brussels, New Delhi, Tehran, Moscow and Beijing, rather than in Kabul or the towns and villages of Afghanistan.

Nevertheless, the dramatic stage upon which the drama has been most visibly played out is Afghanistan itself, and the people who have suffered disproportionately from the conflict have been Afghans. Therefore, the narrative also provides context by examining the nature of the country. However, the purpose of the analysis is not to make an original contribution to the understanding of the country and its peoples *per se* (there is a rich and growing literature on the history, society and politics of this fascinating land). Rather, it is to shed light on how the West fundamentally lost its way in Afghanistan. It is, therefore, above all else a book about policy and strategy.

The initial action in 2001, driven by righteous anger following the events of 9/11, possessed a degree of conceptual clarity with

3

regard to strategic purpose. The Taliban were to be removed; Al Qaeda disrupted, and preferably destroyed; and Afghanistan denied as a base for international '*jihadists*' intent on wreaking destruction across the world. However, the intervention soon became conflated with a more nebulous series of goals and processes. These included, but were not limited to, 'state-building', 'counterinsurgency', 'winning hearts and minds', 'democratization', 'counterterrorism', 'development' and 'regional stabilization'.

Many of these terms are laced with irony, particularly for the two NATO powers that have committed the most blood and treasure to the conflict: the US and the UK. For the British, Afghanistan was one of the few places specifically ruled out as a likely area of military intervention in the Strategic Defence Review initiated by the incoming Blair government. For the US, 'nation-building' and 'counterinsurgency' were types of activity associated in the mind of the Bush administration with the 'quagmires' it believed the State Department had wrought in the former Yugoslavia, and were activities it simply would not conduct. However, the intervening powers took their eye off the ball after the perceived routing of the Taliban and Al Qaeda in 2001, and the subsequent regrouping and entrenchment of the 'insurgency' from 2003 onwards sucked them into the type of long-term, multifaceted commitment they had previously disdained.

The book will argue that at the heart of the problems that the intervention has faced is incoherent strategy. Effective strategy constantly seeks to balance and rebalance ends, ways and means. At the centre of strategy are questions about how desired political objectives (ends) can be achieved (ways) at a cost (means) that is considered tolerable. For states, it is fundamentally related to notions of security and perceptions of threat. It is not, or should not be, a one-time calculation, but a dynamic *process* that continually questions and re-evaluates the extent to which the three elements are in balance. The constant theme running through the book will be questions related to how this process has been managed and conceptualized in the West's intervention in Afghanistan.

Strategic clarity has been an elusive commodity. At times there have been wide variations in the degree of risk and commitment that states are willing to undertake. In particular, it has often manifested itself as a mismatch between the sometimes apocalyptic predictions of the consequences of 'failure' in Afghanistan and the burden some coalition partners have been prepared to bear. This has had a particularly acute effect on NATO internal coherence. Consequently, the imperatives of Alliance institutional survival and credibility have seemed to dominate policy formulation and implementation at the expense of clear, appropriate strategies for Afghanistan itself. The difficulties that NATO has faced in Afghanistan, and indeed the problems NATO politics has caused for the clarity of the intervention itself, will be a recurring theme in the book.

The lack of clarity has been compounded by genuine disagreements on what an 'appropriate strategy' might look like. Whether on the subject of poppy eradication, counterinsurgency tactics, the desirability of negotiating with the Taliban, developmental policy, the approach to corruption within the Afghan government, policy towards Pakistan, Afghan security sector reform or a myriad other issues, different national preferences within the intervening coalition have prevented a unified and coherent approach. In addition, Afghanistan has become something of a laboratory for key Western states in the development of 'comprehensive' or 'interagency' approaches to stabilization and 'state-building'. There has been a belief that, while military activity, at quite high levels of intensity and over a protracted period, is necessary to achieve desired goals in Afghanistan, such activity will not, on its own, be sufficient. The focus has, therefore, been on how to coherently integrate the use of force within a wider political, diplomatic, economic and developmental policy framework. This coordination has proved to be extremely problematic even within individual contributing states, and exponentially problematic at the international level. Thus, the intervention has been marked by continual debates on the best ways to craft a clear strategy for Afghanistan, and on how to coordinate political, military, diplomatic, economic and developmental policy processes, both within and between contributing nations; by disagreements on appropriate approaches to key policy dilemmas; by tensions over 'burden-sharing'; and by the struggle to match contribution to rhetoric.

Some places are relatively forgiving of strategic incoherence. Afghanistan is not one of them. It is a land of contrasts and juxtapositions. A country with such a complex mélange of social and cultural mores that its peoples can be some of the most hospitable in the world to those seeking help or protection, yet can also respond with extraordinary levels of violence against those perceived to have offended against personal honour (often involving breaches that, in many other cultures, would be dismissed as mild rudeness). It is a land fragmented not just by 'tribal' rivalries, but by a labyrinth of sub-tribal groups, clans, family networks and religious and ethnic cleavages, to an extent that the notion of being an 'Afghan' can sometimes seem to have no particular meaning. Yet, despite this, Afghans have a very clear, indeed often xenophobic, sense of the 'foreigner', and this has traditionally manifested itself in repeated, though usually fragmented, resistance to outsiders who seek to impose their will. Even the very climate and topography render the visitor bewildered by the scale of diversity.

If all this were not sufficient to confuse those seeking to shape the political landscape, a combination of fate and the shaky hand of various imperial cartographers has placed Afghanistan at the centre of a maelstrom of complex regional politics. With Iran to the west, Pakistan to the east and south, and former Soviet republics to the north, domestic politics automatically assume regional and often international significance. As if to ensure that no thorny geopolitical issue is left unprovoked, there is even, to the northeast, a small shared border with China. In addition, around 90 per cent of the world's opium supplies are cultivated from Afghan poppies, resulting in the presence of powerful international criminal gangs that interact with, and are often indistinguishable from, local and national political leaders.

To complicate any strategic efforts still further, parts of the porous southern and eastern border with Pakistan cut through traditional Pashtun lands and provide a safe haven for Taliban and Al Qaeda fighters just across the border. To complete this daunting picture, the government in Kabul has attempted to establish itself over a country that has no historical experience of a central government that couples benign intent and behaviour with an ability to exert control over the disparate provinces. Thus, any civilian or military contingency planner seeking to provide a hypothetical scenario to test the efficacy of international strategy would have to possess a fertile imagination to conjure an operating environment more complex than the one that actually pertains in Afghanistan.

The structure of this book is explicitly chronological, so as to provide a clear and accessible narrative that allows the reader to assess the tortuous course of the intervention. However, there will also be thematic threads that run through the narrative to provide analytical depth. These include how the orthodoxies of liberal approaches to governance and development have fared; the scale and nature of the insurgency in Afghanistan and how this is related to assessments of the international terrorist threat; the often incompatible approaches and essential fragility of the coalition leading the intervention; the looming presence of Pakistan; and the nature and fate of President Karzai's government, an officially sovereign democracy compelled by circumstance to live in the shadow of American military power.

The intervention in Afghanistan represents America's longest-ever war, NATO's first major engagement outside Europe, and Britain's most expensive foreign conflict since the Second World War, as well as the most bloody in terms of casualties since Korea. Canada has suffered, per capita, higher casualties than the US. A number of intervening countries, among them the Netherlands, Australia and Denmark, can likewise point to the shattering of unwanted records occasioned by their participation. Thousands of Afghans have died, in a downward spiral inextricably connected with the violent crises that have exploded across the border in Pakistan. It has been, by any criteria, a devastating ten years. This book examines how this disastrous situation has developed and seeks answers to the fundamental question of how the West lost its way in Afghanistan.

CHAPTER ONE

THE GREAT ENIGMA:
Afghanistan in historical context

*There is a strange fascination in living among the Pathans. One secret
of the hold of the North-West frontier is to be found in the tremendous
scenic canvas against which the Pathan plays out his life . . . The weft
and warp of this tapestry is woven into the souls and bodies of the men
who move before it. Much is harsh, but all is drawn in strong tones
that catch the breath, and at times bring tears, almost of pain.*

Sir Olaf Caroe, *The Pathans* (1958)[1]

HAD SIR OLAF not died twenty years earlier, he would doubtless
have offered strong words of advice to the coalition that began to
be assembled in 2001 on the dangers of interfering in the affairs of
the 'Pathans'. However, a perception that the security of powerful
external actors was again threatened by policy decisions made in
Kabul compelled outsiders to intervene once more to try and
impose their will. The prospects for 'success' came burdened with,
and were directly shaped by, the bleak lessons of Afghanistan's own

9

very particular modern history. What retains the capacity to surprise, even ten years after the initial intervention, is the degree of historical illiteracy evident in many of the initial pronouncements on the likely challenges awaiting the intervening powers. This chapter aims to provide a broad historical and social context for the challenges the intervening coalition has faced. It explores both the conditions that led to the rise of the Taliban, and why the Afghanistan of 2001 had come to be such a singularly unforgiving environment for foreign forces seeking to impose their will.

When coalition forces first arrived in Afghanistan to avenge the attacks on America carried out by Al Qaeda on 11 September 2001, academics and journalists the world over speculated wildly about the final outcome – this being, as many commented at the time, only the latest in a long line of foreign military interventions in that country. Most international commentators recalled the relatively recent long war fought by Soviet forces in support of a native Afghan Marxist government, the PDPA (People's Democratic Party of Afghanistan) between 1979 and 1989; far fewer were aware that this had in fact been the second Soviet intervention in that country, the first being a failed covert operation in 1929. The British, meanwhile, among America's keenest allies in 2001, had already formally intervened in Afghanistan on no fewer than three separate occasions. The first Anglo-Afghan War of 1838–42, a second war in 1878–80 and a third conflict in 1919 each helped to shape Afghanistan's modern history, with the last conflict culminating in the emergence of a fully independent Afghan state.

None of these earlier military interventions into Afghanistan had covered themselves with glory. The Soviet intervention of 1979–89 was widely perceived internationally as a disaster, and one that many believed contributed to the collapse of the Soviet Union itself. The three wars that Britain fought in the country had each been marked by varying degrees of tactical failure, the costliest being the first Anglo-Afghan War of 1838–42, in the course of which an entire Anglo-Indian army of over 4,000 men, alongside some 10,000 civilian camp followers, was lost. On each of these three earlier occasions, Britain had quickly taken revenge for initial military reverses and won the final battles of the war, but, suitably intimidated, had then held back from attempting the full-scale military–political administration of the country. Afghanistan between 1880 and 1919 instead became a classic political 'buffer state' between the British and Russian empires, with the most prominent Afghan leader of that period, the 'Iron Amir' Abdur Rahman (r. 1881–1901), receiving a hefty subsidy in return for ceding control of Afghan foreign policy to the British.

Historically, Afghanistan had, therefore, already earned itself a formidable reputation for severely challenging foreign intervention forces. Indeed, in Pakistan in late 2001, pro-Taliban elements, aware of this past, proudly waved banners declaring that Afghanistan was a proven 'empire-killer', a challenge against which America's own current global hegemony would likewise founder. On at least one level, however, this reputation embodies a profound paradox: namely, that Afghanistan's formidable reputation rests not upon the difficulties presented to would-be invaders by its formal military capability, but upon its long political-economic record of profound ungovernability. Overthrowing whatever elite had established itself in Kabul has always proved relatively straightforward – as indeed was the case in 2001. Shaping the behaviour of the Afghan people to the will of the invader, however, has always been far more difficult. Afghanistan, throughout its modern history, has been a structurally weak state; it was this very weakness which had periodically contributed to drawing in foreign intervention forces, the geopolitics of the region rendering neighbouring states unable to tolerate a power vacuum. Afghanistan's main deterrent throughout history has lain not in the massed ranks of its armed forces, but in its formidable natural terrain and proudly independent and warlike people, conditions that greatly favoured classic unconventional 'guerrilla' tactics.

Successive past interventions underlined the purely military challenges of dominating Afghanistan. During the 1980s, Soviet tanks designed for the plains of central Europe or northern Manchuria had struggled in Afghanistan amidst narrow valleys and along poor roads. The story of European-oriented armies experiencing unexpected difficulties had been little different in the nineteenth century, when, during the first Anglo-Afghan War, for example, dense British infantry 'squares', famous for their stoicism in the conventional European conflicts of the day, had simply formed a larger target for the longer-ranged local weapons of Afghan tribesmen. The challenge of actually governing the country was also a testing one, however, even for indigenous rulers. The first truly modern ruler of the country, Amir Abdur Rahman, had advanced the cause of central government after 1881 only by establishing the most savage form of personal dictatorship. Afghanistan, simply, has no historical experience of a central government that couples benign intent and behaviour with an ability to exert control over the disparate provinces.

AFGHAN GOVERNANCE: THE BURDEN OF HISTORY AND TRADITION

Although Afghanistan had first emerged during the eighteenth century under the Durrani dynasty, civil war had repeatedly engulfed the country after the death of the founder of the dynasty, Ahmad Shah, in 1772. Afghan monarchs after Ahmad Shah consistently walked a tightrope of maintaining an imperial governmental structure (including an increasingly professional army, seen as essential to free them from an undesirable dependence on irregular tribal forces) on a relatively small base of tax revenues. Adopting Tsar Peter the Great of Russia as his role model, however, Amir Abdur Rahman after 1881 took it as his personal mission in life to reunite and modernize the country, as well as to entrench the power of the royal family. To this end, he combined substantial military reform with savage repression and the importation of foreign technology. Those who resisted the 'Iron Amir' were subjected to horrific punishments, including mass executions by impalement, being pulled in half, or grotesquely turned into human icicles by being chained in a pit below dripping ice-cold water. The amir was particularly proud of this last punishment as an apt cure for rapists, joking of one offender subjected to this torture that he would 'never be too hot again'.[2] The amir also ensured that hills of human skulls were periodically constructed and publicly displayed, as a way of deterring would-be robbers and rebels. This apparently had only limited success, however, since he calculated that during his reign he had executed 120,000 people.[3]

Overall, therefore, the Iron Amir showed a dedication to extreme violence and social engineering that was truly totalitarian, a factor to which his British paymasters turned a blind eye, particularly when it came to the treatment of Afghan ethnic minorities. During his period in office, large-scale compulsory population resettlement occurred, with non-Pashtun nationalities in the centre and north of the country being particularly singled out for punishment. Small numbers of foreign physicians, engineers and geologists came to Afghanistan, and a few factories were established to manufacture soap, candles and leather goods. Nonetheless, even this form of authoritarian 'modernization' encountered severe limitations, largely because the state remained so poor in terms of capital and capacity, but also because the endeavour was coupled with a strong dose of xenophobia, most clearly reflected at this time in decisions made regarding transport infrastructure.

Conscious of the deterrent value to foreign armies offered by the challenging physical terrain of his realm, the Iron Amir allowed internal road building (which, he recognized, was useful for suppressing indigenous tribal rebellions), but barred external railway lines from crossing onto his territory.[4] Relative backwardness in transportation terms remained a conscious defensive policy in Afghanistan throughout much of the twentieth century. Indeed, not until the 1960s would the Hindu Kush mountain barrier between central and northern Afghanistan be penetrated by the Soviet-built Salang road tunnel. Whatever his own internal successes in building up and maintaining his personal power, however, the pact that he made with the British also permitted the Iron Amir no autonomy in the realm of foreign policy. During the last decades of the nineteenth century, the actual physical borders of Afghanistan were largely finalized according to British whim, creating a geopolitical legacy that further weakened the already severely challenged Afghan central government.

The frontiers established during the Amir Abdur Rahman's reign in the late nineteenth century were to contribute to Afghanistan's problems after September 2001. As a consequence of the British desire that the British and Russian empires should never at any point territorially meet, the eastern frontier of Afghanistan with China emerged as a long, narrow, utterly indefensible, but symbolic strip of land, the so-called 'Wakhan corridor'. British diplomat Sir Mortimer Durand repeated this performance in imperial border-drawing when deciding Afghanistan's southern frontiers. Drawing a line between Afghanistan and what was then British India (now modern-day Pakistan), he cut in half the Pashtun tribes,

Afghanistan's dominant ethnic group, and created at a stroke the so-called 'Pashtunistan' issue which came to dominate Afghan relations with Pakistan, and which remains a vitally important complicating factor in the current intervention.

After 1948, the Durand Line created a nightmare new dilemma almost overnight, given the emergence of the independent Islamic state of Pakistan. Non-recognition by successive Afghan governments of the legality of the Durand Line created decades of Afghan–Pakistani political tension, at the same time as Pakistan itself was left with a wild and almost ungovernable Pashtun-dominated borderland, in the form of the Federally Administered Tribal Areas (FATA). Pakistani governments would in turn come to see the FATA as both a blessing and a curse, since these territories demanded periodic intervention and stabilization by the Pakistani armed forces, yet simultaneously also served as a potential piedmont of political influence into Afghanistan itself. During the 1979–89 Soviet intervention in Afghanistan, the already Pashtun-dominated FATA became a territorial safe haven and training zone for the *mujahidin*, as well as a home for thousands of Afghan refugees sheltered in overcrowded and often unsanitary refugee camps; centres that quickly became the *mujahidin*'s single largest recruiting base.

Afghanistan, as a result of Durand's work, was therefore left with a political–territorial ulcer, one which both sapped its confidence regarding its own territorial integrity, and left an open door to intervention and interference by Pakistani-backed Pashtun political groups further to the south. Against this background, there was no comfort to be drawn from the fact that Pakistan was, if anything, left even more insecure by such colonial-era border settlements, in the form of separatist movements in Baluchistan and the still unresolved Kashmir issue with India.

Indeed, Pakistan's strategic contest with India would become the decisive factor over the longer term in shaping Pakistan's relations with Afghanistan, with the Pakistani General Staff in the 1990s advancing the concept that a pro-Pakistani government in Kabul constituted a vital national security interest, since it would provide Pakistan with 'strategic depth' against India.

ETHNIC TENSIONS AND RIVALRIES

Ethnicity formed another key area of Afghan weakness during its initial emergence as a state in the modern period. Scholars have often pointed to Afghanistan's great tribal diversity as exacerbating its ungovernable nature and proneness to internal crisis, and even the Iron Amir's efforts at centralization between 1881 and 1901 deepened the gulf between town and countryside (by creating a new political elite of civil servants in Kabul) rather than fundamentally transforming the rural balance of power.[5] The Pashtuns constitute the largest and most powerful ethnic group in Afghanistan, but they themselves are subdivided into an estimated sixty major tribes. Each tribe represents a complex social network of mutual assistance, which is then further subdivided down to the village level by the notion of *qawm*, a group founded on kinship and patron–client relationships. *Qawm* networks form dense, informal clusters to provide the social security net that the Afghan state itself never has, via financial loans for start-up investments and small-scale initial running costs. These loans, even in the modern period, are just as liable to be secured by the marrying-off of a daughter in a strategic alliance, or the provision of a young male foot soldier for a local warlord, as by entering into a formal business agreement. During the 1980s, Afghan rural society became effectively atomized by war and forced migration, increasing the relevance of the *qawm* as a local survival strategy. In Afghanistan, therefore, the *qawm* constituted not so much a local substitute for the Western notion of 'civil society' as its complete negation, effectively a product of de-modernization.[6]

The Pashtun tribes based on Afghan territory make up five large tribal confederations – the Durrani, Ghilzai, Ghurghusht, Karlanri and Sarbani, all located in the south of the country. The Pashtuns have traditionally been seen as united by *Pashtunwali*, the pre-Islamic Pashtun tribal code, which demands hospitality and generosity when someone asks for pardon or protection, alongside an absolute obligation to avenge any slights. Tribal politics have also played a frequent role in Afghanistan's internal power shifts. The Durrani dynasty, the traditional founders and rulers of Afghanistan, acquired its name in 1747, with the ascent to the throne of Ahmad Shah Durrani, who renamed his own tribal group (until then designated the Abdali) the Durrani, from the Persian expression 'pearl of pearls'. However, despite close familial ties, the Durrani themselves were prone to frequent internal splits, of which the most famous occurred in 1973, when King Zahir Shah was toppled by his own cousin, ex-Prime Minister Mohammed Daoud. Within the Soviet-backed PDPA, Daoud's successors in government after 1978, tribal politics continued to play a role from the very start, despite the party's ostensibly Marxist nature. The split between Parcham and Khalq factions within the PDPA was also a tribal split between Persian and Pashtun speakers. Nur Mohammad Taraki, leader of the more radically militant Marxist Khalq faction of the PDPA, the group which took the lead in killing Daoud and seizing office in 1978, came from non-elite Ghilzai Pashtun stock. His rival, Babrak Karmal, leader of the more moderate Parcham faction, represented the more overtly royalist Durrani Pashtun. The Ghilzais in

Afghan history have, in fact, been traditionally suspicious of the Durranis and have been rivals for power, with Ghilzai representatives seizing control of the state on no fewer than three separate occasions – in 1721, 1978 and again in 1996, when the Taliban leader Mullah Omar came to power.[7]

Powerful and significant though their role has been in Afghan history, the Pashtuns have often been perceived by Afghanistan's other ethnic minorities as brutal oppressors. Until the rise to power of Abdur Rahman, the very concept of Afghanistan as a nation had been problematic. The British observer Mountstuart Elphinstone remarked in 1809 that 'these people have no name for their country'.[8] Prior to Rahman's accession to the throne, the territory could either be defined in dynastic terms by the Durrani clan, or, from a purely religious perspective, as an isolated Islamic bastion in a sea of infidel kingdoms. Rahman's innovation was to attempt to blend the two world views together by centralizing dynastic power while publicly promoting the importance of *jihad*. Nonetheless, the dynastic state-building project also bore an unmistakable Pashtun character, one that was unfriendly towards Afghanistan's other ethnic groups, most of which reside in the north of the country. Analyses of the precise ethnic balance in Afghanistan are notoriously unreliable, but a recent CIA estimate, viewed as reasonably credible, calculated the population in 2010 at 29,121,286 individuals, subdivided ethnically into 42 per cent Pashtun, 27 per cent Tajik, 9 per cent Hazara, 9 per cent Uzbek, 4 per cent Aimak, 3 per cent Turkmen, 2 per cent Baloch and 4 per cent 'other'.[9]

Ruling such a diverse coalition of tribes and ethnic groups has proved problematic throughout Afghan history. The obvious limitations of the authoritarian modernization model, given Afghanistan's own shortage of resources and significant capital reserves, led Abdur

Rahman's successors after 1919 to gradually abandon his approach to national development and instead to experiment more and more with international aid and client-like relationships, with ever more unhappy results. The outcome was a pattern of increasingly sharp developmental crises that gripped the country.

ECONOMIC WEAKNESS AND DEVELOPMENT CRISES

International intervention forces in 2001 inherited a state that was economically broken, with life expectancy among the lowest in the world, and infant mortality among the highest. However, those who blamed the economic misery so visible in Afghanistan in 2001 purely on Taliban rule and the previous ten-year war against the Soviet-backed Kabul government overlooked the much wider and longer-term history of Afghanistan's failed economic modernization. For much of the twentieth century, Afghanistan was functionally an increasingly weak 'rentier state'; this was typified by the fact that, by the 1970s, tax-gathering accounted for less than 2 per cent of domestic revenue. As a result Afghanistan shared the governance and developmental problems that were common to other aid-dependent states in the world's southern tier. Whereas oil states could manipulate sales volume, Afghanistan had no such control or leverage over levels of foreign aid, and this set the scene for an acute fiscal crisis when aid levels eventually declined.[10]

Afghanistan during the twentieth century was therefore left to attempt modernization by building its internal market on the periphery of the world economy, making what little use it could, given its non-aligned status, of Cold War dynamics to acquire hefty subsidies. A degree of modernization and technical assistance for the army was achieved largely through Soviet support, much as, in the nineteenth century, what little effort had been made to modernize the army occurred under British or Turkish influence. Basic infrastructural improvements also came about largely through foreign aid. During the 1950s and 1960s, the Soviet Union built Kabul airport and the Americans constructed the airport at Kandahar, while, after 1973, Afghan President Daoud spoke symbolically of his long-term desire to continue lighting American cigarettes with Soviet matches.[11] Externally funded developmental projects from 1957 onwards led to a growth in the role of foreign experts, but also often produced only industrialized enclaves, and a politicized and educated student middle class that was increasingly discontented with the contemporary political scene.[12] Afghan Islamists from among the ranks of the latter attempted a state takeover in 1975, but failed on account of their inability to get the Afghan armed forces 'on side'. The PDPA coup of 1978, by contrast, succeeded precisely because of the presence of large cadres of left-leaning Afghan officers who were a legacy of the dominant Soviet role in training, arming and equipping the Afghan armed forces since the 1950s.[13]

THE SOVIET INTERVENTION

The 1978 seizure of power by the PDPA – a pro-Soviet Afghan Marxist party founded in 1965, which, since its foundation, had also been almost permanently divided into two warring factions, Khalq and Parcham (led by the poet Nur Mohammad Taraki and the politician and student leader Babrak Karmal, respectively) – came as something of a shock to the leadership of the Soviet Union. Via Indian mediators, the Soviet Union had encouraged the two warring PDPA factions to reconcile their differences in 1977, but had also explicitly warned against any kind of military adventurism (this despite the Kremlin's own growing political differences with the ruling Daoud regime).[14] On 27 April 1978, Afghan military units loyal to Khalq, and to Taraki's deputy, Hafizullah Amin, in particular, nonetheless responded to the arrest of some leading communists by launching a successful coup, killing Daoud in the presidential palace via an airstrike, and overnight placing the PDPA in power. Thereafter, the Kremlin increasingly found itself forced to intervene to support the PDPA as the latter struggled to consolidate itself in power. Infighting resumed within the PDPA itself and even grew in intensity, while resistance in the countryside to PDPA land reforms led to more violence.

By early 1979 the Soviet Union had provided the PDPA with substantial military equipment and had also deployed some 550 advisers in Afghanistan. It nonetheless continued to refuse requests from the Afghan side for Soviet personnel to take part in active combat operations, rejected between eleven and fourteen requests for direct military intervention (including an explicit PDPA request in March 1979 – when fighting around Herat left 5,000 people dead – for the immediate dispatch of Soviet combat forces), and instead urged the Kabul government to cease internal repression and broaden its political base in the countryside. Soviet Politburo leaders at the time explicitly recognized the fact that Afghanistan was not yet ready for socialism, that 'we can suppress a [*mujahidin*] revolution in Afghanistan only with the aid of our bayonets, and that is for us entirely inadmissible', and that 'our army, [if] it arrives in Afghanistan, will be the aggressor'.[15] Ongoing PDPA factional infighting, however, steadily reduced the Kremlin's freedom of manoeuvre, bound as it was after December 1978 by a strategic alliance pact to support the revolution in Afghanistan.

With Karmal and his Parcham associates already either repressed or effectively exiled abroad, the Khalq faction of the PDPA over the course of 1979 descended into bloody internecine strife. Amin had Taraki smothered to death on 9 October 1979 and personally assumed full dictatorial powers, leading the Soviet KGB to begin to fear either that he was a CIA plant seeking deliberately to undermine the revolution, or that he was preparing to 'do a Sadat on us' (a wholesale defection from the Soviet camp to the United States).[16] In this rapidly deteriorating context, the Soviet Politburo met on 12 December and ratified a formal proposal to intervene in Afghanistan, assassinate Amin in the process, and replace him with the more moderate Babrak Karmal. By 27 December, Amin was dead and some 75,000 Soviet troops were deploying across the territory of Afghanistan.

Moscow's intentions in ordering the deployment of the Limited Contingent of Soviet Forces (LCOSF) to Afghanistan were basically defensive in nature; the Politburo feared the defection of Afghanistan from the socialist camp, the possible subsequent deployment of American missiles there, and the Islamist destabilization of Soviet Central Asia. Nonetheless, the Kremlin's own hopes for a period of rapid stabilization, regime consolidation, and then withdrawal (Brezhnev himself allegedly hoped for a drawdown of Soviet forces by February 1980) were soon confounded.[17]

US President Carter's national security adviser, Zbigniew Brzezinski, was acutely aware of the opportunity to turn Afghanistan into the Soviet Union's Vietnam, and had already persuaded Carter to authorize covert aid to anti-Kabul factions in July 1979, in an attempt to lure in a greater Soviet ground presence.[18] In the wake of President Ronald Reagan's election in 1980, large-scale covert military aid to the *mujahidin* became fully formalized, funnelled via an arms pipeline that incorporated Egypt, Israel, Pakistan and China. American support for the *mujahidin* grew from $30 million in 1980 to a peak of more than \$600 million per year in 1986–89, with Saudi Arabia matching or slightly exceeding American financial support.[19] In the face of this rising tide of foreign-sponsored insurgency, the number of Soviet troops increased to 108,800 by April 1986 – still far too few to truly dominate the countryside, and never comparable to the earlier American commitment of over 500,000 men to Vietnam. However, Soviet forces then began to withdraw in the second half of 1986, in line with General Secretary Gorbachev's resolve to pursue a political solution to the conflict.

The war itself left Afghanistan devastated, however, and compounded its already difficult economic development. Most notably, the Soviet intervention in 1979–89 led to a further increase in Afghanistan's dependency on outside aid. Much of the country's underground *karez* irrigation system was destroyed once the Soviets became aware that its tunnels were also being used as shelter points by local *mujahidin*. By the late 1980s, the country had become heavily dependent on Soviet wheat and fuel imports, and the Soviet government's inability to supply its annual provision of 230,000 tonnes of food aid helped to precipitate the final crisis of the Najibullah regime in 1991.[20]

GEOPOLITICS IN A TOUGH NEIGHBOURHOOD

Afghanistan's relative economic failure and periodic crises, however, are also inextricably linked to the eternal, almost intractable, geopolitical challenges created by the country's key location. Afghanistan's economic impoverishment and 'rentier state' status have periodically drawn neighbours into the country who were concerned at the broader implications of such weakness. The geopolitics of the region have meanwhile ensured that Afghanistan is seen as strategically significant only as a land bridge to somewhere else, a pawn in the chess game of ensuring wider geopolitical stability, or a stage on which broader international and regional rivalries can be played out. Here the earliest conquerors set the tone for much of what followed: Alexander the Great travelled rapidly through the area in 329–327 BC en route to India, with his 'civilizing mission' in Asia leaving behind remarkably few literary or cultural traces in Afghanistan itself, beyond some isolated archaeological ruins, coin hoards, and claims among certain local tribes – the Afridis, for example – that their lineage contained traces of Greek blood.[21]

During the 1980s, many Western commentators speculated wildly that the Soviet Union's only real interest in Afghanistan lay in the fact that it could serve as a transport corridor to warm-water ports, reviving hoary nineteenth-century Anglo-Indian myths about the eternally avaricious nature of Russian aggression. The Soviet presence in Afghanistan was correspondingly presented by the American government after 1979, in highly irrational terms, as posing an immediate threat to the Persian Gulf.[22] In reality, the Soviet Union itself, as recently declassified documents have revealed, intervened in Afghanistan only with great reluctance, having already been caught unawares both by the speed of the PDPA takeover of the country and by the pace of the subsequent tribal backlash. Yurii Andropov, head of the Soviet KGB at the time, lamented:

> once we dreamed of worldwide revolution, now we are not even made happy by one in a neighbouring state . . . if only this [Afghan] revolution had occurred two or three years later . . . on the other hand a revolution is like a close relative, one cannot simply abandon it.[23]

Suspicions regarding the wider geopolitical motivations of external actors – some rather better founded than others – outlasted the withdrawal of Soviet forces from Afghanistan. During the 1990s, the American oil company Unocal, with support from vocal members of the US State Department, opened talks with the Taliban over the construction of a $2 billion gas pipeline from Turkmenistan across Afghanistan to Pakistan and India. Talks stalled following US domestic agitation over the Taliban's record on women's rights, but after 2001 Afghanistan remained a critical component in the strategic 'Silk Road' project advocated by some key US think tanks for stabilizing the wider Eurasian region in a broadly pro-American and pro-free market direction.[24] President Karzai, aware of Afghanistan's historic geopolitical fate, would periodically court Iran, the Shanghai Cooperation Organization (SCO) and the Russian-led Collective Security Treaty Organization (CSTO) as alternative regional security providers to NATO, though his freedom to shape foreign policy rapidly became almost as constrained as Amir Abdur Rahman's had been.

THE SOVIET WITHDRAWAL

By February 1989, the last Soviet armoured columns were pulling out of the Republic of Afghanistan, as part of a negotiated international peace process (the Geneva Accords). Despite post-war claims that they had been humiliatingly defeated, Soviet forces in reality withdrew in good order, and left in place a regime in Kabul with (in principle) more than sufficient military force to defend itself. The Soviets had also managed to complement their military retreat with a facilitative local political agenda from 1986 onwards, in which the recently appointed (and Soviet-backed) Afghan President Mohammad Najibullah publicly went on record as being ready to negotiate with declared enemies as part of a new 'National Reconciliation Policy'.[25]

Though some anticipated a rapid collapse without a large-scale Soviet presence, the Kabul government after 1989 retained colossal quantities of modern military equipment, including SCUD missiles and over 1,000 tanks. In terms of sheer numbers available at the time of withdrawal, the Afghan regular army, which officially stood at 165,000 men, supported by 97,000 Interior Ministry and 57,000 State Security Ministry troops, dwarfed the comparable post-2001 international coalition effort to generate indigenous military forces in Afghanistan, even after nearly ten years of NATO's own 'state-building' campaign.[26] However, the Soviet-trained Afghan armed forces continued to be undermined by corruption and desertion, while the Geneva Accords contained a significant political loop-hole, given that they committed neither the Soviets nor the Americans to reducing military deliveries to their respective clients.

With both the government and the *mujahidin* receiving significant funding from abroad, the internal military–political situation in Afghanistan remained deadlocked, and Najibullah was unable to make much significant progress in his National Reconciliation Policy. Initially there were promising signs. The number of *mujahidin* who defected to the government side rose sharply from 60,000 in 1988 to 125,000 by 1989, while the number of Afghan villages recorded as officially 'under government control' also rose steeply – from 7,265 in 1986 to 11,265 by 1988. However, this latter metric then fell back just as sharply, to 6,100 villages officially 'under government control' by the end of 1989. This meant that, although, by 1990, 25 per cent of all non-government armed units had signed 'reconciliation' agreements and 40 per cent had signed ceasefire agreements, the overall reconciliation process lacked significant forward momentum, an experience that in many ways mirrored NATO's experience in 2009–10.[27] Yet the *mujahidin* also proved incapable of overwhelming the well-armed Afghan regular army, even when occasionally supported by cross-border Pakistani army artillery fire. The key to the collapse of the Soviet-backed government in Afghanistan therefore lay not in some well-organized *mujahidin* military victory, but in the ongoing political disintegration of the Soviet Union itself, with the last official Soviet foreign minister pledging in September 1991 (barely two months before the dissolution of the Soviet Union) to cut off all military and economic aid to Najibullah by January 1992.

By March 1992, UN negotiators had persuaded Najibullah to step aside, with the Afghan president publicly announcing his resignation and willingness to hand over power to a transition government. Reading the writing on the wall, one of Najibullah's most capable military commanders in the north of the country, the Uzbek General Dostum, defected the very next day to ally his 40,000-plus strong military contingent, including artillery and armoured vehicles, with the followers of the indefatigable Tajik insurgent Ahmad Shah Massoud. Kabul fell rapidly to both men's combined forces the following month. Having earlier evacuated his family to India, Najibullah now found his scheduled flight out of the country blockaded, and was reduced to seeking refuge within the tenuous security of the UN compound in Kabul. There he led a confined existence under UN guard until the Taliban broke into the compound some four years later, following which both he and his brother were brutally tortured and murdered, with their mangled bodies then hung from lamp posts in one of the most vivid early displays of the nature of Taliban public justice.

The 1992 collapse of the Najibullah government in the wake of the withdrawal of Soviet military and economic support was followed, with depressing inevitability, by a *mujahidin* civil war over the division of the spoils. The *mujahidin* movement that had emerged during the war against the Soviet-backed PDPA government in Kabul had long been marked by internal divisions. The most obvious was the gulf between the eight predominantly Shi'a *mujahidin* parties based in Iran and the seven predominantly Sunni parties based in Pakistan. These geopolitical distinctions were then further compounded by internal divisions within both fronts between royalists and political moderates on the one hand, and Islamists on the other.[28] Against this backdrop, the Islamist groups in Pakistan possessed an organizational advantage, since they had already established a nascent political infrastructure there prior to 1979.[29] They were also favoured by a powerful actor, a player whose influence and effect on events in both Afghanistan and Pakistan resonate to this day: the Inter-Services Intelligence Directorate (ISI) of the Pakistani military.

THE INFLUENCE OF THE ISI AND *MUJAHIDIN* FRAGMENTATION

The *mujahidin* movement that grew up in the refugee camps in Pakistan rapidly came under the wing of the ISI. Established in 1948 as the successor to the Intelligence Bureau (IB), manned and controlled exclusively by the Pakistani military, and charged since its creation with gathering and analysing both external and internal political intelligence in the region, the ISI by the 1980s had evolved into one of the major players in Pakistan's government, marked out by its large personnel establishment of over 10,000 officers and staff (not counting informants and intelligence assets). The role and scale of the ISI Afghan Bureau's efforts during the 1980s was reflected in the later boast of its main desk chief at the time that, between 1984 and 1987, over 80,000 *mujahidin* passed through ISI training camps, hundreds of thousands of tonnes of weapons and ammunition were distributed, and disruptive operations were planned and carried out in twenty-nine provinces of Afghanistan.[30]

However, as we shall see as the story of the post-2001 intervention unfolds, Afghanistan, like Kashmir, was, in the eyes of the ISI, merely a pawn in the wider struggle against what it perceived to be the Pakistani state's main opponent – India.

During the 1980s, the ISI served as a vital intermediary in funnelling foreign arms and aid, in what rapidly became the largest global covert operation in modern intelligence history. It took care early on to establish a clear division of labour between itself and its American counterparts in the CIA. In particular, the ISI acquired a monopoly over the actual in-theatre distribution of funds and weapons, with arms being issued to the *mujahidin* not only to carry out operations, but also as a reward for success.[31] The Saudi intelligence service under Prince Turki (the GID or, in Arabic, *al-Istakhbarah al-'Amah*) not only helped the CIA and ISI manage this immense pipeline of money and arms, but also coordinated the waves of Arab volunteers who were soon travelling to Pakistan to participate in the international *jihad* against the Soviet-backed regime in Kabul.

On the ground itself, the ISI distributed arms to those groups which it felt most closely conformed to Pakistan's own military and political goals for Afghanistan. The royalist parties quickly lost out in this process, due to Pakistan's insistence, fuelled by its wariness of Pashtun nationalism, that only religiously oriented parties and leaders could operate on its soil. The enormous institutional foot-print of the ISI in Pakistan, and its immense overall political and economic influence in directing this process, reflected Pakistan's own dysfunctional political evolution. Ever since the state's creation, the military had eluded civilian control, and took its self-designated status as guardian of the nation as sufficient justification to frequently seize the reins of power. The Pakistani military dictator General Zia ul-Haq, following his takeover in June 1977 (he famously hanged

Zulfiqar Ali Bhutto, the father of future Prime Minister Benazir Bhutto, in 1979), vigorously pursued the increasing Islamization of Pakistani public and political life, while simultaneously propagating his own grand strategic vision for the wider region. Zia foresaw Afghanistan becoming 'a real Islamic state, part of a pan-Islamic revival that will one day win over the Muslims of the Soviet Union'.[32]

Nor did Iran hesitate to ruthlessly pursue its own national interests with regard to the *mujahidin* factions based on its territory. Afghan moderate nationalists were repressed, but thousands of young Shi'ite Afghan refugees received training in Iranian religious schools aimed at fostering the emergence of a pro-Ayatollah Khomeini camp among Afghan Shi'ites.[33]

During this time, the ISI identified Gulbuddin Hikmatyar's rigidly centralized Hizb-i Islami-yi Afghanistan (HIH – Islamic Party of Afghanistan) as its most favoured client, with the leading ISI coordinator at the time praising Hikmatyar as 'the toughest and most vigorous of all the alliance Leaders'.[34] This marked the beginning of a close relationship between Hikmatyar and elements of the Pakistani security bureaucracy that persists to this day – a further example of a lack of fastidiousness when courting allies deemed useful in Pakistan's strategic calculations. Hikmatyar, it is safe to say, is not a particularly admirable individual. He had been enrolled in Kabul University's engineering faculty, where he failed to shine as a scholar but managed to acquire a brutal reputation through acts such as throwing acid in the faces of unveiled female students. His Leninist-style centralized Islamist party, which established its own military academy but also maintained a parallel layer of religious commissars to keep these same officers in check, nonetheless fully met the ISI's requirement for a disciplined military organization that would do what it was told, and only HIH's subsequent inability to fully mobilize the Pashtun tribal belt later led the ISI to shift its focus to the Taliban.[35]

The fragmentation of the Afghan *mujahidin* – generated by the need both to cultivate external sponsorship and to remain in favour with the ISI – was further compounded by the political and physical distance separating party leaders based in Pakistan or Iran (the 'external front') and field commanders actually fighting within Afghanistan itself (the 'internal front').[36] Consequently, the image of unity which the leaders of the political 'external front' attempted to present to their various foreign backers never reflected the reality of the fighting within Afghanistan itself, which was frequently characterized by 'turf war' struggles between rival factions. For pressing economic reasons, commanders on the ground usually aligned themselves with one or other of the external parties. The Francophile Tajik commander Ahmad Shah Massoud, for example, dubbed the 'Lion of the Panjshir' by the Western press, and probably the most effective *mujahidin* field commander to emerge during the whole course of the war, affiliated himself with Burhanuddin Rabbani's Jama'at-i Islami-yi Afghanistan (JIA). However, the mass of *mujahidin* in the field owed their loyalty to their commander along horizontal lines of local social (*qawm*) networks, rather than along vertical lines of political loyalty. Therefore, when a field commander defected from one party to another, he usually took his men with him.

Most field commanders retained a significant degree of regional autonomy, making local political decisions, recruiting fighters and raising local taxes. Most famously, Massoud unilaterally concluded a personal truce with Soviet forces in 1983. ISI distrust of Massoud's independent ways meant that he was destined to receive only eight examples of the American-supplied Stinger anti-aircraft missile, the single most important and technologically sophisticated weapon provided by foreign aid to the *mujahidin* after 1986. Massoud received his own stock of these weapons only in 1991, and all eight remained unfired when CIA operatives returned to buy them back five years later.[37]

Therefore, despite much retrospective mythologizing about 'all groups fighting for a common cause with uncompromising determination',[38] *mujahidin* inter-party fighting ended up inflicting as many casualties within Afghanistan as Soviet or PDPA military activity, with relations becoming particularly bad between Rabbani's JIA and Hikmatyar's HIH. Against this backdrop, *mujahidin* efforts to establish a unified government in the wake of Najibullah's fall from power always looked fragile. The ISI, with Saudi backing, continued to back Hikmatyar over other leaders. During 1990, Hikmatyar launched two unsuccessful bids to hasten Najibullah's collapse, the second of which – eventually halted by protests from the US State Department – envisaged a massive military assault on Kabul, preceded by a wholly indiscriminate long-range artillery barrage from 40,000 rockets.[39]

Kabul eventually fell to the Massoud–Dostum alliance in April 1992. However, fighting soon broke out within the city between Massoud's forces on one side, and Hikmatyar's HIH on the other. Between May and August 1992, Hikmatyar periodically bombarded Kabul with rockets, killing over 1,500 civilians and, according to the UN, turning more than 500,000 people into refugees. By the end of the year, over 5,000 people had been killed and perhaps a million had fled. Kabul itself, the epicentre of Soviet investment in the country, and formerly a significant modern conurbation (enjoying clean water, gas, electricity, an airport, schools, a university, modern housing, decent roads and an effective sewerage system), was reduced to rubble. In the process, the city was also transformed into a neo-medieval micro-state, whose every inch was disputed and fought over by rival warlord factions.[40]

Caught in the midst of the fighting between Hikmatyar and Massoud around Kabul was the one, notably unsuccessful, attempt to form a coalition government by *mujahidin* moderates. As early as January 1988, Ed McWilliams of the US State Department had voiced concerns that the predominantly secular and well-educated Afghans living in the Communist-controlled regions of the country might so dread the potential social consequences of an extremist like Hikmatyar seizing power that they would support Najibullah remaining in office over the longer term, even in the wake of the Soviet pullout. Such concerns eventually triggered a gradual overall rethink of American policy towards Afghanistan within the State Department, leading to a shift by 1990 towards encouraging the creation of a future governing coalition of Afghan 'moderates', one that excluded both Najibullah, at one end of the political spectrum, and Hikmatyar and extreme Islamist groups at the other.[41] The 'National Commanders Shura' (NCS) of *mujahidin* leaders was then formed in May 1990 in Kunar, with ISI Director General Assad Durrani deliberately excluded from the first talks, and with the initial meetings, consequently, quickly boycotted by Hikmatyar. In brief, the policy appeared to promise the emergence of a nascent 'third movement' in Afghan politics, located between the Najibullah government and the ISI's closest clients.[42]

Those leaders who remained within the NCS were quickly invited by Massoud to Kabul in 1992 to help form a transitional government. In April of that year they agreed to create an interim government with a rotating presidency, within which Massoud served as defence minister, while Sebghatullah Mujadidi served as head of state for two months, and Burhanuddin Rabbani for four months. However, this process brought to the fore long-simmering tensions between the 'external' and 'internal' fronts of the *mujahidin* movement, with a disillusioned Massoud soon declaring that the external front leaders had comprehensively failed to work out a coherent unified programme of government.[43] A multi-polar war of 'all against all' then broke out, involving the Iranian-backed Hizb-i Wahdat (in alliance with local Hazaras), Hikmatyar, Massoud's Tajiks and JIA forces, and Dostum's Uzbek forces, which played all sides, first defecting from Massoud to ally with Hikmatyar, before then ultimately rejoining Massoud's 'Northern Alliance' in the wake of the eventual fall of Kabul to the Taliban.

Those who suffered the most from this civil war were, predictably, the civilian population in Kabul, with the *mujahidin* quickly becoming completely discredited in the eyes of many Afghans as 'worse than the Russians'.[44] However, this chaos also placed under threat Pakistan's rich cross-border trade with the Central Asian states, an energy and economic transit corridor in which Benazir Bhutto's new government, elected to office in the wake of Zia's death in a mysterious aircraft accident in 1988, maintained a strong, and growing, interest. A nexus of concerned power brokers within Pakistan began to view this growing chaos with increasing disquiet. As we shall see later in the chapter, this led to the fateful decision to lend support to a growing force on the Afghan scene: the Taliban.

REGIONAL CRIME AND CORRUPTION

The covert operations of the 1980s had already established a thriving 'black economy' of trucking operations in the region, accompanied by its own 'transport mafia'. Powerful criminal networks forged linkages at this time with local, national and regional power brokers to form a complex nexus that has woven itself into the social, political and economic fabric of the region. By 1989, Afghanistan and Pakistan were already ranked as, respectively, the world's largest and second largest global suppliers of illicit heroin. The heroin market itself had, meanwhile, changed radically since the end of the 1970s. Iranian policy towards opium production, in combination with several successive years of drought in the 'Golden Triangle' of Laos, Thailand, Myanmar and Vietnam, compelled a shift in geographical focus among the drug syndicates of south-east Asia in order to meet ongoing global demand. This change was enhanced by the course of the war in Afghanistan, where the fighting destroyed much of the already fragile local agricultural ecosystem, driving Afghan hill farmers in particular to replace wheat crops, mulberry trees and nut orchards with the sturdier, more easily cultivated opium poppy, while the relatively rich and traditionally more lush Helmand valley became a major hub of the opium trade.[45] Pakistan had 5,000 heroin users in 1980, a number which rocketed to 70,000 by 1983, and to more than 1.3 million addicts less than three years later.[46] CIA–ISI covert operations were therefore deeply intertwined with the more general smuggling economy that now exploded in the region, with Pakistani drug trafficking by 1986 already reckoned to be a $100 billion industry.

The most obvious evidence of the covert arms pipeline doubling as a heroin smuggling route relates to the trucks employed by the Pakistan army's National Logistics Cell (NLC). During most of the 1980s, these trucks would drive up from Karachi loaded with CIA-provided arms, and then perform the return trip loaded with heroin. The trucks were protected from police search by ISI papers. Pakistani officials at the highest levels in government were complicit in this trade, with sixteen military officers arrested in 1986 alone on charges of heroin trafficking. An external Norwegian investigation even tracked the operations of one particular drug syndicate back to General Zia ul-Haq's own personal banker.[47] *Mujahidin* leaders, meanwhile, systematically used heroin profits to help build up their own power bases within and outside the country. Hikmatyar, by the end of the 1980s, had entered into partnership with Pakistani heroin syndicates to invest in their opium processing plants, whilst Massoud and Rabbani also took a share of the new drug-trafficking routes opening up to the north through Tajikistan and Russia to Europe.

Important as the illicit heroin market had become by the 1990s in binding Pakistan and Afghanistan together in a corrupt embrace, trade in licit goods was of equal, if not even greater, importance to the Pakistani informal economy, due to a legislative anomaly dating back four decades. In 1950, in line with international agreements, Pakistan had granted land-locked Afghanistan the right to import duty-free goods through Karachi under the Afghan Transit Trade (ATT) agreement. The normal pattern of trade that arose as a consequence of this deal saw truckers driving up from Karachi to sell a few goods in Kabul, then driving back south to resell left-over stock in Pakistani markets. During the 1990s, however, this loophole in the Pakistani customs system led to a booming trade in cheap fuel, Japanese TVs, camcorders, satellite dishes, electronics, fridge-freezers, air-conditioners and other white goods, all of which flooded the Pakistani marketplace, undercutting and obliterating domestic competition, while simultaneously delivering huge profits to the 'transport mafias' based in Quetta who participated in the trade. The ATT traffic fuelled roaring levels of corruption at the highest levels among Pakistani police, politicians and army officers, who made money from physically protecting and politically defending the trade. The underground economy in Pakistan as a whole exploded as a result, from 15 billion rupees in 1973 to 1,115 billion by 1996, while its share of national GDP rose from 20 per cent to 51 per cent. Towards the end of the 1990s it was estimated that 44 billion rupees' worth of products were being illegally exported from Pakistan to Iran and Afghanistan, and over 67 billion rupees' worth illegally imported.[48]

Inconveniently, the chaos created by *mujahidin* infighting in Afghanistan hampered both the heroin economy and the ATT, with various warlords tapping into both markets to help pay for and equip their respective armies. However, the sheer proliferation of warlord factions, each of them running multiple informal 'customs barriers' that taxed any traffic travelling along the roads they controlled, posed a serious threat to the Quetta transport mafia's profit margins. Pakistani Prime Minister Benazir Bhutto's second administration (1993–96) meanwhile, always suspicious of the ISI, had by now become disillusioned with that agency's Afghanistan policy, and in particular with the evident failure of its chief client, Hikmatyar. Benazir Bhutto's interior minister and adviser on Afghan affairs, the former general Nasirullah Khan Babar, engineered a switch of government support from Hikmatyar to a nascent emerging movement, the Taliban. Babar also created an Afghan Trade Development Cell within the Interior Ministry with the ostensible task of developing a trade route to Central Asia – one employing ex-army lorry drivers from the NLC. The Development Cell also came to provide logistical backing for the Taliban. In what marked a 'civilianization' of Pakistan's covert effort in Afghanistan, the paramilitary Frontier Corps, directly under Babar's control, later helped to set up an internal wireless network for Taliban field commanders, while Pakistan

International Airlines sent in technicians to repair Kandahar airport, as well as the fighter jets and helicopters captured by the Taliban there.[49] Not until the very end of 1994, by contrast, did the ISI itself decisively switch its own support from Hikmatyar to the Taliban.[50] It would be delighted by how quickly its bet was to pay off.

THE TALIBAN CASTS ITS SHADOW

The Taliban, even before 11 September 2001, represented an enigma. The Western intelligence community, though curious, failed to establish a consensus as to the nature of this new phenomenon. Was the Taliban an organic offshoot of the 1980s Afghan *mujahidin*; a tribal coalition; or merely a proxy of the ISI? A dominant Western media image emerged prior to 2001 of the Taliban as backward, medieval, fundamentalist barbarians, more adept at destroying televisions and tape recorders, and persecuting unveiled women, than conducting modern warfare. As we shall see, this portrayal would undergo sharp revision during the subsequent ten years, as dismayed coalition commanders discovered that their Taliban opponents were not only capable of demonstrating remarkable tactical flexibility, but were often more proficient at information warfare than they were themselves.

The roots of the Taliban movement, now semi-mythologized, lay in the network of religious *madrasas* that sprang up in Pakistan's FATA territories during the Islamization campaign that had characterized Zia ul-Haq's reign. In 1956 there were only about 244 *madrasas* in the whole of what was then West Pakistan. By 1988, however, that figure had increased exponentially to 2,891 *madrasas* in Pakistan, of which 1,869 belonged to the puritanical Deobandi movement much favoured by external Saudi sponsors.[51]

These schools, which provided free room and board and a monthly salary with which students could support their families, became a magnet for children from the Afghan refugee camps. The camps themselves, located miles from any town, made it extremely hard to find legitimate civilian jobs. Consequently, students (*talibs*) at these religious schools frequently participated in the anti-Soviet and anti-Najibullah *jihads* as members of the *mujahidin* parties based in Peshawar. They took part in the fighting, managed the religious affairs of the *mujahidin* groups, and performed prayers over the dead. The Taliban were therefore already participants in the 1980s *mujahidin* movement. The future leader of the Taliban movement, Mullah Mohammad Omar, was just one of many *jihadist* war veterans, a member of Khalis' HIK who came to be affiliated, in particular, with the Jama'at Ulema-i Islamiyyah *madrasa* in Karachi.

According to Taliban folklore, the movement's swift development as a major independent force was the result of Omar's moral disgust at *mujahidin* leadership failings, and his subsequent decision, in the spring of 1994, to take up arms and, along with thirty *talib* followers armed with just sixteen rifles between them, liberate two young girls who had been abducted and repeatedly raped by a local warlord commander. In reality, it seems to have originated with outraged religious elders mobilizing their local followers, with Mullah Omar only subsequently meeting the concerned clergy involved and agreeing retrospectively (after several petitions from them) to lead the movement.

In the autumn of 1994, at a meeting of some forty or fifty people at the white mosque in the town of Sangisar in Kandahar province, the Taliban were formally constituted to 'prosecute vice and foster virtue, and . . . stop those who were bleeding the land'.[52] However, it was with its seizure of the truck stop and border district centre of Spin Boldak on 12 October 1994 that the movement first attracted significant media attention and began to acquire military momentum. The accompanying fall of the nearby Pasha arms depot, held by Hikmatyar's HIH forces, provided the movement with a significant supply of weapons, reportedly including 18,000 Kalashnikov assault rifles. Accounts differ over the true quantity of the arms captured after Spin Boldak's fall, and over the true intensity of the fighting there, with some believing that the capture of the arms dump merely provided a convenient cover for substantial fresh weapons supplies from elsewhere. Whatever the full story, eyewitnesses later recorded the Taliban forces gathering outside Kandahar scattering greaseproof wrapping paper everywhere as they broke out hundreds of brand new Kalashnikov rifles in readiness for the fighting that followed.[53]

A wide variety of actors saw potential in the movement, as a means of advancing their disparate interests. These interests were economic as well as political. For example, though the shortest route to Central Asia from Peshawar ran through Kabul, the Salang tunnel and Mazar-i-Sharif, Nasirullah Khan Babar and the Quetta transport mafia became keen advocates for an alternative northwestern route to be opened up via Quetta, Kandahar and Herat, and on to Ashkhabad, the capital of Turkmenistan. The Taliban became the defenders of an advance convoy sent into Afghanistan to symbolically pioneer this route in October 1994. That month its troops attacked and routed a warlord faction that had hijacked the convoy just outside Kandahar and was holding it captive. The truck convoy had itself been organized by the Pakistani army's NLC, and had eighty Pakistani ex-army drivers, as well as an officer from the ISI on board. Two days later, the Taliban swept on to seize Kandahar, demonstrating its utility not only as traffic police, but as an alternative spearhead of Pakistani influence into Afghanistan.[54]

In a further demonstration of its relative skill in addressing external agendas, the Taliban project had by this time also attracted the attention and support of the US oil company Unocal and its Saudi counterpart Delta, with Unocal successfully lobbying Washington to give Islamabad the green light over backing the Taliban, while Delta financed the provision of several hundred Toyota pickup trucks, which were converted into excellent high-speed advance convoys by Taliban troops.[55] Both companies were heavily invested at the time in bringing about the construction of a $2 billion gas pipeline linking Ashkhabad with Pakistan and the Arabian Sea; Delta itself then went on to sign an agreement with Turkmenistan and the Taliban for the construction of the proposed pipeline.[56]

The fall of Kandahar to Taliban forces in November established two methods of operation that went on to become critical to their wider strategic success. First, the Taliban's key potential opponent in Kandahar, Naqib, who commanded an estimated 2,500 men, did not resist, being persuaded to surrender instead, possibly for a bribe. This exemplified the Taliban's skill at exploiting local *qawm* networks to break away weaker and more vulnerable regional commanders, and their ability to threaten militia leaders with separation from their supporters. Money here was arguably of much less importance than local knowledge of the social networks concerned, since Pakistani financial support to the Taliban – even in 1997–98, after they had already substantially consolidated their power – has been estimated at a relatively modest $30 million a year, substantially less, for example, than earlier Soviet subsidies to Najibullah.[57] Secondly, the fall of Kandahar meant that significant quantities of modern military equipment fell into Taliban hands, including tanks and MiG fighter jets. The Taliban therefore quickly demonstrated that they could expand their numbers exponentially, utilizing culturally traditional Afghan *lashkar* formations, and that they could effectively employ modern military equipment.[58] As a result, in the space of less than three weeks, in the words of Anthony Davis, 'a hitherto unknown force had seized control of the country's second city and was estimated to have grown from several hundred to some 2,500–3,000 disciplined and motivated fighters'.[59]

Clashes in January 1995 between Hikmatyar's HIH forces, situated around southern Kabul, and advancing Taliban troops led to yet further Taliban victories. The Taliban had by now grown to a force of at least 10,000 fighters, backed by perhaps as many as a hundred operational tanks. In addition, they had demonstrated a strikingly efficient command and control network, and a willingness to mount daring night operations. The movement also employed a notably accurate artillery arm, serviced by ex-communist regime officers with specialized training (whom the Taliban utilized with apparently not a single moment's cultural hesitation). All this served to turn the Taliban, within the space of a few months, into a devastatingly effective hybrid force.[60] Though driven back from the centre of Kabul by Massoud's air force, which pounded advancing Taliban forces from Mi-35 helicopter gunships and Su-22 jets, the Taliban compensated for what were their first serious military reverses by making striking gains elsewhere in the country.

To the west, following the urgings of the Quetta transport mafia to seize Herat, the Taliban advance had initially ground to a halt against the forces of Ismail Khan. In the meantime, however, Dostum had temporarily defected to the Taliban side, granting it brief access to recently repaired MiG-21 fighter jets. Having paused to consolidate their troops and retrain, the Taliban first skilfully repulsed a thrust by Ismail Khan's troops that overran Helmand and threatened Kandahar itself, before mounting a stunningly successful high-speed counter-attack, employing pickup truck-mounted anti-aircraft cannon and BM-21 multi-barrelled rocket launchers. On 5 September 1995, Herat was abandoned, leaving Kabul and Mazar-i-Sharif as the only major towns still held by Massoud and Rabbani's embattled government.[61] ISI help was suspected by many to have helped coordinate this western campaign, with General Nasirullah Babar conducting a victory tour from Quetta through Kandahar to Herat and back just days after the fall of the town to Taliban forces.[62]

The 1996 campaigning season was dominated by battles around the approaches to Kabul, with the Taliban again relying on a combination of high-speed advances along multiple axes, and the organized defection of waves of significant regional militia commanders. This double line of assault simultaneously disoriented and demoralized their opponents. On 26 September, Massoud elected to abandon Kabul, conducting a skilful retreat that allowed him to preserve and evacuate most of his armour, artillery and air power, but granting the Taliban the ultimate political prize. The Taliban phenomenon had swept all before it thanks to its military and political flexibility.

Foreign commentators struggled to explain the Taliban's achievement, particularly when they compared the skilful and highly adaptive military campaign it had waged with its almost neo-medieval leadership structure. The whole Taliban movement continued to be run by two major councils: the Inner Shura of six members, led by Mullah Omar, and the subordinate nine-member Central Shura.[63] Omar himself remained a recluse, distributing funds from a metal box (on which foreign newspaper correspondents would often find him squatting) and frequently communicating with his subordinates via hand-written scraps of paper. A force that employed motorized vehicles and modern multi-barrelled rocket launchers with devastating effect also outlawed TVs, VCRs, satellite dishes, gambling and the shaving of beards as phenomena that were immoral and against the law of God. Religious sanctions came to be rigidly enforced by the Department for the Preservation of Virtue and the Elimination of Vice, whose young recruits paraded the streets, armed with long sticks, policing the local population and making sure that people attended the mosques for daily prayers. Taliban bureaucracy therefore remained both near-shapeless but also highly functional, defying Western notions of how an effective government should operate.

Though the Taliban were now in control of most of the country, their economic model remained essentially rooted in the parasitic shadow economy, with the bulk of their revenues raised from taxes (*zakat*) on the opium crop and Afghan transit trade. After taking Kabul, the Taliban levied an average of 6,000 rupees (US$150) on a truck travelling from Peshawar to Kabul, and also acquired a stake in the Quetta transport mafia's business, buying trucks or arranging for relatives to do so. Between 1992 and 1995, Afghanistan also produced a steady 2,200–2,400 tonnes of opium annually (rising to 2,800 tonnes in 1997), with the Taliban raking in an estimated $20 million in taxes from the trade.[64]

In the wake of their success in seizing Kabul and Kandahar, the Taliban began to stagnate. Like most revolutionary movements, the zeal and enthusiasm associated with insurrection faded in the face of the more difficult demands of everyday governance. Moreover, as a predominantly Pashtun movement, the Taliban found campaigning in the north of the country against the Shi'ite Hazaras, Dostum's Uzbeks and Massoud's Tajiks altogether harder going. In 1997, the Taliban suffered perhaps their worst defeat. A deal struck with a local commander, allowing their forces to enter Mazar-i-Sharif, rapidly went sour. Caught off guard in the centre of the city, some 600 Taliban were massacred, with ten top Taliban leaders either killed or captured in the bloody street fighting that followed. One of those captured was the Taliban foreign minister. Fighting in the north increasingly took on the characteristics of ethnic terror, verging at times on genocide, with quarter neither asked nor given by either side.

When the Taliban re-took Mazar-i-Sharif in August 1998 (by bribing and arranging defections within Dostum's forces), the UN estimated the subsequent total death toll from Taliban-led revenge massacres at between 5,000 and 6,000, with Shi'ite Hazara troops a particular target. The murder at the same time of eleven Iranian diplomats in the local consulate brought Afghanistan and Iran to the very brink of war. The Taliban's growing intolerance of Afghanistan's ethnic and religious minorities was also on display the following month when, after the siege and fall of the Hazara centre of Bamyan, they used explosives, rocket-propelled grenades (RPGs) and aircraft rockets to destroy and deface the massive local Buddhist statues in the region, declaring them an un-Islamic abomination. As the formerly fluid military front lines became increasingly static, however, the loosely organized *lashkar*-style Taliban military administration found itself struggling to man frontline trenches permanently. During 2001, more and more foreign fighters from the Central Asian republics, Uighur separatists and Arabs from Osama bin Laden's Al Qaeda network were drafted in to meet this requirement.[65]

Nevertheless, the flexibility that the Taliban had displayed in seizing power should have alerted Western forces to their adaptive capacities; that this did not happen was, as we shall see, a failure of both intelligence and imagination. The Taliban possessed unique advantages that later underpinned their effectiveness in fighting NATO forces, in particular an intimate knowledge of local *qawm* networks and a willingness to utilize whatever military technology came to hand. Crucial to their power base and financial structure was their ability to sit athwart a complex and murky nexus of transport mafias, drug smugglers and tribal militias, drawing sufficient income from all sides, through a combination of threats and promises, to maintain substantial field forces. For a movement that had grown from a core of perhaps a hundred men to over ten thousand within two years, dramatic expansion and contraction according to military circumstances also came as second nature. Therefore, none of these factors, when on display over the subsequent ten years, represented any kind of fundamental innovation in the core nature of the Taliban movement.

The Taliban had been forged in the crucible of Afghan and Pakistani politics. For many, their significance was local or, at most, regional. Indeed, the world had displayed remarkably little consistent interest in the affairs of Afghanistan since the withdrawal of Soviet forces. However, in 2001, all that was to change radically. The consequences of the fragmentation of Afghanistan were now about to manifest themselves on the world stage, and in the most dramatic fashion imaginable.

CHAPTER TWO

9/11 AND THE RESPONSE,
11–25 SEPTEMBER 2001

War has been waged against us by stealth and deceit and murder. This nation is peaceful, but fierce when stirred to anger. This conflict was begun on the timing and terms of others; it will end in a way and at an hour of our choosing.
President George W. Bush, Speech at the National Cathedral,
Washington, DC, 14 September 2001

THE HORRIFIC EVENTS of 11 September 2001 in New York City, Washington, DC and Shanksville, Pennsylvania, rocked the US and the world. It is impossible to fully understand the nature of the response from the administration of George W. Bush without grasping the fact that its members saw 9/11 as far more than appalling criminal acts perpetrated by a specific group. There was a strong sense that the attacks were a manifestation of wider global forces and linkages, to which the US needed to respond. This coalesced within the administration's thinking into a belief that a triad of threats had come together to form a potent and dangerous brew that posed an existential threat to the US and the West in general: terrorist groups with a global reach, the proliferation of weapons of mass destruction (WMD), and the malign influence of 'rogue states'. Together, these were seen as constituting as dangerous an environment as anything the Cold War had produced. The natural corollary of such a belief was that new ways of thinking about security policy, and about the role of military power in particular, were required to meet these challenges.

There are a number of elements of this analysis that are open to question. Why, for example, would a 'rogue state' run the gargantuan strategic risk of facilitating a WMD attack on the state with the greatest retaliatory military power the world had ever seen?[1] However, for the administration it meant that a bewildering array of global problems could be fed into this 'threat triad'. The consequence was that clarity, of both purpose and strategy, would be severely undermined during the early stages of the intervention. This set a pattern of inconsistency that was to persist, with fluctuating degrees of egregiousness, for the next decade.

From a very early stage, therefore, the coming intervention in Afghanistan was seen as a necessary, but not a sufficient, response to the attacks. To some extent, this was a natural psychological reaction to the enormity of the events. Meting out revenge on one particular terrorist group seemed inadequate for a country as powerful as the United States. However, it also reflected the temperament of the president himself: George W. Bush considered himself a visionary, comfortable with big 'strategic plays' and scornful of piecemeal, incremental policymaking unworthy of America's greatness.[2]

However, the nature of the response was also shaped by some deeply embedded assumptions and beliefs within the administration about foreign policy and the appropriate role of the military. The first of these was an obsessive, visceral disdain for 'nation-building'. The various peacekeeping operations in the 1990s of which the US had been a part – in the former Yugoslavia and Haiti, for example – were held up by key administration figures as definitive proof of the woolly-mindedness and strategic vacuity of the Clinton administration. The president, Condoleezza Rice (the national security adviser), Dick Cheney (the vice president) and Donald Rumsfeld (the secretary of defense) had all, very publicly, gone on record before and after the 2000 election deploring the use of American military forces for this purpose, and lamenting the waste of political and economic resources on such 'unfocused' and 'ill-judged' adventures. The attitude of the president can be gleaned from an exchange with the US commander of American forces in Kosovo (Brigadier General William David) during a July 2001 visit, at one point of which George Bush wistfully proclaimed, 'We've got to get you out of here.'[3]

The second deeply held belief, shared in particular by the president, Cheney and Rumsfeld, was the need to fundamentally 'transform' the military. This was partly linked to ideas about the appropriate purpose of military activity noted above. American troops were not to be used for 'policing' or for open-ended peacekeeping missions linked to nebulous notions of 'nation-building'. However, the vision went well beyond declarations of intent regarding the type of mission to be conducted. The way in which the US fought its engagements was to be fundamentally revolutionized. The technological innovations that had first been unveiled in the liberation of Kuwait in 1991 (Operation Desert Storm) had been heralded by some military analysts as a 'revolution in military affairs'. These innovations were to be honed and developed in a process that became known as 'transformation'. In his most definitive speech on what this was to entail, President Bush declared in 1999:

> This opportunity is created by a revolution in the technology of war. Power is increasingly defined, not by mass or size, but by mobility and swiftness. Influence is measured in information, safety is gained in stealth, and force is projected on the long arc of precision-guided weapons. This revolution perfectly matches the strengths of our country – the skill of our people and the superiority of our technology. The best way to keep the peace is to redefine war on our terms.[4]

Therefore, warfare and, presumably, the conflict dynamics that spurred it were to be made to conform to the particular technical strengths of the US military; as an example of putting the cart before the horse, this took some beating. The result was a highly technocratic view of the use of force that would come to equate operational victory on the battlefield with strategic and political success; this had predictably mixed results. The man charged with bringing this vision to life was Defense Secretary Donald Rumsfeld. Following the election, he set in motion a military transformation process designed to harness technological advances, in order to produce a leaner, more efficient military that could achieve combat success with fewer planes, vehicles, ships and (particularly) manpower. Rumsfeld threw himself vigorously into this task, and did not trouble to hide his irritation with what he saw as the Pentagon's (particularly the army's) 'obsession' with deploying overwhelming force, conceived in terms of massive quantities of troops and equipment. The direction of US transformation, therefore, was very much towards high-technology, rapidly deployed, short-duration combat missions, in which victory could be achieved quickly and forces speedily withdrawn to avoid the 'nation-building' quagmire that Rumsfeld believed the US State Department, under President Clinton, had wrought in the former Yugoslavia.[5]

These specific policy approaches stemmed from deeply held ideological commitments from some of the key players in the administration. A number of Washington-based think tanks had sprung up in the 1990s, united in their contempt for the manner in which the Clinton administration was conducting policy. One of the most influential was the Project for the New American Century. In June 1997, this organization produced a 'Statement of Principles' designed, as they saw it, to address the drift in US foreign and defence policy. This statement advocated an increase in defence spending and modernization of the armed forces; a call to challenge regimes hostile to US 'interests and values'; a demand that the US accepts its 'unique' role in preserving an international order conducive to its principles and interests; and a call to promote international 'political and economic freedom'.[6]

Of the twenty-five named signatories to these principles, a remarkable number were to gain senior positions in the future Bush administration. These included Dick Cheney, Donald Rumsfeld, Paul Wolfowitz and Zalmay Khalilzad, names that would recur continually as the intervention in Afghanistan unfolded. Further administration stalwarts on the list were Elliott Abrams, I. Lewis (Scooter) Libby and Peter Rodman, as well as Jeb Bush, the future president's younger brother. These principles brought together a number of ideological strands that had significant policy implications: the US should embrace leadership and shape the international order; security should be enhanced by putting America's military, economic and political weight behind the march of global 'democratization', not through inconclusive and draining 'peacekeeping' missions, but by challenging the repressive and dangerous regimes that prevented the natural desire of all peoples to embrace freedom (understood as Western-style liberal democracy). Out of these general principles flowed a number of policy priorities that bordered on the obsessive. In addition to those noted earlier, the need for enhanced national ballistic missile defence became a prominent theme. However, as we shall see, the issue that continued to gnaw away at key administration figures was the unfinished business with Saddam Hussein's Iraq.[7]

A NATION IN SHOCK

Thus, by 11 September 2001, the administration had already formed some strongly held, indeed ideologically rigid views on the nature of the threat environment and the appropriate way in which to engage with it. The events of that day, though they required some reordering of priorities, were seen as confirming rather than altering this basic analysis. However, while this book is critical of many of the policies that have been pursued in Afghanistan, it is important to recognize the significant mitigating circumstances surrounding the initial response to the attacks. Few policymakers have had to conduct their business in such a febrile atmosphere.

The attacks themselves were tailor-made for a twenty-first-century audience, which had grown used to 24/7, real-time media coverage. Amateur footage showed the moment that American Airlines Flight 11 hit the North Tower of the World Trade Center at 0846 (Eastern Daylight Time). By the time United Airlines Flight 175 hit the South Tower, some seventeen minutes later, news crews in the area had managed to get to the scene and filmed the second plane coming in. All around the world, people began to gather around the nearest TV screen as the devastating events unfolded as if scripted by a Hollywood disaster-movie director. The collapse of the South Tower at 0959, followed by the North Tower at 1028, turned the emotional screw still further. Reports began to come in of the crash of United Airlines Flight 93 in Shanksville, Pennsylvania, at 1003. Then, at 1030, American Airlines Flight 77 slammed into the Pentagon in Washington, DC.[8]

The, by now, blanket media coverage captured the shock, terror and confusion of bystanders, as well as the chaos as emergency services rushed to the scenes. Discomfort at the almost voyeuristic experience of witnessing such events as they unfolded was compounded when it became clear that the very moment that President Bush was given the news of the initial attacks had been captured on film. The president had been reading to seven- and eight-year-old children at an elementary school in Florida when first Karl Rove, his senior adviser, and then Andrew Card, the White House chief of staff, whispered in his ear the news of the second plane hitting the World Trade Center. With Card's confirmation of the second crash, it was clear that America was under attack. Presidents and prime ministers are usually afforded the luxury of being given catastrophic news in private – in offices, the back of limousines or on official flights. There is often time for them to recover their composure and to prepare a response before they face the glare of the cameras. That luxury was not given to President Bush, and the look of shock and confusion on his face when given the news would be replayed many times over the following weeks and months.

The president made a short speech at 0930 regarding the 'national tragedy' of the two (at that stage) crashed planes and then boarded Air Force One which was airborne by 0955. On Secret

Service advice, the plane headed not for Washington, but first for Barksdale Air Force Base in Louisiana, and then on to Offutt Air Force Base in Nebraska. Meanwhile the White House and the Capitol building were evacuated and, for the first time in history, all US airports were closed and civilian aircraft grounded. Secretary of Defense Rumsfeld placed the Armed Forces on Defence Condition 3 (DEFCON 3) for the first time since the Yom Kippur War of 1973.[9]

At Barksdale, the president taped a message, aired in the early afternoon, in which he vowed to hunt down and punish those responsible; then, at 1515, following his arrival at Offutt, he conducted a video teleconference with his main advisers. Rejecting his aides' advice, he then ordered Air Force One to return to Washington, DC. The helicopter ride from Andrews Air Force Base to the White House was both dramatic and emotional, as its flight path took it over the smouldering site of the Pentagon building. At 2030 the president gave a national address from the White House which included the memorable line: 'We will make no distinction between the terrorists who committed these acts and those who harbour them.'[10]

The question that reverberated around the world was: who could be responsible for such attacks? For the public, this was initially a puzzle. However, from the moment that the second plane hit the South Tower those who worked in the murky world of counterterrorism had no doubts about the identity of the organization and the main individual behind the attacks. In 1996, the Central Intelligence Agency (CIA) had set up a special 'Usama bin Laden' unit within its Counterterrorism Center; both bin Laden and the organization he had established, Al Qaeda, had been linked to a string of attacks around the world on American and Western interests. Both George Tenet, the CIA director from

1997 to 2004, and Richard Clarke, who was appointed by President Clinton as the first 'National Coordinator for Security, Infrastructure Protection, and Counterterrorism' in 1998 (and who continued in this position under President Bush), as well as a number of other intelligence and terrorism experts, had been issuing increasingly shrill warnings that it was only a matter of time before bin Laden and Al Qaeda launched attacks on the American homeland.[11] That time had arrived.[12]

The draining nature of these events would be compounded, for those planning the policy response over the succeeding weeks and months, by the outpouring of grief. Memorial services, meetings with victims' loved ones, commendations to those who acted hero-ically on the day and a seemingly endless stream of heart-rending tales would keep a finger in the open emotional wounds. However, what ratcheted the tension up more than anything was the fear that the attacks were just the first wave, and could be followed by even more devastating acts. Incessant 'intelligence chatter' suggested that chemical, biological, radiological (so-called 'dirty bombs') and even nuclear attacks were being planned. Such were the fears that Bob Woodward quotes a 'senior administration official' as confirming that covert monitoring teams, capable of detecting nuclear material and chemical and biological warfare agents, were deployed and at work in Washington, New York and six other cities.[13] The British ambassador to Washington, Christopher Meyer, conveyed the nature of the atmosphere within which policy was being made:

> Unless you were living in America at the time it is not easy to imagine the impact on Bush himself. He was responsible for the security of nearly three hundred million American lives. The fear of further atrocity was overwhelming.[14]

THE RESPONSE UNFOLDS

The specific responsibility for the attacks was quickly established. At the president's intelligence briefing on the morning of 12 September, CIA Director Tenet laid out the evidence that was already accumulating and that pointed unequivocally to Osama bin Laden and Al Qaeda. However, over the next days and weeks, this apparently clear line of responsibility was to become clouded, as a range of issues and actors were included in the list of malign factors that required attention as part of the unfolding response. On the evening of 11 September itself, Donald Rumsfeld had encouraged the president and his other key advisers to 'think broadly' about who might share responsibility. Iraq, Libya, Sudan and Iran were specifically mentioned, in addition to Afghanistan.[15]

This set a pattern for both the policy debates within the administration and the communication of its thinking to the American public and the world. While it was obvious from the outset that Al Qaeda in Afghanistan, and the Taliban if it got in the way, would be at least part of the initial focus, the response was clearly going to be broader and more diffuse than this. The implicit question that would plague the intervention over the next ten years was beginning to take shape. How did Afghanistan and its neighbourhood fit into a broader geopolitical vision of change that would increase the security of the US, its allies and the 'international community' more generally? Unfortunately, the answer to this question was never clearly formulated.

This ambiguity dates back to early in the post-9/11 policy response. At a meeting of the National Security Council on 12 September, Secretary of State Colin Powell asserted that 'the goal is terrorism in its broadest sense', beginning with Al Qaeda. Vice President Cheney declared in response that this opened the door to going after states that harboured terrorists, and introduced a soon-to-be-common theme by arguing, 'it's easier to find them than it is to find bin Laden'.[16] In his early speeches, President Bush confirmed that nothing less than terrorism itself was the target. However, he also ruled out neutrality as an acceptable option for those who may have considered it with his 'either you are with us or you are with the terrorists' declaration.[17] Finally, he declared in an early meeting with congressional leaders following the attacks that the enemy was 'a frame of mind'.[18]

In short order, therefore, the threat was conceptualized as being drawn from a list that included an individual (bin Laden), a group (Al Qaeda), a tactic (terrorism), hostile governments, neutral governments, and a state of mind. While some of this can be partly explained by the rhetorical flourishes demanded of a statesman in an hour of crisis, it also reflected an inchoate approach that would undermine the coming intervention in Afghanistan. Bounding a problem that contains so many loosely connected strands becomes impossible. There is no clear way to differentiate the vital from the peripheral; the essential from the desirable; or the threatening from the merely problematic.

The issue that continually resurfaced in the first few days, however, was Iraq. For a number of key figures in the administration, Saddam Hussein and Iraq were an obsession. On the evening of 12 September, Richard Clarke and a few colleagues were invited by the president to examine any possible linkages between the attack and Saddam Hussein. A mystified Clarke blurted out that Al Qaeda was clearly responsible. 'Look into Iraq, Saddam,' shot back an irritated president.[19]

Secretary of Defense Rumsfeld and his influential deputy, Paul Wolfowitz, pushed for Iraq to be included in the initial response from the very first post-attack meetings. This was clearly a corporate line in the civilian upper reaches of the Defense Department. Lieutenant General Greg Newbold, a straight-talking marine and director of operations for the Joint Chiefs of Staff, recalled in a later interview that, upon hearing of the attacks, he had returned immediately from London to a Pentagon whose corridors were still choked with the acrid odour of smoke. On encountering Douglas Feith, the undersecretary of defense for policy and a close associate of Donald Rumsfeld, he sought to reassure him by confirming that no effort was being spared on Afghanistan. Feith's response stunned Newbold: 'Why are you working on Afghanistan? You ought to be working on Iraq.'[20]

The debate about Iraq was a continual theme, and it was clear that it would have to be addressed at the two-day session set up by the president at Camp David from 15 September. However, initial planning for the response in Afghanistan was already under way. This was not conducted on a blank sheet of paper. The CIA's Usama bin Laden unit, set up in 1996, had grown from about a dozen officers to nearly fifty by 9/11.[21] Bin Laden's move from Sudan to Afghanistan in 1996 was the prelude to an increase in the tempo of Al Qaeda's activities, and a more explicit targeting of US interests. The suicide bombings at the US embassies in Tanzania and Kenya on 7 August 1998, which left 224 people dead, including twelve Americans, and the suicide bombing of the American warship USS *Cole* in Yemen on 12 October 2000, which killed seventeen sailors, led to a swelling of recruits in the Al Qaeda-run training camps in eastern Afghanistan.[22]

The reaction in Washington had been to increase efforts to neutralize the threat. A series of interagency plans were developed either to snatch bin Laden or to kill him. President Clinton had ordered cruise missile attacks on a pharmaceutical factory at al-Shifa in Sudan, alleged to be linked to the production of lethal chemical agents, and a camp in Khost, eastern Afghanistan, where intelligence had recently placed bin Laden. Debate rages to this day about whether the Sudanese facility was in reality linked to chemical weapons, and, although intelligence suggests that a dozen or so 'terrorists' were killed at Khost, bin Laden had already left the camp.[23]

Domestic opponents of Clinton poured scorn on the use of cruise missiles, implying that this was mere gesture politics. However, the other options were all proving problematic. A number of 'snatch or kill' schemes reached reasonably advanced stages of planning, but all foundered either on logistical obstacles or nervousness in one agency or another about US casualties, potential 'collateral damage', the likelihood of success, legality questions, or the reaction of Afghanistan's neighbours, in particular the Pakistanis. Any large-scale attempt to target bin Laden or to obliterate the camps using manned bombers or Special Forces would require the active assistance, or at the very least benign acquiescence, of Pakistan.[24] This was never forthcoming. Even the limited cruise missile strike at Khost necessitated the dispatching of the vice chairman of the Joint Chiefs of Staff, General Joe Ralston, to Islamabad to soothe ruffled Pakistani feathers and convince them that the missiles crossing their airspace were not Indian in origin.[25]

There were also significant diplomatic efforts. The Clinton administration attempted to convince the Taliban to hand over bin Laden, and made strenuous efforts to persuade Pakistan to cooperate in shutting down Al Qaeda's activities and to facilitate the capture of bin Laden – either directly or through its influence with the Taliban. All these efforts were to no avail, for the simple reason that such entreaties offered little strategic advantage for either the Taliban or the Pakistanis. The US, by this stage, had shown no appetite for taking the level of political, diplomatic, military and economic risk required to change these strategic calculations.

As far as the Taliban was concerned, Al Qaeda offered the prospect of a final Taliban victory over the Northern Alliance. The popular Western image of bin Laden as a robed 'fakir' squatting in a dusty cave in the mountains was not his image in eastern and southern Afghanistan. Nicknamed the 'Sheikh', he and his entourage travelled round in top-of-the-range four-wheel drives and dispensed money from what must have seemed to the poverty-stricken population a bottomless pit. He supplied the Taliban not just with significant financial support, but also with cadres of fanatical, experienced fighters. In return, the Taliban ceded control of the training camps in eastern Afghanistan to Al Qaeda and provided the latter with the sort of secure base that was a terrorist's dream.

For the Pakistanis, the Taliban and its spiritual leader, Mullah Omar, appeared to offer the perfect solution to Pakistan's 'Afghan problems'. Pakistan's interests were deemed to lie in having a rabidly anti-Indian government in Kabul that was Pashtun dominated, but sufficiently religiously austere to ensure that no hint of nationalist fervour would be created to inflame the 'Pashtunistan' question. If this government was willing to maintain the licit and illicit trade networks that had mushroomed, and was also committed to training and facilitating Kashmiri insurgents in Afghan camps, then all boxes appeared to be ticked.

This was a deeply embedded strategic calculation within the Pakistani security bureaucracy, and there is little evidence that its basic premises are much changed to this day. The last element also explains why the Pakistanis, and the ISI in particular, were willing to tolerate the influx of foreign fighters, even at the risk of attracting baleful attention from the Americans and others.

Apart from sharing the burden of supporting the Taliban, Al Qaeda's presence implicitly offered the Pakistanis the prospect of enhancing the capability of Kashmiri insurgents. The ISI believed, not very presciently, that it could effectively manage this new actor on the Afghan scene and maintain its dominant influence over the Taliban. Al Qaeda, therefore, became the hub of extremist activity in the region and established particularly close contacts with Pakistani domestic groups, including an elaborate logistics network – a connection the Pakistan government would come to regret.

The outgoing Clinton administration recommended that combating Al Qaeda should be a major priority for the new Bush government. In a conversation between the two men a month before Bush's inauguration, President Clinton suggested that Al Qaeda, Middle East diplomacy, North Korea and the South Asian nuclear competition should all be afforded higher priority than Iraq or national ballistic missile defence – the main foreign-policy themes of the Bush campaign.[26] The counterterrorism community also waded in to try and shape the attitude of the new administration. Various briefings by Tenet, Clarke and others to Condoleezza Rice highlighted the threat from Al Qaeda. Following on from previous practice, the new administration made further representations to the Taliban and the Pakistanis in the hope of facilitating the capture of bin Laden and the removal of the camps. In June 2001, Rice held a heated meeting with Abdul Sattar, the Pakistani foreign minister, in which Al Qaeda dominated the discussion. In early August, President Bush wrote a personal letter to Pakistani President Musharraf, also urging action against Al Qaeda.[27] Many of the plans that had been developed, to various stages of maturity, under the Clinton administration were dusted off. The bureaucracy was moving, but at bureaucratic speed.

The first formal meeting of the National Security Council's Principals Committee devoted specifically to Al Qaeda took place on 4 September, only a week before the attacks.[28] The committee approved a draft National Security Presidential Directive (NSPD) whose objectives were the elimination of the Al Qaeda network and its sanctuaries.[29] With bitterly ironic timing, the very day before the attacks the Deputies Committee[30] agreed a three-phase strategy. First, continue diplomatic pressure. Second, combine this with covert action to support anti-Taliban Afghans and attack Al Qaeda bases. Third, if all else fails try 'covert action to topple the Taliban leadership from within'.[31]

There was more than one bitterly ironic aspect to the unfolding tragedy. The first, to be seen more clearly in retrospect, was that an event that would have such a seminal effect on Afghanistan featured no Afghans in its planning or execution. The second concerned the identity of the middle-aged gentleman with the distinguished military bearing who was ensconced with Porter Goss, chairman of the House of Representatives Permanent Select Committee on Intelligence, and others in a breakfast meeting on Capitol Hill on the morning of 11 September. This was none other than General Mahmood Ahmad, head of the ISI.

Seldom can any senior official's position have changed so swiftly or so profoundly. General Ahmad had met a number of Washington 'movers and shakers', including the CIA director on 9 September. His attitude had been consistent: he was immovable on support for the Taliban and would make no commitment on cooperation over Al Qaeda. However, while being driven back from his 11 September meeting on Capitol Hill, his attention was drawn to the pall of smoke rising from the Pentagon.[32] The next major meeting he attended in Washington was conducted in a rather different tone.

President Bush had delegated to the State Department the job of bringing Pakistan 'on side' for the inevitable conflict to come. On 13 September, Richard Armitage, Colin Powell's deputy, summoned the Pakistani ambassador, Dr Maleeha Lodhi, and General Ahmad to the State Department. He laid out seven 'non-negotiable' steps the Pakistanis must take. These required the ending of all logistical support for Al Qaeda and public condemnation of the terrorist acts. In addition, fuel shipments were to be cut to the Taliban and recruits prevented from reaching Afghanistan. Basing, overflight and territorial-access rights were to be provided to US military forces and intelligence agencies, alongside active cooperation in the intelligence-gathering effort. Finally, if it continued to harbour Al Qaeda, the Pakistanis were required to break off all relations with the Taliban government.[33]

By the next day, President Musharraf had agreed to all seven demands. This represented, on the face of it, nothing less than the abandonment of Pakistan's Afghanistan policy. However, as always, the reality was rather more complex. The acceptance had followed a difficult meeting between Musharraf and his key military advisers. The deciding arguments, apparently, were that India would step into any vacuum if US–Pakistan relations ruptured irrevocably, at worst threatening Pakistan's existence, and at best fatally undermining the struggle in Kashmir. In addition, strong hints had been emerging from Washington that Pakistan itself 'would be at risk' from American action.[34]

It was clear that support (at least overt support) for the Taliban, let alone Al Qaeda, would have to cease. As we will see later in the book, this did not reflect a fundamental change in Pakistan's basic strategic beliefs – only recognition of the deep quandary in which it found itself. Musharraf immediately set about making the best of a phenomenally bad job. He conveyed to Washington, via the US embassy in Islamabad, that he would require a *quid pro quo* to mitigate the significant domestic backlash that acceptance of the US terms would occasion. Attention immediately turned to the sanctions that Pakistan was under due to the 1999 military coup and its nuclear weapons programme. The Bush administration quickly engineered the lifting of all sanctions and the resumption of aid flows.

Musharraf played his hand in terms of relations with Washington quite skilfully. A pattern developed in which he would point to the delicacy of his domestic position (with the spectre of 'Islamic extremism' to the fore) and the consequent need for Washington to avoid pushing him too hard. The irony of this, given the Pakistani military's traditional embrace of radical Islam both domestically and in Afghanistan, seemed to be lost on some in the Bush administration.[35] Soon, the logistical and basing support that Pakistan was to provide would be indispensable. This, combined with the desire not to stir up volatile Pakistani domestic politics, would significantly inhibit US robustness in dealing with Pakistan. As we shall see in the next chapter, this had very important consequences.

The two-day session scheduled to begin at Camp David on 15 September included the pivotal meetings that shaped the initial response. A number of issues had already begun to be highlighted even before the participants gathered.[36] A Defense Department briefing paper put together for the meetings argued that there were three priorities for initial action in the soon-to-be-launched 'war on terror'. These were Al Qaeda, Iraq and the Taliban. Interestingly, given the way the intervention in Afghanistan was to unfold over the next decade, only Al Qaeda and Iraq, not the Taliban, were deemed to be 'strategic threats' to the US.[37] In addition, while the Pakistani acceptance of the seven demands articulated by Armitage appeared to ameliorate some of the pressing logistical hurdles, the pre-Camp David indications of the state of military planning for action in Afghanistan had been received with very little enthusiasm by the administration.

US Central Command (CENTCOM), the geographical command responsible for the Afghan theatre and, significantly, Iraq, under the command of General Tommy Franks, had been forced to admit that there was no plan on the shelf for the invasion of the country.[38] All the indications were that a major invasion of Afghanistan by US forces would require months to prepare and would need to overcome daunting problems, given the inaccessible, landlocked geography of the country and the 'difficult' geopolitical relationships in the neighbourhood. This irritated the administration, since a large-scale build-up of military forces over a protracted period of time was the very thing that 'transformation' was designed to avoid. Furthermore, there would be serious domestic political consequences if several months elapsed before any sign of action that the American people would be likely to consider proportionate to the trauma inflicted on them. Something credible had to be done much sooner.

As expected, however, the first morning was dominated by Iraq. Rumsfeld raised the issue of including an attack on Iraq in the first stages of the response; but it was his deputy, Paul Wolfowitz, who really pressed home the argument. Powell countered – with what would later prove to be great prescience – that the solidarity and support shown by coalition partners and allies would evaporate if Iraq was hit at this stage. Rumsfeld responded with what would be a recurring theme of his contributions to the debates: that Afghanistan had little in the way of good targets for the military, whereas Iraq was replete with them. It appears that, at some point in the late morning, Bush indicated that there had been sufficient debate on Iraq and that attention should focus on Afghanistan.[39] This was the point at which it became clear that Iraq would not be part of the first wave of response; but the unspoken assumption was that it would most certainly return to the agenda at some point in the future. Few would have predicted just how soon that would be.

The most dramatic presentation came from CIA Director George Tenet. He articulated a plan, first mooted to the president two days before, that would involve inserting a number of CIA teams into northern Afghanistan to link up with key Northern Alliance (NA) commanders currently fighting the Taliban. The idea was that the CIA teams, armed with millions of dollars, would strengthen the sinews of the NA and set the scene for the arrival of US and coalition Special Forces, which would coordinate and direct massive US airpower onto Taliban and Al Qaeda positions, support NA ground offensives and hunt Al Qaeda suspects. It was hoped that this would be enough to turn the tide of battle, which had reached something of a stalemate, and facilitate both the overthrow of the Taliban (should it fail to turn against Al Qaeda, as the US was demanding) and the death or capture of bin Laden and his lieutenants.

This was a daring plan, not least because it was feared that the assassination six days before (on 9 September) of Ahmad Shah Massoud, the charismatic leader of the NA, would lead to demoralization, fragmentation and infighting in what had always been a shaky coalition of mostly Tajik, Uzbek and Hazara warlords with a long history of fighting among themselves and changing sides for tactical advantage.[40] However, the plan had a number of attractions. Specifically, it could be put into effect quickly, and it did not necessitate a large US commitment of ground forces. Given the likely alternatives emanating from CENTCOM, this guaranteed that the plan would receive an enthusiastic presidential welcome. George Bush pronounced himself delighted, and Donald Rumsfeld expressed guarded support. The defense secretary was slightly ambivalent because, while the plan was certainly 'transformational', with its light footprint and supposedly 'innovative' marriage of Special Forces, indigenous fighters and high-technology airpower, it promised to give the CIA an uncomfortable degree of authority in the early stages of the campaign.[41] Two days later, on 17 September, the president signed a Memorandum of Notification authorizing the CIA to put into effect the plan unveiled at Camp David.

For the next three weeks or so, meetings involving the key players in the administration fell into a fairly predictable pattern. At some point, the president would assert that, whatever happened, US forces must not be involved in 'nation-building'; Donald Rumsfeld would concur and lament the absence of lucrative 'target-sets' to hit in Afghanistan; and all would caution against falling into the Soviet trap of committing large numbers of troops and thus stimulating the Afghans' propensity for resisting foreign invaders. Taken together, these admonitions would provide a powerful inhibition to effective strategic thinking and, in particular, agility and adaptation as circumstances changed. It was strategy by metaphor and analogy. Thus, the enemy was 'Clintonian nation-building', and success was to be achieved by understanding that 'the general rule was to study what the Soviets had done and do the opposite'.[42] The preoccupations of the defense secretary were particularly dispiriting. While the constant focus on the absence of useful things to hit in Afghanistan was partly code for 'we should be in Iraq', it also reflected an obsession with the 'transformation' agenda and the appropriate function of the military; as if geopolitics could be reduced to a comparative analysis of tactical target lists.

This became increasingly significant, given the balance of power and influence within the administration. The senior members of the Bush team had a long and complex personal history of inter-relationships. Donald Rumsfeld had the distinction of being both the youngest and the oldest defense secretary. His stint in the job under President Gerald Ford, between 1975 and 1977, coincided with Dick Cheney's role as Ford's chief of staff. Indeed, the Cheney–Rumsfeld connection went back over thirty years, beginning with a notably unsuccessful job interview for Cheney with then Congressman Rumsfeld in 1968. However, the relationship improved and Rumsfeld became something of a mentor for Cheney in the Nixon administration, and also later when Cheney was a deputy assistant to President Ford while Rumsfeld was chief of staff. By the time of the Bush election victory in 2000 they had a close working relationship.

Colin Powell also had a long association with Dick Cheney. Cheney was President George H.W. Bush's defense secretary when Powell was the chairman of the Joint Chiefs of Staff during Operation Desert Storm. While this relationship was reasonably amicable, if never close, Powell's dealings with Paul Wolfowitz were more difficult. The pair had locked horns on more than one occasion when Wolfowitz was the undersecretary of defense for policy in the George H.W. Bush administration, and Powell made it known that he did not want Wolfowitz to serve as his deputy at the State Department in 2000, though Wolfowitz was keen to take the job. Powell had not worked closely with Rumsfeld prior to the formation of the 2000 administration because the latter had spent much of the 1980s and 1990s in the private sector. However, to add to the entanglements, Richard Armitage, whom Powell chose as his deputy on the basis of their close association going back to the days when they both worked under Defense Secretary Caspar

Weinberger in the first Reagan administration, had a less than positive relationship with Donald Rumsfeld.[43] Condoleezza Rice had also served in the George H.W. Bush administration, but had worked almost exclusively on policy towards the Soviet Union, and so had not been drawn into some of the more difficult inter-personal spats that had been simmering between her future colleagues.

Thus, the foreign policy team that President Bush began to assemble in 2000 came with a degree of personal baggage. This would prove to be significant when it came to the jockeying for influence within the White House. All administrations are shaped by who can most successfully command the presidential ear. Colin Powell would find that he had the most difficult task in this regard. Powell had launched his autobiography in a blaze of publicity in 1995, stimulating a protracted frenzy about whether he might tilt at the presidency.[44] Given his background as national security adviser in the second Reagan administration and chairman of the Joint Chiefs of Staff in the succeeding Bush administration, and his image as an all-action African-American hero, he was an attrac-tive potential candidate. For George W. Bush, therefore, he had been viewed more as a rival than a potential colleague. The Powell appointment was a signal that the foreign policy team was to be an experienced, heavyweight collection, but suspicion of Powell's motives and actions never quite evaporated.

Bush was personally much closer to Rice, Cheney and Rumsfeld. In time, he would come to lean increasingly on the experience and stature of the Cheney–Rumsfeld combination. Both men had already been dubbed in the press as the most powerful vice president and defense secretary in history. Such was the perception of Cheney's influence, in particular, that it spawned some black humour. Given his history of heart trouble, one of the beltway-insider jokes that periodically appear and are difficult to source suggested that George Bush was 'a heartbeat away from the presidency'. While George Bush was never as lacking in authority as this 'joke' suggests, it indicates the perception of Cheney's influence.

The most important institutional tension, in terms of the administration's Afghanistan policy, would be between the State Department and the Defense Department. Although, as noted above, Powell and Rumsfeld had relatively little direct history of animosity before 2000, the relationship was quick to deteriorate. Early on, the question of US commitments in Bosnia became an issue. Rumsfeld wanted an immediate withdrawal of American troops; Powell cautioned against this for fear of putting a strain on relations with key NATO allies. The State Department's 'victory' in this early dispute poured fuel on an already raging fire within the Defense Secretary about the iniquities of 'nation-building' and the suspect attitude of the State Department.[45]

Mutual recriminations between the Pentagon and the State Department became semi-institutionalized and were to be at their worst over Iraq. However, the influence of Rumsfeld, magnified by his closeness to Cheney and doubts over Powell that periodically resurfaced, ensured that Afghanistan policy increasingly became driven by the Pentagon. An additional factor was Powell's reluctance to take a strong stance on military issues. He was conscious that, given his senior military background, other members of the administration would be particularly sensitive to perceptions that he was seeking to influence defence matters. All these factors coalesced to ensure that, in the first few years of the Afghanistan intervention, the foreign policy of the Bush administration was shaped by the dominance of the Department of Defense to an extent that had few parallels in US political history.

OPERATION ENDURING FREEDOM BEGINS

The military intervention in Afghanistan was imminent. The Pentagon ventured the codename Operation 'Infinite Justice', believing that it captured just the right mix of steely resolve and legitimate intention. However, when it was gently pointed out that Muslims tended to see 'justice' – particularly of the 'infinite' variety – as more appropriately dispensed by Allah than by CENTCOM, the name was quickly changed to Operation 'Enduring Freedom'. Although the CIA plan called for a relatively small number of American ground forces, there were still some planning headaches to overcome. There was a pressing need for overflight agreements and for contiguous basing and access rights, so that CIA and Special Forces teams could be introduced and resupplied. Furthermore, once manned aerial bombing began in earnest, there would also be the requirement for bases that enabled Combat Search and Rescue (CSAR) missions to be launched for any downed pilots.

The problem was less acute in the south, as it was confidently expected that Oman would provide facilities, US carriers in the Arabian Sea could enable a 'lily-pad' approach, and, most importantly, Pakistan had secretly agreed to provide basing and access rights for US personnel. There were greater difficulties, however, in the north of the country.[46] Although Putin had surprised the world by supporting, in principle, 'temporary' US bases in the Central Asian countries bordering Afghanistan, securing the formal rights was proving tricky.[47] The Americans were particularly keen to use the old Soviet air base at Karshi-Khanabad (K2) in Uzbekistan. However, Uzbek President Islam Karimov was driving a hard bargain.

Karimov was concerned about a backlash from the Islamic Movement of Uzbekistan (IMU), the Islamist group that was conducting an anti-government terrorist campaign and seeking Karimov's overthrow. He was keen to ensure that the US was interested in a long-term strategic partnership, rather than a tactical short-term one that would eventually leave him at the mercy of his considerable number of enemies. The prospect of an extensive aid package was also attractive. Karimov's refusal to commit to a formal agreement was causing increasing angst among American military planners, to such an extent that Rumsfeld himself was forced to visit Tashkent, on 5 October, to offer the sort of commitments the Uzbek president was seeking. Finally, on 12 October, a formal agreement was signed that hinted at American security guarantees for Uzbekistan and a significant aid package.[48]

However, events were already moving forward. While the Bush administration worked out its policy response, all eyes were shifting from Washington to the mountains and plains of Afghanistan. Al Qaeda had announced itself to a largely ignorant world on 11 September 2001. A little more than two weeks later, Americans were about to enter Afghanistan in deadly earnest.

CHAPTER THREE

'BOOTS ON THE GROUND':
From the arrival of the CIA to the emergency Loya Jirga, 26 September 2001–June 2002

Gentlemen, I want to give you your marching orders, and I want to make them very clear. I have discussed this with the President and he is in full agreement. You are to convince the Northern Alliance to work with us and to accept US military forces into the Panjshir Valley so that we can utilize that area as a base for our operations. But, beyond that your mission is to exert all efforts to find Usama bin Ladin and his senior lieutenants and to kill them . . . I don't want bin Ladin and his thugs captured, I want them dead . . . They must be killed. I want to see photos of their heads on pikes. I want bin Ladin's head shipped back in a box filled with dry ice. I want to be able to show bin Ladin's head to the President. I promised him I would do that . . . Have I made myself clear?[1]

Cofer Black, director of the CIA's Counterterrorism Center, briefing the first CIA team to enter Afghanistan after 9/11

ON 26 SEPTEMBER, a lone helicopter took off from Dushanbe in Tajikistan. At 1445 it deposited the first seven-man CIA team into the Panjshir valley of north-east Afghanistan. This team, code-named 'Jawbreaker', was led by a fifty-nine-year-old CIA veteran, Gary Schroen. The team members brought with them an array of communications equipment, and the small matter of $3 million in cash (Schroen, according to his own account, was to spend a total of $5 million during his forty days in Afghanistan). This second element was to be the CIA's most potent weapon, and represented the first tranche of a multi-million-dollar effort to co-opt Afghan allies to the fight against the Taliban and Al Qaeda.[2]

As noted above, Cofer Black, director of the CIA's Counterterrorism Center had, a week earlier, given Gary Schroen and his colleagues an admirably clear outline of the mission for the Jawbreaker teams that were to be deployed in Afghanistan. On the night of their arrival, Schroen met Aref Sarwari, who had been head of the intelligence operation of slain Northern Alliance leader Ahmad Shah Massoud, and handed over $500,000. The following night he met General Mohammed Fahim, the Tajik commander who had taken over the leadership of the NA from Massoud, and Dr Abdullah Abdullah, the NA 'foreign minister'. The sum handed over to Fahim was a cool $1million.

This was by no means the first contact between the CIA and NA commanders. Over the previous months and years there had been periodic attempts to build an intelligence relationship. Indeed, between February and March 2001, five CIA teams had visited the Panjshir valley to liaise with the various groupings.[3] However, this was their first meeting post-9/11 and the atmosphere was energized.

The Afghans' questions were pointed. What was the US plan? How long would the US stay? How did the NA fit into the plan? Schroen convinced them that the US was there to bring down the Taliban and eliminate Al Qaeda, and that the Americans recognized the place of the NA as the only credible Afghan force currently opposing the Taliban.[4]

The difficult issue for Fahim concerned indications from Schroen that the CIA intended to provide direct support to specific NA commanders, such as the Uzbek General Rashid Dostum and Ismail Khan, the Tajik commander from Herat. Fahim wanted everything coordinated through him. However, he possessed neither the charisma nor the deep respect that Massoud had commanded, and it was clear that the CIA was not going to subcontract the war in the north and west to Fahim simply so that he could consolidate his personal position.

This issue introduced the Americans to what would be a recurring problem. The complex internal politics and rivalries between key NA commanders would require constant 'finessing' from the CIA and Special Forces teams over the next few weeks. This became clear when the second Jawbreaker team (Team Alpha), inserted on 16 October, was sent to liaise with General Dostum, who was operating around Mazar-i-Sharif. The team found that there were three NA commanders conducting operations in this geographical area, the others being General Mohammed Atta, a Tajik commander, and General Mohaqqeq, a Hazara. Relations between them were strained, particularly between Dostum and Atta. Eventually, Team Alpha and the Special Forces personnel complementing it had to split into two – one element with Dostum, the other with Atta.[5]

Partly, these recurring tensions had to do with the long and complex history of local rivalries. However, they also reflected the levels of money the CIA was directing towards local warlords. Having a dedicated CIA team became a sure route to significant riches. While some money was spent on supplies and logistic requirements for the fighting, a significant proportion also acted as seed money for future business interests.[6] The huge profits from these interests would end up in property in Afghanistan, international bank accounts, business buy-ups, or even as stake money for drugs and other smuggling operations. Little, if any, would find its way through taxation into the coffers of the future Afghan government. CIA dollars were further entrenching the power and influence of the northern warlords. This was to constrain, still more, the range of credible political options once fighting had ceased.

Washington, too, was gearing up for action. The president had used his 20 September address to the joint session of Congress to publicly outline three demands of the Taliban: to release all foreign nationals; close all terrorist training camps; and hand over every terrorist. There was little confidence within the administration that the Taliban would comply, but the ISI encouraged the belief that there were hitherto hidden elements of 'moderate' Taliban ready to oppose Mullah Omar and hand over bin Laden.

The ISI was in a difficult position. In the immediate post-9/11 period the organization was trying to regain its balance after the surprise of the attacks and the fast pace of unfolding events. It is doubtful whether, in this early period, the ISI had reconciled itself to abandoning Mullah Omar. Indeed, the Taliban ambassador to Islamabad, Mullah Abdul Salam Zaeef, recalls a post-9/11 meeting with General Mahmood Ahmad at the embassy, during which the general pledged Pakistan's (or at least the ISI's) solidarity with the Taliban in the coming *jihad* against America.[7] However, as the Taliban's position worsened, and after Musharraf had bowed to intense US pressure to sack Ahmad, Zaeef notes a further meeting, at which senior ISI figures suggested that 'moderate' Taliban should move against the more 'fundamentalist' sections of the movement, and replace Mullah Omar.[8] It was clear, by this later stage, that the ISI was desperately casting around for any solution that would save the Taliban in some form, and forestall the strategic nightmare of a total NA victory.[9] Nevertheless, it is extremely unlikely that the ISI's conception of who was 'moderate' and 'fundamentalist' would chime with the understanding of these terms in Washington. The evidence suggests that the ISI was engaged in no more than tactical sparring. For example, its new-found concern with 'fundamentalism' is difficult to square with the fact that the organization had spent the previous five years assidu-ously searching out ideologically unsound elements in the Taliban and giving them up to Mullah Omar. Zaeef poured scorn on such overtures.

There was also no sign of progress on the US demand that all terrorists should be handed over – most importantly, of course, bin Laden. The explanation most often advanced for the refusal of the Taliban to produce bin Laden is that the honour code of *Pashtunwali* prevented it. While this code would certainly have inclined the Taliban to resist such demands, too little attention is paid to the comparable power relationship. It would have been no easy task, by September 2001, for the Taliban leadership to 'turn over' bin Laden, even had it so wished. He commanded a hard core of fanatical and battle-hardened followers, whose numbers were to swell exponentially in the immediate aftermath of 9/11, with foreign recruits eager to join the *jihad* against the Americans. These recruits were to perform more robustly in the battles to come than most of the indigenous Afghans.[10] British journalist Christina Lamb conducted a number of interviews with defecting Talibs in late September. The comments of one cast doubt on the conventional wisdom:

We laughed when we heard the Americans asking Mullah Omar to hand over Osama bin Laden . . . The Americans are crazy. It is Osama bin Laden that can hand over Mullah Omar – not the other way around.[11]

It was clear, at an early stage, that demands to sweep aside the Taliban leadership and turn over key Al Qaeda members were unlikely to bear fruit. Matters would have to be settled by force.

AMERICAN AIR POWER ENTERS THE FRAY

After a number of delayed starts, US air power was about to enter the fray in earnest. On 7 October, President Bush addressed the nation and confirmed that, because the Taliban had failed to comply with his demands, air operations were under way. For the Jawbreaker team on the ground, and certainly for the NA commanders, the initial results were a disappointment. On the first day, thirty-one targets were struck across the country, by a combination of aircraft and Tomahawk Land Attack Missiles (TLAMs), including a number launched from British submarines; but these were generally static sites, such as the Taliban's rudimentary air defence systems, tank repair facilities and storage depots. While damaging these sites had some use, the list was largely exhausted after the first couple of days. As Donald Rumsfeld had frequently opined, Afghanistan was not a rich environment for the traditional types of air target. The NA commanders had been expecting the US Air Force to bomb Taliban and Al Qaeda frontline combat positions.[12]

For the next few weeks the pattern continued. In the early stages, there was still only one CIA team in the country and, therefore, there were no ground forces to direct aircraft onto targets.

Without ground confirmation that sites were clear of civilians, and with no laser-guided equipment to pinpoint enemy positions, pilots were reduced to hitting the type of traditional command-and-control and logistical sites that would be important in a war between major states, but that were much less significant in the Afghan context. A further complication was that the CIA was not allowed to employ the Special Operations Forces Laser Acquisition Marker (SOFLAM) because only military personnel were permitted to use it.[13]

It was not until mid- to late October, when more Special Forces and CIA teams were introduced, that the air campaign began the switch to supporting NA forces on the ground. When this change in targeting occurred, the effect was dramatic. By early November, about 80 per cent of air sorties were directly supporting NA, CIA and Special Forces teams in combat.[14] Although assessing combat numbers is a very inexact science in Afghanistan, most estimates put the Taliban strength at between 40,000 and 60,000, of whom between a fifth and a quarter were 'foreign fighters' – either Al Qaeda or part of the recent influx of *jihadists* arrived to take on the Americans.[15] Ranged against them were approximately 20,000 NA troops, often tied to their individual commanders more by personal and kinship bonds than by any sense of a broad, coherent movement.[16] However, the expertise of the CIA and Special Forces teams, and the devastating effects of modern airpower, were to render this numerical disparity irrelevant.

A key series of battles raged around Mazar-i-Sharif. General Dostum's forces attacked through the Darya Suf river valley to the east and General Mohaqqeq's pushed through the Darya Balkh river valley to the west. Meanwhile, General Atta's troops surrounded the village of Akopunk further west. The key battle was on 5 November and was typical of the warfare being conducted. The Taliban and its allies had dug into fortified defensive positions in strength, awaiting an attack from Dostum. Such scenarios had been commonplace in the civil war, and usually ended in a bloody stalemate. This time a US Special Forces team identified the Taliban positions for attacking aircraft. Incoming MC-130 planes dropped two BLU-82 bombs two minutes apart. These 15,000 lb monsters (with the innocent-sounding nickname of 'Daisy Cutters') obliterated the fixed Taliban positions in a devastating fireball and shockwave. General Dostum and his men then launched a cavalry charge on horseback to finish off the few, badly disorientated, surviving enemy troops.[17] By 10 November, Mazar had fallen.

A similar story was unfolding further east, where the NA commander, Bismullah Khan, supported by a Special Forces team and ubiquitous air power, had driven the Taliban out of Taloqan. There were now two Taliban forces in headlong retreat. The first was heading east from Mazar, and the other was heading west from Taloqan. Both were converging on the city of Kunduz, soon to be the last remaining Taliban stronghold in the north.

The speed of events as they had unfolded since the end of October had caught both Washington and Islamabad by surprise. Up until then, there had been much talk of 'quagmires' and 'hunkering down' for the winter. Many pundits in Pakistan had confidently predicted that the Americans would face a long, bloody struggle to get rid of the Taliban. This basic analysis was shared by the ISI. Indeed, even as the Pakistanis were providing logistical and intelligence support to the US, other ISI officers were organizing a major supply operation for the Taliban by utilizing the army's National Logistics Cell trucking fleet.[18] This was before, during and after Musharraf had sacked General Ahmad as head of the ISI on 7 October, in an attempt to increase his own credibility and influence with the US in the coming conflict. The unfolding rout of the Taliban was turning into a strategic disaster for the Pakistanis. However, worse was to come.

In Washington, the rapidly developing situation on the ground was a more pleasant surprise, but it still necessitated some important decisions. The question of Kabul came to dominate discussion within the administration. The Pakistanis were desperate to avoid the NA occupying the city. Their fear was that this would pre-empt negotiations about Afghanistan's political future, and at the same time institutionalize non-Pashtun (and anti-Pakistani) control of the capital. A series of forlorn requests went out from Washington to NA commanders, pleading with them to desist from entering Kabul until a UN or 'Pashtun' force could join them to avoid the perception of NA domination.[19] The rather obvious problem with this approach was that neither a coherent Pashtun nor a UN force was currently available, or likely to be available any time soon. Events on the ground were simply moving too fast to put such measures in place. On 11 November, Bamiyan fell, and on 13 November the Taliban abandoned Kabul. General Fahim quickly moved a sizeable force into the city to 'maintain order'. On the same day, Ismail Khan's forces captured Herat in the west.

Meanwhile, the city of Kunduz was under siege from NA generals Dostum, Daoud and Baryalai Khan. Thousands of Taliban and Al Qaeda fighters were trapped in its environs, and there were strong and persistent rumours from multiple sources that a large number of Pakistani advisers and ISI officers were amongst them.[20] Despite denials at the time from both the US and the Pakistani governments, it is now widely believed that an informal agreement was reached at the highest level that allowed Pakistan to complete the evacuation of its personnel. In the few days around 23 November, two planes, probably making multiple sorties, flew in and out of Kunduz, ferrying passengers to Pakistan.[21]

Most of the controversy about this incident now surrounds the question of who else, apart from Pakistani officials, also got out this way. It is impossible to verify the claims and counterclaims, but it seems unlikely that key allies of the ISI, whether Taliban or Al Qaeda, would have been refused places on the planes. Their knowledge of ISI activities, or even their very presence, could have become an embarrassment for the Pakistanis if captured. This incident reveals two things. First, elements of the Pakistani security bureaucracy were playing a double game with the Americans and had not abandoned the Taliban or fundamentally revised their strategic calculations. Second, Musharraf was perceived as an indispensable asset by the US administration, which was clearly willing to make many concessions to maintain his support. Kunduz finally fell on 26 November.

THE CAMPAIGN IN THE SOUTH AND EAST

None of the main Uzbek and Tajik commanders of the NA had either the motivation or the capability to pursue the Taliban, or to hunt Al Qaeda in the south and east. These majority-Pashtun areas would be highly resistant to what would inevitably be seen as an NA attempt to take over the whole of Afghanistan. The presence of Fahim or Dostum, for example – figures who had acquired a fearsome reputation – would stimulate major Pashtun resistance and cause uproar in relations with the Pakistanis. In any case, with the seizure of Kabul, all the NA objectives had been largely achieved, and there was no motivation for senior NA figures to venture south or east. The problem the coalition faced was that there appeared little evidence, in the early stages of the conflict, to indicate that the Pashtun tribes in these areas were, themselves, preparing to rise up against the Taliban.

The model that had worked so well in the north and west appeared to be foundering on the social and political dynamics of southern and eastern Afghanistan. Only four groups of actors had wielded significant power there for some time: the Taliban; Al Qaeda; the ISI; and the complex web of transport mafias and drug barons interacting with minor local thugs and warlords. Decades of war had atomized traditional village, district and even tribal leadership structures.

The search for any anti-Taliban Pashtuns of 'influence' who had somehow kept off the Taliban and ISI radar was proving frustrating. To survive, all had been forced either to leave the country or to make accommodations with the Taliban. Neither the CIA nor the British intelligence service, MI6, could identify many influential Pashtuns to stimulate an anti-Taliban rising. They fell back on responding to suggestions coming from the ISI or empowering the local thugs and warlords noted above. This was to have a disastrous impact on the subsequent political dynamics of Afghanistan.

However, one figure of substance did emerge, who was neither a predatory warlord nor a stooge of the ISI: this was Hamid Karzai. A very senior figure in the Popalzai tribe of the Durrani Pashtuns, Karzai's background placed him firmly within the Pashtun tribal elite. Born in the village of Karz, near Kandahar, Karzai emerged on the national scene during the Soviet occupation, when he became a senior figure in the Afghan National Liberation Front, led by Sebghatullah Mujadidi. However, based as he was in Pakistan, his role was advisory and diplomatic, and did not include significant battlefield experience – the traditional source of influence for an aspiring leader in Afghanistan's violent recent history. He was deputy foreign minister from 1992 to 1994 in the Rabbani government, but resigned as the *mujahidin* descended into internecine conflict. Karzai was initially sympathetic to the Taliban, and briefly considered acting as their representative at the UN, but became disillusioned both by the glaring excesses of the movement and the manner in which it was increasingly manipulated by the ISI. He established himself in Quetta, in the Pakistani province of Balochistan, and began to use the international contacts he had built up over the years to draw attention to the increasing brutality of the Taliban, and to agitate for a national Loya Jirga.

Inevitably, this attracted baleful attention from both the Taliban and the ISI. In 1999, his father, Abdul Ahad Karzai, the then chief of the Popalzai and a significant anti-Taliban figure in his own right, was assassinated by Taliban agents. To this day, Hamid Karzai believes that the ISI also had a hand in the murder.[22] He enhanced his reputation by leading the convoy of family members and tribal leaders from Quetta to Kandahar, where the family grave site was located. This was a considerable personal risk, but the Taliban calculated that interference or violence against the funeral arrangements of such a notable tribal dignitary would be a propaganda disaster.

Therefore, by October 2001, Karzai had become a significant Pashtun, anti-Taliban figure. However, the CIA was slow to take seriously his credentials as a potential leader of a southern uprising. Although reasonably well known to the agency, even before 9/11, he was viewed as a somewhat cerebral character, who, while urbane and charming, commanded no significant military capabilities of his own, and had no direct military experience. Nevertheless, contacts were re-established, and when Karzai, on 9 October, entered Afghanistan from Balochistan, it is claimed riding pillion on a motorcycle, he carried with him a CIA-issued satellite phone.[23]

His ultimate destination was Tarin Kowt, the capital of Uruzghan province, where he intended to rendezvous with a few hundred armed supporters. This was a direct challenge to Mullah Omar. Tarin Kowt was only 25 miles east of the Taliban leader's traditional family base and 70 miles north of Kandahar, the spiritual home of the Taliban and their de facto capital. The fact that Karzai was originally from the Kandahar area made the challenge all the more personal and would be sure to trigger a furious response should Karzai's presence be detected.

Within a few days, Karzai's supporters had seized the airfield at Tarin Kowt; but in doing so they revealed their presence. The Taliban sent a sizeable force up from Kandahar to intercept them. Soon Karzai and his men were surrounded and in deep trouble. Accounts of what happened next differ. The CIA director at the time, George Tenet, is adamant that Karzai requested extraction on 3 November and was airlifted out on the night of 4–5 November and flown to Pakistan. Ahmed Rashid, by contrast, quotes Karzai as saying that he eluded the Taliban and only left the area at the CIA's request, and that he was then flown to an airfield in Helmand province. A clue as to which account is more persuasive might be gleaned from Tenet's assertion that Karzai was extremely keen for his extraction to remain secret, so as not to demoralize his men and undermine his reputation.[24]

However, all are agreed that on 14 November Karzai returned to Tarin Kowt, supported by a six-man CIA team (codenamed 'Echo'), a dozen Special Forces personnel, and a Joint Special Operations Command (JSOC) unit containing three men.[25] He immediately set about rallying local fighters to rise up against the Taliban. On 16 November a large Taliban force of approximately five hundred was spotted advancing on the area. Over the next two days fierce skirmishes ensued, and at one point it appeared that Karzai's forces would be overrun. However, the US Special Forces team called in a series of air strikes on the Taliban convoy and positions, and by the end of 18 November some 300 Talibs lay dead, with the remainder fleeing in disarray.

This was an important military victory that helped unhinge the Taliban position in the south; but of even more significance was the effect it had on Karzai's reputation. He could now claim to be a military, as well as a political, leader, and his increased credibility would soon place him at the centre of events in Afghanistan. The immediate consequence was that he could now rally local forces for the push towards the main objective – Kandahar.[26]

As Karzai's group, with its American complement, moved towards Kandahar from the north, another force was approaching from the south. This force was commanded by a Pashtun warlord called Gul Agha Sherzai, who was destined to become something of a symbol for the corruption and failed governance of southern Afghanistan after the conflict. Sherzai had been governor of Kandahar from 1992, before fleeing in the face of Taliban pressure in 1994. The ISI permitted him to establish himself in Quetta, where it offered some protection, maintained a careful eye on his activities, and kept its options open. When the CIA came calling, demanding likely candidates to stimulate a Pashtun uprising in the south, the Pakistanis were able to produce Sherzai. Now, loaded with CIA dollars and supported by US Special Forces, he had raised a militia and was heading back to reclaim Kandahar. Fierce battles raged to the north and south of the city until, on 6 December, Mullah Omar and his key lieutenants fled.[27]

Sherzai installed himself in the city and became the de facto provincial governor, a position that Karzai would later be compelled to endorse, despite an expressed preference for another candidate. Sherzai put his CIA windfall, and the continued patronage of the agency, to use by financing business interests that, by one estimate, generated an income that exceeded $1.5 million per month. This figure was accumulated by providing US bases with goods and services, including the supply of a local workforce. Sherzai claimed fees both directly from the US military for supplying this labour and from the workers themselves by taking a chunk of their salaries.[28] The figure is also strongly rumoured to have been swelled by participation in the drugs trade. Sherzai was exactly the type of political leader that the politically sensitive southern provinces and districts did not need. He would ruthlessly favour his own tribe, the Barakzai Pashtuns, and provided, as one observer put it, the most egregious example of an appointment made for political expediency rather than on merit.[29] However, he is a shrewd political operator and survivor, and is still influential to this day. Indeed, his influence grew to the extent that he was widely tipped as a presidential candidate for the 2009 elections, before withdrawing in May of that year. His standing was enhanced by being named Radio Free Afghanistan's 'Person of the Year' in 2008 – an award that (to adapt Tom Lehrer's famous phrase) probably marked the moment satire died.[30]

While the Taliban was being routed in the south, events in the east of the country were even more dramatic and would later prove to be highly controversial. CIA attempts to put together a credible 'Eastern Alliance' that would mirror the success of the north were proving to be something of an embarrassment. The one potential commander of stature, a Pashtun with a national profile called Abdul Haq, had, rather recklessly, entered Afghanistan with only a small group of companions. Rejecting the offer of a CIA phone (he had a mutually suspicious relationship with the agency) he was captured, tortured and hanged by the Taliban on 25 October.[31] As a consequence, the CIA was forced to be even less discerning in its choice of ally than in other parts of the country.

The result was that it empowered a series of thugs and minor warlords, whose influence rested almost entirely on what they could buy with CIA dollars, and whose motivation stemmed exclusively from the same source. Three 'commanders' would form the bulk of the 'Eastern Alliance'. These were Hazrat Ali, Haji Zaman and Haji Zahir. Hazrat Ali, in particular, was the archetype of what would come to be called the 'American warlords' – 'leaders' who had little independent influence, but whose power grew on the back of American patronage.[32] A major obstacle to positive change in Afghanistan, they enhanced their power by preying on the local population and enriched themselves by political corruption and outright criminality. The better-known 'warlord' figures such as Fahim, Dostum and Khan, while acquiring deserved reputations for ruthlessness and brutality, could at least lay some claim to a genuine support base. The 'American warlords', many of whom were former Taliban sympathizers, bought support by cultivating American patronage as intelligence 'assets' deemed helpful in tracking down Al Qaeda and Taliban fighters.

Hazrat Ali was a minor figure, loosely associated with the NA, from the small Pashai tribe of north-east Afghanistan. This tribe, which is sprinkled through the mountainous areas of the Hindu Kush, is rather looked down upon by the Pashtuns of the plains around Jalalabad. Indeed, the Pashai in general, and Ali in particular, are often referred to by the Pashto insult *shurrhi*: the nearest English colloquial translation is probably 'hillbilly'. Yet, he would come to be the dominant figure in post-Taliban Jalalabad politics purely on the back of the support of the CIA and the US military. Such was the American largesse that, soon after the fall of the

Taliban, he was able to field a militia of some 18,000. Ali, Zaman and Zahir spent an inordinate amount of time bickering and attempting to maximize their share of the spoils. In one indicative incident, as the fighting raged the 'Eastern Alliance' set up a checkpoint and charged US Special Forces soldiers $50 each to go through.[33]

The rapid recruitment of Ali, Zahir and Zaman was spurred by intelligence reports claiming that bin Laden had fled Kabul just before its fall and was heading towards Jalalabad.[34] Gary Berntsen, who had taken over from Schroen as the senior CIA ground commander, quickly decided to send a CIA team (codenamed 'Juliet') in pursuit, guided by Hazrat Ali's nephew and ten companions. That evening, 18 November, they arrived in the city.[35] Over the next week, bin Laden, along with about 1,000–1,500 men, moved south towards Tora Bora, the cave complex of the White Mountains, about 30 miles south-east of Jalalabad. This is a harsh area – about 36 square miles of caves, peaks and rugged rock formations at high altitude – that bin Laden knew well from his anti-Soviet days.[36] During the last week of November, Team Juliet called in air strikes on bin Laden's position in the Milawa valley, with the result that he and his followers retreated further into the caves and mountains. The scene was set for one of the most controversial episodes of the entire intervention.

ESCAPE FROM TORA BORA

Bin Laden and his followers were apparently trapped in the forbidding caves. However, American commanders on the ground were uneasy. There were only a few dozen Special Forces personnel in the area, mostly American, with perhaps a dozen British and a handful of other nationalities. While this was sufficient to call in heavy air bombardments, it was not nearly enough to conduct effective ground combat and to block the possible escape routes over the border into Pakistan. The vast bulk of the forces were followers of Hazrat Ali, Haji Zaman and Haji Zahir. Zaman was positioned to the west, Ali to the centre, and Zahir to the east. The Pakistanis had issued tentative assurances that their Frontier Force troops would block off escape routes to the rear. None of these deployments or promises filled Berntsen with confidence.

The 'Eastern Alliance' was proving to be thoroughly unreliable. A US Delta Force commander in the area, who was later to write an account under the pseudonym 'Dalton Fury', recalled that 95 per cent of the fighters had never heard of 9/11 and couldn't care less. In addition, many of their families had benefited monetarily from bin Laden and Al Qaeda, and the former was something of a hero in the region. If this was not enough, the battles were in the middle of Ramadan, and the fighters had a habit, if home was near, of returning at night to their families to break their fast together, and were obviously hungry and weakened during the day.[37] Their only motivation, as noted above, was money, and many of them would prove happy to switch their services to a higher bidder. In addition, there was no evidence that the Pakistani troops had deployed right into the mountain passes to block the escape, or that they would prove reliable even if they did, given the close relationship those border troops had previously established with the Taliban and Al Qaeda.

Given all this, Berntsen made strenuous, repeated and increasingly desperate pleas for more US forces to be deployed to do the job. What was required was a classic 'block and sweep' operation that would, as the term implies, block off escape routes while sweeping through the cave system, ferreting out the Al Qaeda fighters.[38] Berntsen requested that a Battalion of Rangers (about 800) be immediately sent to the area.[39] He did not receive a formal reply. His boss, Henry Crumpton, head of special operations for the CIA's Counterterrorism Center, made personal requests to General Tommy Franks, head of CENTCOM, to send the more than 1,000 US marines who were currently idling and itching for action south-west of Kandahar. In addition, there were a further 1,000 troops from the army's 10th Mountain Division divided between a base in Uzbekistan and Bagram Air Base near Kabul.[40] As early as the end of November, Crumpton went to the White House to brief President Bush and Dick Cheney, repeated the request he had made to Franks, and spoke as bluntly as it is possible to do to a president, explaining that the Pakistanis were unreliable, the local Afghans demotivated and 'we are going to lose our prey if we're not careful'.[41]

It was clear that something of an obsession had developed in the White House, Pentagon and CENTCOM with regard to minimizing the number of US troops on the ground. Soon, a new metaphor would be added to the list of aphorisms and analogies that took the place of strategic clarity: a 'light footprint'. Rumsfeld and Franks were in total agreement on the need to minimize as far as possible the presence of US forces, and would stick rigidly to this approach, come what may.[42] The atmosphere this created within the US command can be gauged from the comments of Maj. Gen. Warren Edwards, a senior officer in CENTCOM:

The message was strong from the national level down: We are not going to repeat the mistakes of the Soviets. We are not going to go in with large conventional forces ... This was so embedded in our decision-making process, in our psyche ... There was a constant – in our mind – disconnect between mission and assets allowed to be available to do the mission.[43]

Fierce aerial bombardments continued, causing significant casualties even among those fighters dug into the cave complexes; but the topography provided many secure hiding places.

Virtually all accounts now agree that on or around 16 December, bin Laden, accompanied by a complement of bodyguards and fighters, slipped out of the Tora Bora region and crossed the border to disappear into the remote, inaccessible areas of the Pakistani tribal agencies. This was achieved by the liberal distribution of bribes to some 'Eastern Alliance' fighters, the few Pakistani border guards who were actually near the action and Pashtun guides who had crossed from Pakistan to meet their clients.[44]

In the following months and years, Rumsfeld and Franks would cast doubt on whether bin Laden had even been in Tora Bora at this period. However, their protestations lack all credibility. American forces in place at the time recall hearing bin Laden's voice over the short-wave radios Al Qaeda was using for communication, and having this confirmed by translators who had heard his voice before. Frequent references to the 'Sheikh' also came over the radio traffic. All intelligence reports also point to his being in the area, and bin Laden himself later admitted that he was in Tora Bora at this time. The key point, however, is that Rumsfeld, Franks, Cheney and President Bush himself were all told repeatedly that he was in the area, and that unless action was taken he might escape.

None of this is meant to suggest that, even if US forces had been dispatched, the capture or killing of bin Laden would have been easy. There were formidable logistical problems in swiftly moving a force of 2,000–3,000 troops, given the terrain, altitude and availability of airlift assets. Yet if the will had been there in the higher command, these problems could have been overcome, and it is highly probable, if not certain, that bin Laden would have met his end, one way or another, at Tora Bora. While this would not have ended the Al Qaeda threat, the fact that he survived, escaped and is still at large today has built the mythology and attractiveness of the bin Laden and Al Qaeda 'brand' around the world for potential terrorists.

FINDING A POLITICAL SETTLEMENT

As the pace of military events on the ground quickened from late October, attention in Washington turned to what post-conflict Afghanistan would look like. These debates took on a familiar character. The US would not be involved in 'nation-building' or 'social engineering' and there would be no large-scale American military presence in the country. The goal was to be the pursuit of Al Qaeda, as part of a broader 'Global War on Terror'. These rigid presumptions shaped all the debates about Afghanistan's political future within the Bush administration. However, rather than aiding the construction of a flexible, clear-headed policy approach, the metaphors and analogies that resurfaced again and again had the effect of shutting down the possibility of a systematic analysis of the relationship between the political configuration of post-conflict Afghanistan and the broader goal of enhancing US and international security.

As events at Tora Bora demonstrate, even the superficially clear objective of pursuing, killing or capturing bin Laden and his lieutenants had become obscured and hampered by competing imperatives and assumptions. A familiar issue reappeared on the agenda.

On 27 November General Franks received a phone call from Donald Rumsfeld, demanding to know, in the name of the president, the current position regarding military planning. The concern was not about future plans for the still ongoing conflict in Afghanistan – but for Iraq.[45] From this point, not only would the Afghan theatre be increasingly starved of key capabilities such as surveillance assets, Special Forces personnel, helicopters and transport planes, but some already there would be withdrawn to prepare for operations in Iraq. Even more important than the practical consequences was the mindset they revealed. Afghanistan, as early as the end of November, was beginning to slip down the list of priorities in Washington. The threat triad of terrorist groups, 'rogue' states and proliferation of WMD was being seen increasingly through the prism of a common solution: regime change. Afghanistan's regime had been removed; next on the list was Iraq's. Not only did this play to the high-tech strengths of the US military, important in an increasingly Pentagon-driven foreign policy, but it also condensed a myriad complex problems into a workable and easily understood solution. Yet, as we have seen, it competed directly with other goals, such as the pursuit of Al Qaeda itself and the stabilization of a country and region that was at the heart of the terrorist threat to the US, and to the West in general.

However, before these big strategic plays could be fully put into effect, there was still the 'irritating' problem of Afghanistan's future to be dealt with. On 13 November, at that day's National Security Council (NSC) meeting, President Bush set the scene:

> We will not stay. We don't do police work. We need a core of a coalition of the willing . . . and then pass these tasks on to others.[46]

It had already been agreed that the UN should 'handle' Kabul – a sure sign, given the Bush administration's previous and subsequent antipathy to the organization, that the political make-up of post-conflict Afghanistan was not a high priority. The basic shape of an acceptable solution had been agreed within the White House. A broad-based government was required, including participation from across the ethnic and tribal mix; and, given the history of Afghanistan, a Pashtun figurehead would probably be needed to lead an interim administration. The task of bringing this about was given to the State Department, and Colin Powell recruited Ambassador James Dobbins, a highly experienced diplomat who had overseen US post-conflict diplomatic efforts in Haiti, Bosnia and Kosovo.

Meanwhile, on the same day as the NSC meeting, the UN-appointed chief envoy to Afghanistan, the Algerian Lakhdar Brahimi, laid out a plan to the Security Council that pointed the way forward to a political transition process in Afghanistan. It called for a conference between selected Afghan factions that would agree the shape of an interim government and consent to the dispatch of an international force to Kabul to provide security.[47] This meeting would begin two weeks later in Bonn. While the fighting was still raging in Afghanistan, therefore, the immediate future of the country was going to be decided 3,000 miles away in Germany.

THE BONN CONFERENCE

It would have been difficult to find a more incongruous setting to bring together Afghan factions. The conference venue, the Petersberg, is an imposing guest house on top of a tree-lined hill with a stunning view of the river Rhine. Four groups had received invitations. The Northern Alliance was represented by 'Interior Minister' Younis Qanooni and was dominated, to the intense irritation of Dostum and Ismail Khan (neither of whom was present), by Tajiks.[48] The 'Rome group', made up largely of émigré Pashtuns loyal to the former King Mohammed Zahir Shah, had built a reputation for conducting the types of activities common to most émigré groups – bickering and plotting. This was the group with which Hamid Karzai was associated. The 'Cyprus group', so called because it had held a number of meetings on the island, contained Hazaras and Pashtuns and was nominally pro-Iranian.[49] The final faction, known as the 'Peshawar group', consisted of Pashtun exiles who had congregated in the Pakistan city of Peshawar. The Cyprus and Peshawar groups would prove to be relatively peripheral to the outcome of the conference.

There were also a number of national delegations in attendance, although they were not permitted to enter the meeting room when the Afghan factions were in formal session. The most important delegations in terms of influence were the American, Russian, Iranian, Indian and Pakistani. Pakistan's position was difficult. With the partial exception of the Peshawar group, all the Afghan factions and most of the national delegations were hostile to Islamabad. Pakistan's main chance of influencing the outcome would be by voicing its concerns to the Americans – a stunning reversal in the normal balance of influence in Afghan affairs.

There were a number of significant absentees. The Taliban had, most definitely, not been invited, but Pashtun participation was in any case skewed. There were few participants from the present-day south or east of the country. This reflected, as noted above, the fate of anti-Taliban Pashtuns of influence over the preceding years. The consequence was that representation was dominated by émigrés and the majority of Pashtuns at the conference had little recent experience of contemporary Afghanistan. In addition, neither President Burhanuddin Rabbani, who still nominally held Afghanistan's seat in the UN General Assembly, nor the former king was in attendance, although their influence would be felt at key points of the conference.

The first order of business was to agree a head of the interim administration. All recognized, even the NA, that this must be a Pashtun. Indeed, it was the NA 'foreign minister', Abdullah Abdullah, who, according to Dobbins, first pushed the candidacy of the one Pashtun figure likely to gain acceptance from all sides – Hamid Karzai. Dobbins would hear the same name from a wide variety of actors, including the Iranians, Indians, Russians, Turks and even the Pakistanis, and concluded that Abdullah Abdullah had lobbied on Karzai's behalf.[50]

It is not difficult to discern why Karzai's candidacy generated near unanimous approval by the end of the conference. While a number of the groups had other favoured candidates (including, ironically, many of Karzai's own royalist group, who agitated for a restoration of the monarchy), he was the least bad option for all sides. Karzai had impeccable tribal credentials; had not been associated with any major human-rights abuses; was urbane, with a degree of personal charm; had met most of the key players; did not have a reputation, at this stage, for gross personal corruption; and was intelligent and well educated. While in many post-conflict settings that curriculum vitae would be a starting point to develop support, decades of war and disruption ensured that, in the Afghanistan of November 2001, it was virtually unique. Therefore, while Karzai was engaged in pitched battles with the Taliban north of Kandahar, he was being put forward as the agreed candidate to head the interim government. The news was telephoned to him on 5 December. Seemingly as always in

Afghanistan, even this straightforward act was surrounded with high drama. Five minutes before Karzai received the call, an American B-52 mistakenly dropped a 2,000 lb bomb on his position, killing three US Special Forces soldiers, three of Karzai's own men, and very nearly Karzai himself.[51]

The division of ministries between the various factions would prove to be more difficult to negotiate. The NA seemed to be very keen on the maxim 'to the victor the spoils'. While Washington may have perceived the military successes in the north as a testament to the dominance of air power and the subtlety of the CIA and Special Forces, the NA saw it very much as *its* victory. Consequently, it was disinclined to give many concessions to the other factions gathered at Bonn, many of whom it viewed as effete intellectuals who had lived in comfort outside Afghanistan while its members suffered immeasurable hardships fighting within it.

Brahimi suggested that all the factions submit a list of potential ministers. At this point Rabbani, watching events from Kabul, and presumably growing increasingly alarmed that he was being marginalized, managed to deadlock the NA leadership back in Afghanistan and refused to issue the instructions that would allow Qanooni to present the list. It looked as if the conference would have to adjourn. However, according to James Dobbins' account, the Russian ambassador broke the logjam by firmly indicating to the NA that Russian aid would cease unless agreement was reached. Qanooni was allowed to present his list and Rabbani's influence never recovered.

When the NA list was presented, it provoked another mini-crisis. The NA negotiators were demanding 75 per cent of the ministries, including the interior, foreign affairs and defence portfolios. This time it was the Iranian representative, Javad Zarif, who took Qanooni aside for a private 'chat'. Finally, the NA agreed to withdraw its nominations for two ministries and consent to the addition of three new portfolios that would be run by other factions at the conference.[52] However, Qanooni would take over the interior ministry; Abdullah Abdullah foreign affairs; and Fahim defence.

These positive interventions by Russian and Iranian officials reflected a remarkable aspect of the conference. There was a coincidence of interests between the Russians, Iranians, Indians and Americans that was highly unusual. Only the Pakistanis, sullenly sulking in the margins, felt that their national interests would not be furthered by the type of agreement taking shape. The Iranians with their massive Afghan refugee problem, burgeoning drug crisis and history of hostile relations with the Taliban, played an extremely positive role in the conference. Indeed, Dobbins would later report to Washington that a diplomatic door with the Iranians appeared to be opening and that they seemed to be hinting at a rapprochement. This was studiously ignored by the administration.[53] Within two months, President Bush would use his State of the Union address to include Iran in his famous 'axis of evil'.

The US delegation was divided on the question of the Iranian role, with the Pentagon's representatives becoming highly agitated at any indication of cooperation between US and Iranian delegates. The Defense Department officials who were part of Dobbins' team, Bill Luti, Harold Rohde and Larry Franklin, appeared to view their role as semi-autonomous emissaries of Donald Rumsfeld rather than part of a coherent US diplomatic effort. This became dramatically illustrated a few weeks later, when rumours began to circulate that US officials were developing contacts with Iranian opposition groups, designed to finance a programme to overthrow the government in Tehran. It transpired that Rohde and Franklin were putting together a $25 million effort to bankroll opposition groups, and that some of the scoping meetings had taken place, with Luti included, in Rome during the Bonn conference.

Amazingly, all this was taking place without the knowledge of either the State Department or the CIA and, absent the required presidential and congressional notifications, would probably have been illegal. CIA Director Tenet records that when Colin Powell heard about the scheme he 'hit the roof' and set about trying to close it down, something he seems to have achieved by threatening to take the matter straight to the president.[54] This incident strengthens the view that something approaching a parallel foreign policy, on selected issues, was emanating from the Pentagon: a tendency that would be repeatedly seen in policy towards Afghanistan.

The entire American mission to Bonn had an unusual feel to it. Apart from the scheme noted above, perhaps the most incredible aspect was that, on many issues on the table at the conference, Dobbins had received no written instructions from Washington. The ambassador was, to an extent, freewheeling – not because of any impropriety, but because there was little engagement from Washington on the key issues being debated. This is the best indication that the post-conflict configuration of Afghanistan politics and society was of peripheral interest to the key players in the Bush administration, with the partial exception of Colin Powell, with whom Dobbins' relationship remained strong.

On 6 December, as bin Laden was under siege in Tora Bora, the agreement was finally hammered out. The interim administration, headed by Karzai and to be established on 22 December, would contain twenty-nine ministries. Some were created simply to ensure broad participation in government. The NA would hold sixteen of the portfolios, including the key posts noted above of interior, defence and foreign affairs. An emergency Loya Jirga was to be called within six months, to decide on a transitional administration, and this would govern until elections could be held, within two years at the latest. In a nod to the royalists, the emergency Loya Jirga would be opened by the king. Within eighteen months of the establishment of the transitional administration, a further Loya Jirga would be established to draft the new constitution. The agreement also called for the establishment of an International Security Force to maintain security in Kabul, and furthermore held out the possibility of this force's remit being widened to include other areas of Afghanistan.[55] The operation of this force would provide a significant area of controversy.

THE AFTERMATH

Back in Afghanistan, American and coalition force levels were gradually increasing, but were strictly capped by Rumsfeld and Franks. The perception was that the conflict had entered a 'mopping-up' phase, with coalition military units working through the newly empowered warlord network to pursue Taliban remnants and Al Qaeda suspects. These relatively small conventional force numbers led inevitably to an over-reliance on air power to compensate. The predictable result was a constant stream of civilian casualties. One notable event epitomized the problem. On 22 December, a convoy of Karzai's supporters and friends was en route to his inauguration ceremony when it was mistakenly attacked by an American aircraft, killing dozens. The circumstances would become wearily familiar. At first General Franks denied the incident had happened, thus infuriating the local population further. It then transpired that the intelligence leading to the attack had been provided by local warlords, and had been deliberately misleading in order to further personal feuds by manipulating the US Air Force into attacking competitors.[56] Such events, which continually recurred over the following weeks, months and years, would erode the support of the local population both for the coalition and for the Karzai government.

The following month, an international conference was held in Tokyo, on 21–22 January 2002, which brought states together to set up an aid package for Afghanistan. Nearly fifty countries attended, and the rhetoric soared. Declaratory statements about the good the international community would bring to Afghanistan spewed forth from the conference floor. However, in the end only $5 billion worth of pledges was secured, of which $290 million (or 5 per cent) was pledged by the US. Dobbins scathingly contrasts this with the scale of aid packages that went to the former Yugoslavia: 'In their first year of reconstruction, Bosnians received sixteen times more international assistance than did Afghans. Kosovars received eight times more.'[57] Furthermore, the $5 billion were only pledges, and there was a worrying lack of detail about when and in what form the aid would arrive. It was the first sign that aid from the international community was likely to be low in terms of quantity and slow in terms of arrival.

One of the main items on the agenda at Tokyo was reform of the Afghan police, army, prisons and courts. This 'Security Sector Reform' strand is well recognized as a fundamental aspect of post-conflict stabilization. In Tokyo, a 'lead nation' approach was adopted, with particular countries taking on the responsibility for each sector. As we shall see in the next chapter, the results would be, to say the least, disappointing. Taken in the round, therefore, the results from Tokyo seemed to suggest a worrying trend. The desire for a 'light footprint' approach came to dominate the jargon and analyses of what was deemed necessary from the international community in Afghanistan.

THE PROVISION OF SECURITY

On 20 December, the UN authorized the dispatch of the International Security Assistance Force (ISAF) agreed at Bonn. The force would be commanded by a British officer, Major-General John McColl. UK forces would make up the bulk of its complement, but there were representatives of eighteen countries. It would grow in strength, in its initial manifestation, to nearly 5,000. While its initial deployment was only to Kabul, there were provisions in the Bonn agreement for this to expand beyond the city to other urban centres. The debate about this potential broadening of ISAF's mission became highly controversial.

The security situation outside Kabul was extremely poor. Not only were combat operations against the Taliban and Al Qaeda continuing, but the warlords and criminal gangs, many of them recipients of CIA and US military dollars, were battling for their share of the drugs market, smuggling operations and control of territory, or were simply shaking down the population. On all sides, including from Karzai and Brahimi, the call went out for ISAF's mission to be expanded and quickly. There were numerous deputations to Karzai from Afghans themselves complaining about the deteriorating security situation and demanding that ISAF broaden its presence outside of Kabul. Repeatedly, these requests were vetoed by the Bush administration.[58]

Apart from the general aversion to such security operations, the opposition from the administration was based on two main factors. The first was the fear that an expanded international presence in Afghanistan would hamper the counterterrorism mission being conducted by US forces. The warlords and militias, which a broadened ISAF force might have been expected to seek to disarm, were deemed indispensable in providing intelligence and support in the hunt for Al Qaeda. The second concern was that, even if no American troops were formally involved in ISAF, it would still soak up US assets, as the mission would require logistical, airlift, surveillance and intelligence support and, *in extremis*, American reinforcement if missions turned sour. This factor grew in salience as assets began to be quietly redeployed to meet the requirements of the coming invasion of Iraq. Therefore, not only would the administration not provide troops for security-building missions, but it would seek to prevent anyone else from doing so, too.

General McColl would later estimate that a force of about 20,000 would have provided a reasonable security presence in key locations. He recognized the logic and pressing need for such a security presence but was, of course, entirely dependent on the judgement of his political masters.[59] However, the Americans were not the only ones reluctant to put together such a force. A number of countries, including the British, were decidedly queasy at the thought of committing their troops to such an expanded mission. Unlike the Bush administration, their objections were not ideological or a matter of principle; most saw the logic of such a force, but had practical fears about becoming embroiled in an open-ended, complex commitment.

Their tentativeness would have far-reaching consequences. In post-conflict stabilization scenarios the window of opportunity to provide a basic foundation of security is usually small, to the extent that (as Iraq would demonstrate all too soon) it can be measured in months. Security vacuums tend to be filled, in one way or another. Such was the case in Afghanistan through 2002. The result was predictable. Warlords, from the traditional 'big beasts' of the north and west to the new 'American warlords' of the south and east, consolidated their power and influence. The chance to marginalize corrupt local power brokers was lost. Ordinary Afghans, who had seen this all too often, accommodated themselves to local realities and kept their heads down. By the time the international coalition began, at least rhetorically, to place 'state-building' at the heart of its approach, the security situation was already deeply compromised and warlord influence virtually institutionalized.

In March, a major contingent of foreign fighters, similar in size to the force at Tora Bora, was identified in the Shah-i-Kot valley in eastern Afghanistan. The fighters, many of whom were experienced Al Qaeda combatants, were again dug in to heavily fortified and inaccessible positions at high altitude. This time, however, there were American conventional forces from the 10th Mountain and 101st Airborne Divisions present, as well as Special Forces from Britain, Canada, Australia, Germany, Denmark, France and the US. The resulting operation (codenamed 'Anaconda') led to fierce fighting for seven days from 2 March, with sporadic engagements lasting until 18 March. The defenders fought fanatically but took heavy casualties, and finally the remnants scattered and fled. This was dubbed at the time, not very presciently, as the last major combat operation of the Afghan conflict.[60]

Although this was not recognized at the time, Operation Anaconda was an indicator of the future fighting to come. The US and its allies were taken aback at the ferocity and fanaticism with which the enemy engaged them. Significant reinforcements had to be drafted in and resistance continued well beyond the point at which victory seemed to have been secured. The casualness with which many of the fighters faced probable death should perhaps have given the allies pause before their confident declaration that major combat operations were at an end.

Despite the security situation in the countryside and towns outside Kabul, the resilience of the Afghan people was on display. As the date of the emergency Loya Jirga (LJ) approached, there was a palpable sense of optimism that life was going to improve for ordinary Afghans. The LJ was scheduled to run from 6 to 10 June 2002. It would be conducted under the auspices of a Karzai-appointed commission, headed by a lawyer – Ismael Qasimyar. People in local districts would elect twenty members, who would in turn elect the delegate they wished to send to the LJ.

There was a significant degree of intimidation, both in the local electoral processes and towards the selected delegates. Most of this was conducted by warlords seeking to exert their influence, and eight candidates were killed, with more attacked, kidnapped and threatened.[61] Nevertheless, when upwards of 1,500 delegates gathered in Kabul, there was a joyous mood. However, when the business of the Loya Jirga began, hard-nosed politics dominated. A late bid by the royalist groupings to put the king up as a challenger to Karzai for the presidency was quashed under the combined pressure of a threatened NA walkout and the 'persuasion' of President Bush's special envoy to Afghanistan, Zalmay Khalilzad.

In the end, Karzai won a resounding victory and was appointed president until national elections could be held in 2004. The cabinet he put together reflected the status quo. All the main NA figures retained their positions, with the exception of Qanooni, who was persuaded to cede his position as interior minister (although he would take the education portfolio) to assuage Pashtun concerns of under-representation.[62] The LJ ended with an even greater sense of optimism that threatened to become unrealistic. Expectations of what could be quickly achieved had not been helped by a line in a speech two months before by President Bush at the Virginia Military Institute, in which he used the term 'Marshall Plan' in a way that implied, but did not promise, that a similar plan was heading Afghanistan's way. This was seized on by many of the Afghan elite as proof that a massive aid effort would soon be launched. It was not to be.

THE SCENE IS SET

June 2002 was probably the high-water mark of optimism and hope in post-Taliban Afghanistan. However, the trends and forces that would dominate the next nine years of conflict were already in place. The manner in which the Taliban government had been removed entrenched the power and influence of both the traditional warlords of the NA in the north and west, and the new breed of 'American warlords' in the south and east. Karzai would come under criticism for not doing more to undermine the warlord power base when he came to office. One of the shrewdest external observers of the Afghan scene, Antonio Giustozzi, argues that Karzai should have been more forceful and gambled by taking on the warlords.[63] However, while Karzai will come under significant criticism in later chapters of this book for some of his major failings, he was in a very difficult position in relation to the warlords in the early months of power.

There was little prospect of the NA not being accorded the lion's share of the ministries at Bonn, given the prominent role it had played in overthrowing the Taliban. For Karzai to have sought to undermine the positions of Fahim, Dostum and Khan, for example, would have been hugely risky. Similarly, Karzai had very little practical influence over the regional power brokers who had entrenched themselves in the south and east. To force a confrontation, he would have had to be confident that the one military power capable of ensuring the disarmament and neutering of the warlords – the US – was willing to play such a role. All the evidence – in terms not just of policy statements, but also of policy actions – suggested there was no chance of such an outcome. Indeed, when the question of the future Afghan security forces came on the agenda, Bob Woodward quotes Rumsfeld, in the spring of 2002, questioning 'why they couldn't just let the Afghan warlords create an army'.[64] The evidence suggested the opposite of what Karzai would have required to establish effective government: that the US was actively seeking to maintain a warlord network, through which it could work to pursue Al Qaeda.

The long-term effect of warlord influence would undoubtedly be disastrous, but Karzai was highly constrained in the early months. He had to choose between constructing a merit-based government that would promote solely on ability and include a high proportion of Afghan technocrats returned from abroad, and trying to use government appointments as a way of keeping the disparate and potentially violent political factions in balance. Inevitably, he erred towards the latter; but with no guarantee (or even likelihood) of international military support if he chose the path of confrontation, this was understandable. The result was that heads of ministries used their portfolios to provide opportunities for their supporters and to enhance their personal positions. Meanwhile, Kabul would become disconnected from the provinces and districts where local power brokers would hold sway. Stuck in the middle and slowly squeezed were the hopes of the Afghan people.

What the nine months from the intervention in Afghanistan to the Loya Jirga had shown most of all, however, was the lack of strategic clarity in the Bush administration. Events would subsequently reveal that it was not alone in this failing, but it was stark nevertheless. Even the superficially clear aim of 'getting' Al Qaeda became opaque. George Bush kept a photo array of the twenty-two most wanted terrorists in his desk, and diligently crossed off names as news came through of a capture or death.[65] Yet at the moment when the number one name on that chart was at the mercy of the US, competing obsessions, assumptions and preconceived ideas had conspired to paralyse effective action.

Donald Rumsfeld would assert, with more than a little hubris, that the operations had revealed just the sort of flexibility that the 'transformation' agenda was all about. He specifically referred to the operation in Mazar-i-Sharif as the exemplar.[66] However, that battle had more in common with traditional warfare than with any new paradigm. The 'flexibility' was displayed at the tactical level by the CIA and Special Forces teams on the ground, both of which performed very effectively in this and future battles. When the high command and national leadership were called on to think in an agile manner, at Tora Bora, they failed the test miserably. Indeed, the defining feature of the debates in Washington was an *absence* of strategic agility. Metaphors and analogies regarding 'nation-building', 'light footprints' and 'wars by committee' combined with a series of obsessions relating to Iraq and the appropriate role of the military to produce a highly rigid and inflexible decision-making process.[67]

The key question had still not been systematically addressed, either by the US administration or by any other of the intervening coalition partners: how did Afghanistan fit into a broader regional and global geopolitical vision that would enhance international security? This broad question suggested a series of others. Was the Taliban the 'enemy' or was it simply, as originally envisaged, just an obstacle in the way of getting to Al Qaeda? What sort of social and political arrangements for Afghanistan did the intervening powers wish to see? How much blood and treasure were they willing to expend to bring their vision about?

While the eyes of the world began to shift towards the inexorable march of events in Iraq, Afghanistan faced the future. A
seething Pakistan was licking its wounds, while the routed Taliban
and Al Qaeda survivors either went back to their homes or
regrouped in the border areas. The confident declaration that
Operation Anaconda was the last major combat operation of the
intervention in Afghanistan would be revealed as a startling failure
of perception.

CHAPTER FOUR

'TAKING THE EYE OFF THE BALL?' THE ROOTS OF TALIBAN REVIVAL IN AFGHANISTAN, 2002–05

Between the spring of 2002 and 2006 I saw nothing but progress. Afghanistan never would be Switzerland, but it was on the road to becoming a normal developing country.[1]

WITH THE ENDING of formal operations against the Taliban in March 2002, international attention on events in Afghanistan quickly shrank against the backdrop of the run-up to, and outbreak of, coalition military operations against Iraq from March 2003 onwards. Coalition efforts in Afghanistan at this time were low key by comparison, and initially subdivided between the 18,000 members of the American-led military command, Operation Enduring Freedom (OEF), and the 4,500-strong European-led ISAF. Among the main events in Afghanistan that captured international media attention during this time were the adoption of what subsequently proved to be a fatally flawed new Afghan constitution in January 2004, the holding of Afghan presidential

111

elections, which brought Hamid Karzai to office that same October, and parliamentary elections the following year. These broader political developments followed a hectic constitutional timetable that was itself dictated by the doctrines of 'liberal peace theory', an agenda that brought its own problems.[2] Not until the London Conference of January 2006, which revisited the Bonn agreement to produce the policy document known as the Afghan Compact, would international attention again begin to refocus on Afghanistan, in light of both the new stage inaugurated by the adoption of the Afghan National Development Strategy (ANDS) and the rapidly deteriorating security situation across the country as a whole.

However, despite the relative media neglect at the time, the period 2002–05 in Afghanistan was pregnant with developments destined to carry weightier longer-term consequences. The majority of these trends – contrary to most of the analysis that occurred at the time and even since – were in fact dangerously malign.

TREADING LIGHTLY WHILE NOT BUILDING NATIONS

The political–military approach to Afghanistan taken by the international community in general, and by the United States in particular, was, during this period, dictated by two funda-mental and overarching factors. The first was the 'light footprint' approach, outlined in the previous chapter and advocated by the Bush administration and, for different reasons, UN representative Lakhdar Brahimi. Second, and linked to this, was the US govern-ment's own fundamental lack of interest in nation-building, with the accompanying devolution of such nation-building tasks as did occur to others in the coalition, non-governmental organizations (NGOs), private interests and the diarchy formed between Hamid

Karzai and Washington's own unofficial 'viceroy' in Afghanistan during 2003–05, US Ambassador Zalmay Khalilzad.

The Bush administration's distaste for nation-building, soon destined to attract such international opprobrium in the wake of the unfolding disaster apparent in Iraq from 2004 onwards, was already highly visible in both its public and its private statements and actions regarding Afghanistan from as early as 2002. At the first international donors' conference in Tokyo in early 2002, which raised just $5 billion in assistance for Afghanistan (a smaller per capita disbursement than either Bosnia or Kosovo had received), Washington pledged only $290 million of assistance. It was outbid within that same forum by Iran (itself, of course, ironically about to be relegated to President Bush's infamous 'Axis of Evil'), which pledged $540 million.[3]

Force structuring on the ground further reflected these in-built prejudices. The whole purpose of ISAF was, after all, to provide the diplomatic cover of a 'peacekeeping' force, which would then leave American troops free, as part of OEF, to concentrate on purely military ground combat operations. A small military footprint was also widely considered crucial both to avoid provoking heightened Afghan resistance and for engineering an early exit from the country. The incoming XVIII Airborne Corps commander in 2002, Lieutenant-General Dan McNeill, was accordingly explicitly warned by senior Pentagon officials to avoid 'anything that looks like permanence. We are in and out of there in a hurry.'[4]

Secretary of Defense Donald Rumsfeld had already opined to the *New York Times*, in February 2002, that a large peacekeeping force outside Kabul was simply unnecessary. His view, as we shall see, would be modified somewhat later, as he simultaneously became more sanguine about progress in Afghanistan, and preoccupied by the implication for American force deployments as events in Iraq unfolded. In 2002, however, the prevailing American view was that resources could be better spent on building up an Afghan National Army (ANA). This latter force, Rumsfeld subsequently envisaged, would expand to a maximum of 45,000–52,000 men. Initial calls in 2002 by his Afghan counterpart, Marshal Fahim, for a force of 200,000–250,000 men were rejected outright, and subsequent calls by the Afghan Defence Ministry in 2005 for a force of 70,000 troops were again also initially rejected as economically unsustainable.[5]

Such a position becomes even more deeply ironic in retrospect, when American policy radically switched in 2008–09 towards supporting the build-up of a massive standing force of 260,000 men, correspondingly dooming the ANA to a wholly unrealistic programme of sudden and artificially accelerated expansion.[6] In 2002–06, however, the reluctance of the Bush administration to take on a larger peacekeeping commitment, conjoined with the all-too-evident sluggishness of the aid-distribution process and the diversion of a great many military resources and intelligence-gathering assets to the war in Iraq, condemned Afghanistan in the interim to a minor hell of broken promises and shattered illusions: the perfect breeding ground, in fact, for a Taliban revival. If the Afghan people were looking for a coordinated and coherent coalition response, they were to be sorely disappointed.

NATO IN CRISIS

In late 2002 and early 2003 the transatlantic relationship was in disarray. The issue at the heart of the tension was Iraq. The evident desire of some in the Bush administration to overthrow the regime of Saddam Hussein by military force – a desire only superficially masked by the palaver over weapons inspections and

UN resolutions – had split Western powers.[7] In particular, the vehement and very public opposition of France and Germany had generated a mixture of intense irritation and contempt among many of George Bush's key advisers.[8]

Weeks of simmering tension exploded into public acrimony when Donald Rumsfeld, in a January 2003 press conference with foreign reporters in Washington, introduced the construct of 'Old and New Europe' into political debate. Wrongly portrayed by some as a 'gaffe' (Rumsfeld was perfectly well aware of the likely effects), his comments caused something approaching apoplexy in Berlin and Paris.[9] The implication that the Bush administration saw France and Germany as 'has-beens' in terms of diplomatic influence led to a flurry of highly undiplomatic exchanges. Oil was poured on the flames by the media and various politicians, as vituperation hurtled to and fro across the Atlantic. US media scorn was especially focused on the French, with a number of colourful phrases and insults gaining wide currency.[10] The ire of the Bush administration, however, was equally directed towards the Germans. To an extent, French prickliness was already 'priced in' to the diplomatic calculations. Germany, by contrast, had gained a reputation, particularly within NATO, as a consensus builder, and so the strength of the opposition from Berlin was an unwelcome surprise. Diplomatic relations were not helped by an apparently tense personal relationship between George Bush and German Chancellor Gerhard Schroeder, or by a reported comment of the German justice minister which appeared to liken the American president to Adolf Hitler.[11]

For diplomats in NATO, these were difficult times as they tried desperately to prevent the various intergovernmental tensions from spilling over into Alliance deliberations. Many analysts had been predicting since the end of the Cold War that, without the glue provided by the Soviet threat, NATO would eventually succumb to internal splits and a perception of irrelevance. Warning signals were flashing all over Brussels. Any hope that NATO could be insulated from the wider political fallout over Iraq was comprehensively ended in February 2003. The immediate issue, which had been bubbling away for about a month, surrounded attempts to get formal approval for NATO planning to bolster Turkish defences should war with Iraq come to pass. The Bush administration was keen to gain Turkey's support for the coming invasion, and wished to address Turkish fears by providing concrete assistance, such as anti-missile capabilities and aerial surveillance assets, as well as encouraging an expression of NATO solidarity. However, when the issue came before the North Atlantic Council, Germany, France and Belgium objected; under NATO's principle of 'consensus', this represented nothing short of a veto. The refusal to extend support to a member state facing a potential threat went to the heart of the Alliance's solidarity principle and plunged NATO into deep crisis.[12] While diplomatic manoeuvring resolved the specific issue, the political damage was huge, with more than one observer predicting that NATO was unlikely to recover.[13]

However, as war in Iraq became a fait accompli and the initial major combat operations went well, some of the heat was drawn from the issue and the desire grew in most governments to begin to repair the severe diplomatic damage that had been caused, not least to NATO. A number of factors came together to suggest that Afghanistan could provide a means of solidifying the Alliance. In particular, there was a shift of mood in the Bush administration. The growing confidence through 2003 that the mission in Afghanistan was now largely one of stabilization and reconstruction (apart from the focused anti-terrorist activities run by the

Americans) led Rumsfeld and Cheney, in particular, to be more sanguine than they had been in early 2002 about an international 'peacekeeping' effort. There were also certain advantages, from an American perspective, to be derived from NATO taking on the role. First, some of the cost of operations could be shifted on to Alliance partners. Second, NATO could provide US troops with a degree of distance from 'nation-building' while still maintaining American influence through the Alliance chain of command. Third, Afghanistan would be less of a 'distraction' from what was seen, at this stage, as the main effort in the 'war on terror' – Iraq.

A NATO commitment in Afghanistan also looked attractive to America's European partners. It was clearly going to be impossible to agree a substantial Alliance role in Iraq, but there was a palpable desire to get the transatlantic relationship back on track.[14] Going to Afghanistan seemed to offer, from the perspective of mid-2003, a relatively pain-free way of regaining American favour and getting NATO politics back on course.[15] Consequently, representations were made to the UN and the Karzai government and, in return, a joint 'request' was made to transfer ISAF leadership in Kabul to NATO – an invitation the Alliance graciously accepted. This turned what had latterly become a somewhat ad-hoc operation, consisting of six-monthly rotations of often unenthusiastic national commands, into a NATO mission. On 11 August 2003, the Alliance formally took over leadership of ISAF.

For Afghanistan to serve the function assigned to it – stabilizing NATO – the Alliance mission needed to be couched in terms of stabilizing Afghanistan. Operating solely in and around Kabul would not be sufficiently impressive or ambitious to provide the foundation needed to rebuild confidence in NATO. As the previous chapter illustrated, there had been continual pressure from a number of sources, particularly the Karzai government, for

ISAF to extend its remit and support the provision of security across the country. In the early stages, this had been blocked by the Bush administration, and by the fact that various other states had been happy to express support for the idea, but reluctant to provide actual forces. The coincidence of factors noted above now made the rollout of ISAF, under NATO command, politically viable and desirable.

Consequently, in October 2003 a UN Security Council Resolution (UNSCR 1510) was passed, formally mandating wider ISAF operations, initially in the north and west of Afghanistan. It was clear that NATO's intention behind the scenes was that eventually the Alliance would operate in the whole of the country. This was formally confirmed in the main communiqué issued at the Istanbul Summit in June 2004. The plan was for a four-phase 'anti-clockwise' rollout, beginning with the north, then the west, followed by what was recognized as the more challenging south, and finally the east. It was also made abundantly clear what was considered to be at stake. Both the previous secretary general of NATO, Lord Robertson, and his successor, General Jaap de Hoop Scheffer, stated unambiguously in early 2004 that nothing less than the credibility of NATO as a military alliance was on the line in Afghanistan.[16]

The move north, beginning with the December 2003 takeover of the military component of the German Provincial Reconstruction Team (PRT) at Kunduz, went reasonably smoothly, being completed on 1 October 2004. NATO was now firmly committed to the intervention, with its 'credibility on the line'. As we shall see, the initial confidence that Afghanistan could provide a straightforward solution to the Alliance's internal problems would be progressively sapped. Yet, even in this earlier period, the international efforts in Afghanistan, within which NATO was now a leading player, were becoming increasingly incoherent.

SECURITY SECTOR REFORM

The job of security sector reform (SSR) in Afghanistan was, in the wake of the Tokyo donor conference of January 2002, tasked out to five 'lead nations', each of whom took on an individual security 'pillar' to deliver institution building in a specific area. The overarching 'roof' of Afghan governance was intended to rest atop each of these five pillars. The US took on mentorship of the ANA, Germany was allocated the Afghan National Police (ANP), Italy the task of judicial reform, Japan the role of supervising the demobilization, disarmament and reintegration of armed groups (DDR), and the UK adopted the counter-narcotics brief. This emphasis on high-speed institution-building was itself a carry-over from 'liberal peace theory', as well as what some now advocated as the essential process of 'institutionalization before liberalization' – the conjoined necessity for an explicitly 'non-liberal' transition in order to embed market structures, the rule of law and a sound business framework, prior to accelerated, but carefully controlled, elections.[17] In practice, however, the institution-building framework in Afghanistan failed almost from the outset, while the emphasis the process gave to top-down governmental structures (which in practice remained largely abstract and corrupt) meant that the everyday needs of the Afghan people continued to be poorly served. The most damning testament to this fundamentally mismanaged approach was that, far from improving, basic indicators of development actually fell in Afghanistan between 2003 and 2005; life expectancy fell from an already dire 44.5 to 43.1 years, and adult literacy from 28.7 to 23.5 per cent.[18] Against this grim human security backdrop, very few, if any, of the institution-focused security sector reform pillars then made any significant progress of their own between 2002 and 2005 either.

The 'lead nation' approach was notable from the very outset for its lack of coordination, and for the absence of an Afghan voice in decision-making. No national fiscal process was established to oversee where resources would be targeted, and lead nations tended to manage funds either directly or through private contractors, rather than through the Afghan government. This led to donors working in isolation from each other, despite the acknowledged utility of coordinating their efforts to avoid overlap. In practice, most funding was targeted at the ANA, with the unfortunate result that, by 2005, Afghan soldiers were being paid substantially higher salaries (an ordinary infantryman, for example, was on $75 a month) than civil servants ($40 a month) and the Afghan police.[19] Dramatic economic expansion in Kabul meanwhile had brought about an inflationary scenario, whereby the rent of a primitive three-room mud house was $200 a month, and a monthly salary of $40–50 went only halfway towards the cost of even a basic one-kilowatt diesel generator. Afghanistan was rapidly acquiring a rather expensive army, without any sustainable bureaucracy behind it. This was a particular tragedy, given that, in these first few years, the country was in fact blessed with a relatively large number (280,000) of civil servants. However, the lure of working for NGOs based in Kabul, which paid Afghan support staff up to $1,000 a month, rendered work for the Afghan government itself one of the most economically unattractive prospects in town, with predictably devastating wider structural consequences.[20]

Recruitment to the ANA had begun in May 2002, and was initially dogged by high desertion rates (running at 22 per cent in 2003). Increased pay and improved standards of living were introduced to help address this, bringing the desertion rate down to 1.2 per cent by 2004; but lax discipline, a rudimentary ten-week initial training programme, and a culture of corruption continued to render the ANA a rather unreliable and expensive coalition ally. Meanwhile, the almost complete neglect of logistics, communications and organic artillery, armour and air support assets (areas that had been much earlier addressed, albeit imperfectly, by the ANA's Soviet-backed predecessor) also supports the contention of one Western analyst that these troops, for all their considerable initial start-up expenses, were, for much of their first decade of existence, being prepared and trained purely as an 'auxiliary force' to support coalition/NATO forces – an orientation that, of course, raised severe doubts about their ability to act autonomously or to handle any subsequent transition towards assuming a lead role.[21]

Even in this scenario, though, the already high running costs associated with bringing down desertion within the ANA also placed a serious question mark over its own longer-term sustainability, even without factoring in the future provision of more expensive weapons platforms and associated training programmes. In the fiscal year 2004–05 alone, the ANA cost $171 million to sustain, the equivalent of about 25 per cent of the Afghan government's entire operating budget or, to put it another way, approximately 63 per cent of the country's entire domestic revenue for that period. After 2006, when the ANA began to be provided with $2 billion of heavy weaponry by the Americans, its annual running costs at full strength were projected to rise to $1 billion, or 17 per cent of Afghan GDP. Much of this equipment was unnecessarily expensive and impractical, a procurement trend symbolized by the 2007 decision to substitute US Humvees for local pickup trucks and to replace the ubiquitous (and regionally easily sourced) AK-47 with the logistically fussy and high-maintenance American M-16 assault rifle.[22] The fact that the emerging multi-ethnic (though Tajik-dominated) ANA, for all its deep structural problems, was nonetheless regarded by most observers as the main 'success story' of the SSR process in Afghanistan during this period only becomes comprehensible when one then compares it to the progress made in 2002–05 in reforming the judiciary, countering narcotics, or setting up the Afghan National Police.

The Afghan National Highway Police, for example, formed in 2003, soon gained a reputation for being involved in smuggling and for soliciting bribes, and had to be almost completely disbanded in 2006. The disappointing progress in this field overall was, in large part, the natural result of a process that had been, almost from the very start, characterized, in the words of one analyst, by two different but conterminous approaches to police-building: '[o]ne cautious and rational, building on what already existed and extending outwards, and the other bold and sweeping, attempting to tackle a number of pressing problems all at the same time.'[23]

The initial German approach to Afghan police development in 2002 had centred on 'training the trainer' by attempting to turn the most physically and intellectually promising candidates into model specimens for others to follow, though they also only ever anticipated conducting this approach on an extremely modest scale. Consequently, though Germany rapidly established a police academy in Kabul, just forty-one German officers were sent out to train 3,500 Afghan officers over three years; the Afghan candidates selected for such specialized treatment then inevitably struggled to reintegrate within their units once they were posted to the provinces. Such an approach also failed to address the yawning gap in terms of infrastructure and equipment that faced the ANP, deficiencies ranging from radios and body armour to basic housing, suitable prisons and even transport vehicles, particularly in the south of the country.

American impatience with the German approach led the US State Department in 2003 to take over the bulk of Afghan police training, a shift marked by the appointment of an American-trained Afghan technocrat, Ali Ahmad Jalali, to head the Afghan Interior Ministry in 2003–05. DynCorp, the Texas-based private security company allocated a $24 million contract and tasked with turning matters round, then quickly went to the other extreme by focusing on quantity ('output') to the detriment of quality. DynCorp employed American police officers with no knowledge of Afghanistan to run three-week training courses for Afghan officers, with no follow-up training or mentoring, and with no substantial improvement in either basic equipment or logistics. The consequence was that, in the words of Ahmed Rashid, '[b]etween 2003 and 2005, the United States was to spend some $860 million in training forty thousand policemen, but the results were almost totally useless'.[24] The ANP continued to lack vehicles and radios, and remained entrenched in a culture of drug abuse and corruption. It was regularly outfought by its Taliban or drug-trafficker opponents, not least because, as late as 2005–06, its officers were equipped with only Kalashnikov assault rifles and limited quantities of ammunition, while its opponents were armed with multi-barrelled mobile rocket launchers and machine guns. DynCorp itself admitted in 2005 that the Afghan police urgently required an additional 48,500 side arms, 10,000 assault rifles, 6,250 machine guns and 7,400 vehicles; it also acknowledged that criminal suspects continued to be detained in private residences because 'most police stations lack secure holding facilities or reliable electricity or drinking water, and have only rudimentary office furniture and equipment'.[25] Symbolic, in fact, of the disdain with which the ANP continued to be treated by successive stakeholders in the SSR process were the procurement policies aimed at supplying and equipping them. As late as 2008, Afghan police were still being issued forty-year-old rifle ammunition and rusting

Kalashnikov assault rifles, sourced from the ageing and unreliable stockpiles of strictly second-order ex-Eastern Bloc countries like Albania and Poland.[26]

The UK-owned counter-narcotics programme was another obvious failure within the early five-pillar SSR process. The initial UK plan centred on offering Afghan farmers $350 for each *jerib* (unit of area) of poppy that they themselves eliminated. There was a fund of $36.75 million of UK aid and $35 million of international aid allocated to this programme.[27] Yet in 2002, Afghanistan still produced 3,400 tonnes of opium and was the source of about 90 per cent of the heroin consumed in the UK; by 2003 it was producing 3,600 tonnes, and in 2004 a crop of 4,200 tonnes was recorded. With the previous absolute record harvest for annual opium production in Afghanistan since 1990 having been the 4,565 tonnes recorded in 1996, this was clearly an unhealthy trend, and in fact that Taliban-era record would soon be surpassed – in 2007 Afghanistan produced 8,200 tonnes of opium, more than was produced in the whole world the previous year.[28] This growth, in its initial stages, was equally dramatic in terms of its geographical scale – in the 1930s, poppy had only been grown in three Afghan provinces, and even in 1994 it was grown in only eight; yet by 2003 it was already being grown and cultivated in twenty-eight of Afghanistan's thirty-two provinces.[29]

The initial UK programme was soon suspended as its ineffectiveness became apparent. The overall campaign had quickly fallen victim to the intersecting problems of money flowing to corrupt middlemen without results; the perverse incentive structure itself causing more poppy to be grown in the north of the country simply in order to qualify for the eradication payouts; the payouts being too small to offer a significant financial stimulus; and, finally, the available funds themselves rapidly running out. By 2004, the focus had switched instead to interdiction, via targeting large drug traffickers and heroin laboratories. Yet interdiction as carried out by UK- and US-trained Afghan forces was also bedevilled by local corruption and the associated capacity of large traffickers to bribe and deflect the focus onto small traders and local rivals. Against this backdrop, US policy began to shift independently towards advocating a policy of actual physical eradication via crop spraying, a position not supported by either the UK or the Afghan government.[30]

With UK and US approaches towards counter-narcotics now diverging (much as US and German efforts regarding police building had already done), US-backed efforts at actual eradication received their first test in 2005, when the UN recorded a slight drop in poppy production due to an alternative livelihood initiative (in which farmers were paid to grow alternative crops) unfolding in several key provinces. Good weather, however, also meant that relative opium productivity actually increased, from 32 kilograms per hectare in 2004, to a yield of 39 kilograms per hectare in 2005. The year 2006 would then see the counter-narcotics gains of the previous year largely reversed, as a new record harvest of 6,100 tonnes was recorded. The initially stated UK goal of reducing opium cultivation by 70 per cent by 2008 and by 100 per cent by 2013 was beginning to look like a cruel joke.

The overall economic significance of this trade can best be appreciated if one considers that in 2005 – a 'good' year in relative terms for the Western counter-narcotics campaign (largely through the gains made in Nangarhar province – gains quickly lost by a lack of follow-through aid and support) – opium exports still earned Afghanistan $2.7 billion, or 'just' 52 per cent of the country's overall GDP of $5.2 billion, as opposed to 61 per cent of overall GDP the previous year.[31]

This explosion in the drugs economy was a product of the highly under-policed nature of the state, the profitable market conditions both regionally and globally (in 2005 an Afghan farmer, the lowest economic link in the chain, could still achieve a 'farm gate' price for raw unprocessed opium that was between ten and thirty times what he would get for wheat) and the economic interests of the warlords in the Northern Alliance who had initially facilitated Karzai's accession to power in Kabul. Not coincidentally, up until late 2003 this last group also formed an important, though informal, centrepiece of US strategy for securing the country's outer provinces on an administrative shoestring.[32] Transit fees from both legal and illegal traffic during this period continued to provide individual warlords with a substantial source of income: around Herat alone, for example, local warlord Ismail Khan was calculated to be able to tap into customs revenues on the border with Iran that were worth over \$100 million, and he personally maintained a core military force of around 3,000 armed men on the proceeds. Not until 2004, as part of a re-centralization drive, would the able new Afghan finance minister, Ashraf Ghani, attempt to redirect the massive revenues raised from this border trade back into the treasury in Kabul. However, after Ismail Khan was deposed in 2005 by government forces, there was a decline in the level of services and administrative aid disbursed to the local population in the Herat region, generating, if anything, a poor advertisement for the central government's legitimacy and efficiency.[33]

Most warlords in practice, however, evaded Ismail Khan's fate by successfully re-entrenching their political influence, largely by obtaining government posts in the 2004 national elections to the Loya Jirga via vote rigging, bribery and death threats. Calls by local Afghans for such individuals to be tried for previous war crimes were, by contrast, deliberately censored and ignored.[34] The explosion in the drug economy was also matched by an increasing professionalization in drug production that appeared to herald Afghanistan's imminent transformation into a full-blown narco-state. The trade in chemical precursors needed for heroin production, for example, encapsulated increasing attempts by producers within Afghanistan to climb up the value-chain of opiate trafficking between their country and the Western market, with the aim of capturing some of the profits made along the way.[35] In 1996, Afghanistan exported about 25 per cent of its product as heroin, and 75 per cent as unprocessed opium. By 2006, these proportions had been roughly reversed, with the country now exporting about 75 per cent heroin or morphine (another high value-added product) and only about 25 per cent raw opium. This shift in turn required the import of around 7,000–9,000 tonnes of chemical precursors into Afghanistan, in order to supply the laboratories converting around 3,000 tonnes of opium into heroin. These changed export ratios bore testimony to an increasingly sophisticated and transnational network emerging right under the nose of the international coalition's deeply conflicted and ineffective counter-narcotics policy.[36]

The drugs economy played an important role in the very rapid licit growth visible in Afghanistan during this period, with profits from the industry being reinvested in shops, minibuses, cars, motorbikes, satellite dishes and electric generators. Both the IMF and the World Bank in fact warned that *successful* counter-narcotics efforts might have a negative effect on Afghanistan's overall balance of payments, net GDP growth and government revenue.[37] The economic impact of drug-eradication programmes also helps underline the hidden centrality of the illicit economy to what might otherwise appear a remarkably healthy wave of year-on-year national recovery, levelling out at, on average, 8 per cent per annum GDP growth after 2003. Nangarhar province, for example, in the wake of the 2005 poppy-eradication drive conducted there, suffered devastating pauperization due to the lack of follow-through economic support, with local farmers who were now unable to repay their debts reduced to selling daughters as young as three as brides, or absconding to Pakistan. Poppy cultivation in Nangarhar in 2006 correspondingly increased by 346 per cent, the highest rate recorded anywhere in the country, and by an additional 285 per cent in 2007, restoring poppy production there to almost pre-eradication-campaign levels by the end of the year.[38]

Kabul itself was transformed by a wave of ostentatious new hotels (including the five-star Serena in the centre of town, which offered rooms starting at $275 a night) and palatial private residences, dubbed 'poppy palaces' by the locals. These were joined by Chinese brothels and shopping malls selling $4,000 watches and giant flat-screen televisions – all marks of conspicuous consumption on a scale inconceivable without an understanding of the profits being made behind the scenes from heroin trafficking, along with the net liquidity that it provided.

The failure of the counter-narcotics programme in these early years, together with a poorly delivered aid programme, burdened Afghanistan with a primitive two-track economy, characterized, as one study put it, by 'opulence amidst destitution'.[39] It led educated and literate Afghans to graduate towards work in the NGOs and hotels clustered within the economic bubble of Kabul, while the average citizen found it easier to obtain a mobile phone (distributed in their thousands for free as part of the West's 'democratization' project, but also, of course, an invaluable 'dual use' asset in the international drugs trade) than to access clean drinking water or even basic health care.

Against this backdrop, the disarmament and demobilization of armed groups, conducted under the financial aegis of the Japanese government, also enjoyed painfully slow and even misleading progress during these first five years, largely due to its interconnection with the associated 'policing' and 'counter-narcotics' problems. While the international community dealt with these issues as separate reform pillars, the ongoing prevalence of the existing 'war economy' meant that they remained fatally intertwined. Consequently, failures in each area had a tendency to compound and magnify failures in each neighbouring area of the SSR process.

Initial progress in demobilization, disarmament and reintegration (DDR) was slow, with around 100,000 irregular militia forces still in the country, as against around 70,000 regular troops one year after the Bonn agreement.[40] The DDR stage of the Afghan New Beginnings Programme (ANBP), targeting combatants belonging to semi-formal military units that still existed outside the ANA, was formally completed by July 2005, and was then succeeded by the Disbandment of Illegal Armed Groups (DIAG) programme slated to run through to 2007. Results, however, remained modest, with just 13,576 of the 20,411 weapons of different types collected by May 2006 being subsequently redistributed as still usable – a stark indication of the poor condition, low value and limited utility of many of the arms that were being surrendered. Returns of usable weapons also diminished over time, with 66.5 per cent of the weapons amnestied in the first eleven months of the DIAG programme being recorded as still in working condition, compared to only 49 per cent of weapons handed in over the following year. In January 2006, it was calculated that there were still at least 2,753 armed groups in the country, totalling nearly 180,000 men, and at least 90 of the 249 candidates who gained seats in parliament following elections in 2007 were also recognized militia leaders.[41]

While such amnesties, therefore, proved effective in securely stockpiling local collections of heavier military equipment like tanks, artillery and armoured personnel carriers – assets that were intrinsically both more expensive to maintain and harder to conceal from inspectors – the DDR process made only a minimal impression on stemming the tide of rocket launchers, explosives, mines and small arms which still flooded the country, and likewise failed to politically disenfranchise prominent local militia commanders. The whole DDR and associated DIAG process was then almost completely derailed when, in February 2006, proposals were brought forward to establish 'auxiliary' police units – a programme that, in conjunction with initiatives by President Karzai, led to an experiment between 2006 and 2008 in remobilizing and co-opting Afghan village militias. This programme itself marked yet another swing, this time from centralization back towards decentralization, in the international community's wildly inconsistent stabilization and reconstruction effort in Afghanistan. In a broader sense of course, this phenomenon again also dramatically underscored the ongoing and more general intellectual vacuum at the heart of Western liberal peace theory.[42]

A CORRUPT AFGHAN REALITY OR A FAILED WESTERN MODEL?

The fundamental problem contributing to the failure of all these processes – the ineffectiveness of police reform, the conjoined 'bureaucratic façade' of the DDR process, and the failure of the counter-narcotics drive – was, as early as 2004, being laid by American scholar Barnett Rubin at the door of local Afghan networks, whose alleged resilience undermined the establishment and functioning of stronger formal state institutions. This meant that Afghan institutions like the Ministry of Defence remained mere buildings rather than well-functioning bureaucracies in the Western sense – empty formal structures, into which successive owners then brought their own pre-existing networks of followers and hangers-on. Political actors like Marshal Fahim, with their own powerful pre-existing transnational networks of patronage, would therefore use these ministries for their own ends, while Western-educated Afghan technocrats like Ali Ahmad Jalali in the Interior Ministry, or Ashraf Ghani in the Finance Ministry, no matter how intellectually able, struggled to make progress because of their lack of authentic local networks. The accelerated timetable produced by the Bonn agreement had, in practice, therefore led to the ironic outcome that, in Rubin's assessment, Afghanistan by 2004 had developed a dysfunctional system of 'government without institutions'.[43]

Though this conclusion might seem to lay emphasis on Afghan society's own weaknesses as a consequence of decades of civil war, these problems are in fact better understood as being compounded by Western policy in Afghanistan in 2002–05. Ironically, regional developments can best be seen here not as a result of the formal *absence* or *weakness* of state building, but rather as a consequence of the decentralized, and economically highly privatized, 'liberal peace' agenda. This external strategic direction in fact encouraged the very rapid construction of exactly the *wrong kind* of state, at least when measured against the absolute functional efficiency of the traditional Westphalian model. Warlordism and the absence of an effective bureaucracy were the absolutely natural by-products of an externally dictated and implicitly decentralizing economic agenda, which declared coolly that 'consensus [exists] on the principle that the state should be the enabler rather than the provider of economic growth'.[44]

This externally imposed determination to keep the state in Afghanistan as an abstract, politically disenfranchised facilitator, rather than consciously to encourage the emergence of a robust, independent economic actor – a pattern reflected in the decision to leave reconstruction largely to the global private sector – was dictated by Western neoliberal economic theory that bore remarkably little correlation to how war-torn states had in practice been reconstructed in the recent past. Such an approach rejected not only the 1950s Gerschenkron theoretical model of initial state-led economic takeoff (one variant of which involved using tariff barriers to foster 'infant industries' in order to overcome relative backwardness), but also the real-life examples provided by Keynesianism in the UK, by central planning in Stalinist Russia, or by the massive monopolistic and indigenous *zaibatsu* concerns of post-war Japan. It was, in short, a purely ideological formula, remarkably uninformed by history.[45]

Such policies fostered consequences that were, from the point of view of Afghanistan's own core national interests and stability, even more destructive and politically harmful than they had already proven to be in post-1991 Russia and Eastern Europe. Paradoxically, accelerated democratic elections, conducted in order to please Western sponsors and to complete the Bonn process, re-entrenched known warlords in office, while the dissemination of international aid demonstrated the continuing advantages to be gained from controlling roads, bribing and infiltrating the police, and maintaining personal militias and weapon stockpiles. The illicit drug economy had been effectively pump-primed by a relatively recent Taliban crackdown which pushed up the market value, as well as by the hundreds of thousands of dollars disbursed by the CIA to buy off local actors in 2001. This provided the perfect form of financial liquidity for a Western-imposed economic model in which the state was meant either to disappear completely, or to provide only the bare minimum of regulation. In Afghanistan the Western framework of a 'liberal peace' therefore repeated in practice the consequences that it had already wrought in sub-Saharan Africa and other parts of Asia: political and economic liberalization in practice generated destabilizing side-effects in war-shattered states, which then actually perpetuated instability.[46]

Further compounding the failure of the top-down institution-building process by 2002–05 was the extremely lethargic and inefficient economic reconstruction process itself. There can be no more effective testament to this than the recorded declines in basic Afghan literacy and life expectancy mentioned earlier. Part of the difficulty was generated by the differences that soon ballooned between pledges (political commitments), commitments (expenditure contracts) and disbursements (actual spend) within the international community's aid programme for Afghanistan. With the time between pledges and actual spending typically twelve to thirty-six months, and many large infrastructure projects having an expenditure cycle of five to seven years from conception to conclusion, what was inherently an already slow process (in relative terms) was then further damaged by weak Afghan government capacity and local corruption.[47]

In January 2006, as part of the Afghan Compact, a policy document setting out relations between the international community and Afghanistan for the next five years, the London Conference established a new post-Bonn economic aid package for Afghanistan, pledged to disburse $10.5 billion over the course of five years. Yet these pledges remained declarations rather than guarantees. At two previous conferences – Tokyo in 2002 and Berlin in 2004 – donors had pledged a total of just $13.4 billion towards reconstruction costs (costs which the Afghan government and World Bank had themselves estimated at $27.5 billion over seven years). Against that already unimpressive fiscal backdrop, however, by February 2005 international aid donors had only implemented $3.3 billion in reconstruction projects.[48] The Afghan Compact was viewed in retrospect by many of its key implementers as having been less successful than hoped for when it came to providing a clean break with the past. Dr Peter Middlebrook, who was involved in the Compact's development, admitted later that he ultimately remained deeply dissatisfied by the proliferation of benchmarks (ninety pages' worth of which blighted early draft versions), as well as by the weak compliance and conditionalities embodied in the final document, and a weak accountability framework. In his view, if any major reforms were successful, they had been so 'in spite, not because of the compact'.[49]

As the previous chapter noted, right from the beginning, aid in general was a distinct second priority to the military effort. Between 2001 and 2008, the US government appropriated $127 billion for the war in Afghanistan, and the US military spent nearly $100 million a day; by contrast, the full scale of international aid provided there amounted to just $7 million a day. Put another way, and focusing on the US as easily the largest single international aid donor (at one-third of all aid provided), this meant that, between 2001 and 2005, the United States spent eleven times more on military operations in Afghanistan than it did on reconstruction, humanitarian aid, economic assistance and the training of Afghan security forces combined.[50] At the end of 2005, the US ambassador in Kabul, Ronald Neumann, attempted to rectify at least some of this imbalance by having his embassy pull together a specific USAID (Agency for International Development) request for $873 million over 2007 and 2008 to facilitate road building, electrical power generation and agriculture. After weeks of scrutiny by the Washington-based Office of Management and Budget (OMB), however, only $32 million of additional economic expenditure was eventually authorized.[51]

US donations in particular were also marked by their emphasis on overpriced technical assistance and by the tying of aid to the purchase of American-sourced products and services. While Sweden, Norway, Ireland and the UK each deliberately abstained from drawing up aid agreements with such clauses, a full 70 per cent of US aid was made conditional upon US goods and services being purchased or employed, leading to the related phenomenon of what some have called 'phantom aid'.[52] The cost of delivering aid was consequently driven up, both by the rising security costs generated by an escalating insurgency and by the unrelated but contingent tendency of some of the largest donor states – Japan, Germany and America, in particular – to contract out aid delivery to their own private companies. Typical in this regard was the $665 million in contracts allocated by Washington up until September 2006 to the US firm Louis Berger, in order to build roads, dams, schools and other infrastructure in Afghanistan. The company received a contract to construct the Kabul–Kandahar Highway at a fixed cost of $700,000 per kilometre, despite rival bids from other international companies to carry out the work for $250,000 per kilometre, and it eventually delivered a narrow, two-lane, shoulderless highway at a final cost of $1 million per mile, with the finished product already visibly crumbling by 2006.[53]

Similar results were observable in the 2002 USAID programme to build or refurbish as many as 1,000 schools and hospital clinics by the end of 2004. By September 2004, the $73 million project subcontracted to Louis Berger had produced only 100 finished projects, many of them refurbished buildings, in a process that was again accompanied by astronomical associated construction costs (allocating, for example, $226,000 per site for health clinics, which Afghan and European non-profit groups had estimated could be delivered for $40,000–60,000 apiece). Pressure to complete work to present a success story in time for the 2004 Afghan elections led to the widespread use of low-grade and substandard materials, even as a simultaneous obsession with constructing earthquake-proof buildings drove the introduction of advanced roof designs that were subsequently plagued by structural failures and skyrocketing replacement and maintenance costs.[54]

Former Afghan foreign minister and 2009 presidential candidate Dr Abdullah Abdullah subsequently commented acerbically regarding the overall nature of this reconstruction process, that 'international contracts tend to be subcontracted several times, with each person taking a piece of the pie. The result is that only about $30,000 of an international donation of $100,000 will end up being applied to the actual project.'[55] Moreover, the fact that so much aid was directly implemented or contracted by donors was politically corrosive for Afghanistan itself. As Barnett Rubin pointed out at the time, a government 'which cannot report to its parliament about public expenditure can hardly be called democratic, no matter how many elections it holds'.[56]

PROVINCIAL RECONSTRUCTION TEAMS

Aid delivery during these early years was further shaped by a new experiment in CIMIC (civil–military cooperation), involving the growing deployment by various coalition military forces of provincial reconstruction teams (PRTs). First formally established in early 2003 as the brainchild of combined US–UK efforts, PRTs were initially generally composed of sixty to a hundred soldiers working alongside Afghan advisers, as well as representatives of

US and other foreign aid agencies. They were set up with the explicit aim of spreading the 'ISAF effect' outside Kabul itself, via such localized 'capacity-building' exercises as school construction, disarmament, the repair of irrigation works, the provision of seed supplies, and engagement in local conflict mediation. They were therefore comparable in some ways to the agitprop units established by the Afghan government during the Soviet occupation in the 1980s – efforts that had earlier also attempted to expand sustainable zones of pro-government stability in the rural provinces by distributing wheat, sugar, soap and manufactured products, as well as blankets, free medical aid, electric pumps, cooking oil and kerosene.[57]

In contrast to the agitprop units of the Soviet era, however, the multinational PRTs remained dogged by inconsistent mission statements and procedures, internal civil–military tensions, and often limited resources, and they also remained a source of controversy for the numerous NGOs which were also operating in the country by now, not least due to the implicit politicization and militarization of aid delivery. US-run PRTs, for example, made no bones about threatening to withhold critical aid or infrastructure support if local communities did not cooperate in turning over Taliban insurgents. Before long, three generic (and distinct) models had also emerged for how a PRT should be organized, further complicating the situation. The 'German' model – embodied by the German-led PRT in Kunduz, which, at 420 personnel by 2008, was easily the largest PRT in the country – contained a high proportion of civilians, but was also marked by little civil–military coordination or links with local government. By contrast, American PRTs, of 50–100 personnel, lacked civilian specialists and, at least initially, also performed poorly in assessing regional needs, focusing on large projects instead. Finally, the third variety of PRT – the 'UK' model – emphasized equilibrium between civilian and military personnel, as well as the need to operate through local Afghan politicians.[58]

On top of generic organizational differences, individual sponsoring nations then of course also tended to organize PRTs according to their own particular agendas, leading to numerous anomalies and to the imposition of national caveats and rules of engagement regarding what individual teams could and could not do. This soon repeated the related national 'stove piping' that afflicted the overall NATO–ISAF effort, and resulted in the complete lack of any unified operational strategy for their deployment. German PRTs, for example, remained strictly divided, both administratively and physically, between military and civilians, with civilians reporting directly to Berlin; the Norwegian and Finnish PRTs, by contrast, physically integrated civilians directly into their local PRT 'Command Group', leading at times to an open clash of mindsets on the ground itself. But there were then yet further differences between the Norwegians and the Finns, with the Norwegian PRT representatives seeing themselves in classic neoliberal economic terms as 'enablers' of reconstruction, while the Finnish representatives emphasized a more direct, hands-on, neo-Keynesian approach.[59]

The apparent utility of PRTs to the military counterinsurgency effort was nonetheless underlined when Lieutenant-General Barno (the OEF commander), shortly after taking post in November 2003, backed the expansion of the existing programme as part of his encouragement for an overall doctrinal shift within OEF from 'counterterrorism' to 'counterinsurgency'. This increased PRT numbers from eight to fourteen in the space of less than a year, and subsequent further expansion then led to no fewer than twenty-two PRTs operating in various parts of Afghanistan by 2005. PRTs, however, had a specific functional application for the Americans that was not necessarily shared by other members of the coalition. To US eyes, PRTs, as unified civil–military rural action teams, bore a passing resemblance to the CORDS (Civil Operations and Revolutionary Development Support) programme that had been rolled out in Vietnam in the late 1960s. It was no coincidence that the CORDS experience was now being fed into an increasingly prevalent US narrative about that earlier conflict – one that alleged that America had in fact been on the verge of winning in Vietnam, thanks to a more effective counterinsurgency doctrine, before the armed forces were then betrayed by a collapse in domestic support for the war.[60] The consequent American preference after 2003 for employing PRTs in Afghanistan for immediate military–political objectives (objectives that had a focus on 'hearts and minds') via the delivery of so-called 'quick-impact projects', such as the construction of small local wells, continued to sit ill with the thinking of the wider international development community. Critics argued that such projects continued to delay the building-up of indigenous Afghan capacity, corroded the political neutrality and impartiality of aid delivery, and also remained poorly correlated to the wider regional picture, thereby actively impeding healthy and sustainable longer-term economic development.[61]

ELECTIONS AND CONSTITUTIONS

The Afghan presidential elections of 2004 had been widely touted by the American administration as a major watershed of 'progress' and 'success' in the country, perhaps because they simultaneously marked the symbolic official end of the Bonn process, enshrined the Bush administration's own 'democratization' agenda, and coincided with domestic elections in the United States itself. In reality, however, the deeply flawed Afghan constitution under which these elections occurred embodied in microcosm the wider developmental crisis that was now beginning to grip the Afghan state.

The Afghan elections themselves were largely shaped by Zalmay Khalilzad, the US ambassador in Afghanistan until April 2005, who in the preceding months orchestrated a redoubled reconstruction effort that came to be dubbed, without any apparent hint of irony, 'accelerating success'. This programme was aimed in particular at the establishment of a 'thriving private sector', which Khalilzad proclaimed to be 'as important as rebuilding infrastructure, schools, and clinics'. The broader failure of this reconstruction effort, as well as the catastrophic social inequalities that it introduced and entrenched, has already been outlined above.[62] Khalilzad was also instrumental, however, in stage-managing the acceptance of a heavily American-influenced new Afghan constitution in January 2004, a document so flawed that the International Crisis Group, a Brussels-based think tank, remarked of the initial draft that it 'would fail to provide meaningful democratic governance, including power-sharing, a system of checks and balances, or mechanisms for increasing the representation of ethnic, regional and other minority groups'.[63] Though subsequent drafts of the constitution underwent minor amendments, the resulting document nonetheless continued to commit Afghanistan to holding extremely frequent, highly expensive elections (at least six per decade, with the associated danger of voter fatigue), and also generated an ineffective and corrupt legislature, as well as an over-centralized presidential administration.[64]

The most striking anomaly of the new constitutional arrangements, however, was the setup Karzai himself, following his election to office, then adopted for the subsequent elections to the two-chamber Afghan National Assembly. Here, Karzai opted for the 'single non-transferable vote' system, previously only employed in isolated instances, such as in Japan between 1948 and 1993, the Pitcairn Islands, Jordan and Puerto Rico. By allocating seats to provinces in accordance with their estimated populations, this system actively worked against the emergence of coherent national political parties. The upshot was a strongly presidential system, by which Karzai kept the power to distribute favours and operate with relative autonomy, as long as he retained the support of various warlords, religious elders and drug traffickers. By 2009, when Karzai won a second term on the basis of massive vote-rigging, even American commentators began to recognize that the Afghan constitutional system was deeply flawed, to the point where it was actively undermining the establishment of longer-term political stability.[65]

THE RETURN OF THE TALIBAN

Although international commentators would not begin until nearly 2008 to investigate the possible concrete links between state failure, aid ineffectiveness and escalating insurgency, it is nonetheless perhaps unsurprising that, given the chaotic backdrop outlined above, the Taliban revival in Afghanistan during these years took root and prospered.[66] Preliminary evidence of Taliban reorganization began to become apparent as early as 2002, and by 2003 the first 'spike' in insurgent attacks was being noticed, with long-range stand-off harassing attacks, utilizing salvoes of 107mm or 122mm Chinese rockets. These were soon supplemented by bolder ambushes, targeted assassinations, organized propaganda in the form of *shabnama*, or 'night letters' (proclamations pinned on doors or in public spaces), and full-scale assaults on isolated outposts by as many as 400 fighters at a time. In general, meanwhile, up to

2,000 Taliban fighters were calculated to be acting on both sides of the Afghan–Pakistan border by May 2003.[67]

Taliban numbers were usually composed of two layers – a 'hard core' of fighters, predominantly recruited in the *madrasas* of Pakistan and supplemented by mercenaries and foreign fighters (among them Chechens, Central Asian Uzbeks and Arabs) and, secondly, a Pashtun village network in Afghanistan itself, which the Taliban sought to develop and expand via the influence of local Islamic clergy. Within the 'hard core' existed the so-called 'Kandahari network', with at least four indigenous sub-elements, a strongly ideologically committed current dubbed by some commentators 'the Islamic Movement of the Taliban'. Within the more loosely affiliated village network existed groups that took up arms in reaction against the post-2001 political settlement and with the associated division of power and scarce local resources that had followed.[68] The total number of Taliban fighters rose steadily during the very years when Afghanistan itself was supposedly 'on track', in Ann Marlowe's words, to becoming a 'normal developing country', with the ranks of active fighters growing to 9,500 by 2004, 12,500 by 2005 and 17,000 in 2006. By 2010, the number of Taliban fighters in Afghanistan itself had risen to an estimated 25,000, although exact figures are impossible to verify.[69]

Taliban expansion was facilitated by the re-entrenchment of command and control structures, as well as by some preliminary forms of shadow governance. The first real steps in this direction came in March 2003, when Mullah Omar appointed a Leadership Council (*Rahbari Shura*) in the Pakistani city of Quetta, composed initially of ten, then of twelve, eighteen and finally thirty-three members. Mullah Omar himself, as the spiritual leader (literally the *amir ul-mu'menin*, or 'leader of the faithful') continued to provide a cohesive core around which the movement coalesced.

The trauma of defeat in 2001 apparently contributed to a split within the Taliban, with one group based in southern Afghanistan, dubbing itself the *Jaish-ul Muslimeen* (Army of Muslims), breaking away in September 2003. In December 2004, however, the leader of *Jaish*, Akhbar Agha, was arrested in Pakistan, and by June 2005 the remaining members of the movement had merged back into the mainstream Taliban.[70]

The Taliban movement itself formed four insurgent councils below the level of the main Leadership Council for directing operations in specific geographical areas of Afghanistan. The Quetta Shura – whose membership overlapped with the Leadership Council, but which also appears to be a distinct organization – took responsibility for 'Greater Kandahar' and areas further west up to Herat; the Peshawar Shura took responsibility for eastern Afghanistan; the Miramshah Shura responsibility for Loya Paktia and provinces north towards Kabul; and the Gergi Jangal Shura responsibility for Helmand province.[71] Within this overarching organizational structure, however, there were also at least three distinct organizational sub-components.

The first and most obvious of these was the nascent emergence after 2002 of a new, formally separate, organization, the Tehrik-i-Taliban Pakistan (TTP), established in the FATA territories of Pakistan in response to Pakistani army incursions in that region, and a group whose main agenda remains its conflict with the Pakistani government in Islamabad. The Pakistani army's activities from 2002 onwards in the border region, aimed at 'rooting out' Al Qaeda-affiliated foreign fighters, generated considerable local resentment and passive resistance. Active hostilities began on 8 January 2004, when Nek Mohammad, the first Pakistani Taliban leader, issued orders to treat Pakistani soldiers as legitimate targets (he was himself killed by an American airstrike in June of that same year). From December 2007 up until his death in August 2009, the diminutive (5ft 2in tall) but charismatic Baitullah Mehsud then became the self-proclaimed *amir* of this movement, which, in December 2007, was also formally launched as an umbrella organization that embraced thirteen hitherto disparate local militant groups under a command Shura of forty senior leaders. The TTP by 2007 could muster an estimated 30,000 fighters from across all seven tribal agencies, as well as from the settled districts of Swat, Bannu, Tank, Lakki Marwat, Dera Ismail Khan, Kohistan, Buner and the Malakand division.[72] Whilst the 'Afghan' Taliban's goals remained confined to liberating their country from Western domination, the Pakistani Taliban also maintained close links to Al Qaeda and the broader jihadist agenda of attacking Western influence across the region, leading some to speculate by 2009 that a split was emerging between the two movements.[73] At the time of writing, however, the TTP must still be considered an important manpower resource for the Afghan Taliban to draw upon.

Second in importance in terms of the overall insurgency efforts were the longer-term consequences of Gulbuddin Hikmatyar's return to Afghanistan from Iran in February 2002. In September of that same year, following a failed assassination attempt on him by the CIA, Hikmatyar released a tape publicly proclaiming a *jihad* against the United States. His Hizb-i Islami-yi (HIH) organization thereafter revived its activities in south-eastern Afghanistan, and there was already speculation by mid-2003 that his substantial experience, charisma and organizational abilities were contributing to the insurgency's growing cohesion and relative efficiency. Although loosely a Taliban ally, Hikmatyar maintained a distinct and separate organizational structure. By 2008, he had already become a sufficiently powerful opposition player for the Karzai government to attempt to engage him in independent peace talks.[74]

Third, and more obviously closely affiliated with the Taliban (but still regarded by some Western analysts as a semi-independent sub-faction), is the so-called 'Haqqani network', based in Loya Paktia and centred around the *mujahidin* veteran Jalaluddin Haqqani. By 2010, there was mention of the Karzai government attempting individual peace talks with Haqqani, much as it had attempted earlier with Hikmatyar. Like Hikmatyar, Haqqani possesses the prestige and experience of having been one of the earliest Afghan Islamists (he had participated in the Pakistani-sponsored coup attempt against the Daoud government in 1975), and he also had a solid record as an ISI asset fighting boldly against the Soviets in the 1980s. However, he reconciled much more quickly with the Taliban than Hikmatyar, crossing sides in 1995 and being appointed the Taliban's minister for tribal and frontier affairs in 1998.[75] Old age and illness have since reduced Jalaluddin Haqqani's participation in day-to-day operations, but leadership of his network has passed to his son, Serajuddin, while Jalaluddin Haqqani retains a seat on the Taliban Leadership Council.

Making use of decades of on-the-ground knowledge, the Haqqani network after 2003 was able to rebuild its presence in Paktia province, mirroring the Taliban's wider success in rebuilding its influence within southern Afghanistan 'from the ground up', even as the NATO coalition largely failed in its attempt to entrench top-down governance institutions.[76] Basking in his father's prestige, meanwhile, Serajuddin Haqqani has also come to embody a generational changing of the guard, with the emergence of a younger group of charismatic insurgent leadership. Conducting personal online interviews, and reportedly enjoying the closest links to Al Qaeda of any major Taliban leader, Serajuddin Haqqani has also staged some of the most skilful and professional terrorist attacks on representatives of the Kabul, Indian and American governments right in the heart of the Afghan capital itself.[77]

Against this backdrop, by 2006 the Taliban was capable of organizing annual strategic conferences to agree a common approach for upcoming campaigning seasons. By then it had also formulated a universal *Layeha* (Manual of Military Rules), printed in a format small enough for each individual Taliban fighter to carry into battle. This new rule book, or codex, contained explicit prohibitions against robbery, indiscipline, the harassment of 'innocent people' and the selling of weapons or equipment.[78] Command and control of this 'network of networks' nonetheless remained relatively rudimentary, with village cells of Taliban activists permitted a good deal of autonomy, and specific verbal instructions communicated via a courier network. The Taliban's experiments with coordination using mobile phones quickly revealed the dangers of signals intelligence (SIGINT) interdiction by NATO forces, leading them to fall back on short-range radios, motorbike couriers, or even torch signalling. The limitations of such a system for coordinating large units of men became apparent in September 2006, when the Taliban's attempts to deliberately bring about a relatively large-scale ground battle on terrain of their own choosing just outside Kandahar were ruthlessly punished by American airpower.[79]

However difficult it remained for the Taliban to transition successfully from ambushes to something that more closely resembled regular warfare, the years 2002–06 were nonetheless critical to their general revival, in terms both of re-establishing a recognized chain of command, and of generating a viable logistical infrastructure in southern Afghanistan itself. The latter required long-range infiltration by insurgent units from Pakistan, establishing influence at the village level by means of threats, 'night letters' and charitable acts, and subsequently selecting safe houses for the storage of the heavier weaponry – machine guns, RPGs, recoilless guns and mortars – which could not be moved quickly or in large quantities in daylight.[80]

The Taliban's reliance on small teams to establish forward operating bases and spread their political influence by increments bore some important similarities to its initial strategy for rapidly escalating their presence in Afghanistan in 1994–96, but the continuing flexibility of their overall approach also allowed the incorporation of certain new individual elements, such as suicide bombers, increasingly powerful and sophisticated improvised explosive devices (IEDs), and a more skilful and effective propaganda arm. The latter effort now included printed magazines, websites such as Al Emarah (The Emirate – updated daily in five languages), cassettes, the creation of corporate-style branding logos for official Taliban publications, and DVD propaganda videos. It also incorporated extensive briefing by a variety of eloquent media spokesmen who, operating after January 2007 under the aliases Qari Yousaf or Zabihullah Mujahid for security purposes, regularly updated the international press by telephone or text messaging on the course of Taliban operations.[81]

OPTIMISM AND DENIAL

As we have seen, the reconstruction effort during this period was underfunded, corruption-riddled and disorganized, the result of strategic disorganization within the international donor community and the unevenness (and in many cases actual stagnation) of security sector reform. Oddly, however, the prevailing mood in the West was optimistic, and there was a commonly held belief that the Taliban military threat was on the wane. Indeed, at a time when the situation in Iraq began to worsen dramatically in the face of an escalating insurgency in 2005–06, the efforts of coalition forces in Afghanistan were, by contrast, proudly held up by one American armed forces journal as 'the war we're winning'.[82] One prominent American reporter meanwhile declared the Taliban in March 2005 to be a 'busted flush', its leadership 'beginning to split', and quoted Major-General Eric Olson, OEF commander at the time, opining that the Taliban were 'a force in decline'.

Behind the scenes, American intelligence agencies were reportedly equally optimistic in portraying the Taliban as a force so weakened that it had ceased to pose a threat. Secretary of State for Defense Donald Rumsfeld had visited Afghanistan in May 2003 and, in a variation on President Bush's infamous (and near-simultaneous) 'mission accomplished' speech in Iraq, declared that major combat operations in Afghanistan were over, signalling that a more peaceful era of security, stabilization and reconstruction had begun.[83] Another typical American analysis from the autumn of 2005 stated that the overall situation in Afghanistan had evolved to the point where 'guarded optimism is justified' and that a 'large infusion of Western soldiery is not necessary', suggesting instead that the main remaining obstacle to complete stability was the correct coordination of governance institutions.[84] An assessment by the Strategic Studies Institute of the US Army War College from April 2005 was similarly dismissive of the Taliban threat. It portrayed warlords as the main remaining problem, with the Taliban/Al Qaeda coalition dismissed as an insurgency that had been effectively 'defanged'; insurgent 'remnants' might possibly be able to continue 'low level' activities for many years, but this threat was supposedly also becoming more and more manageable by the Afghan police.[85]

As we shall see, events in 2006–09 quickly demonstrated just how dangerously delusional this American (and more broadly coalition-led) intelligence assessment of the level of progress in Afghanistan had become. In retrospect, metrics of violence pointed to a steady rise in resistance to the coalition presence. Suicide attacks, for example, increased from just one or two in 2002–03 to 140 by 2007, whilst between 2005 and 2006 the number of remotely detonated bombings more than doubled – from 530 to 1,297 – and the number of armed attacks nearly tripled, with direct fire attacks increasing from 1,347 to 3,824. Between 2005 and 2006 as well, the number of attacks on Afghan forces rose from 713 to 2,892 and on coalition forces from 919 to 2,496; and the number of attacks on Afghan government officials increased 2.5 times. Attacks on Afghan forces therefore increased by more than 300 per cent, while, according to contested figures, between 4,000 and 4,400 Afghans overall, both civilian and combatant, also died in conflict-related violence in 2006 – more than double the number for 2005, and more than for any other single year since 2001.[86]

THE BARNO THESIS

The rapidly deteriorating security situation from 2006 onwards led to a degree of historical revisionism when commentators reflected on the optimism that had preceded it. An increasingly influential critique in Washington circles was produced by Lieutenant-General David Barno, the key American commander on the ground during the period 2003–05. By 2007, he was retrospectively blaming the reverses experienced after 2005 not on the inaccurate intelligence and blind optimism of his own tenure, but on NATO's assumption of overall leadership of the military effort in Afghanistan in October 2006. This shift, it was claimed, imposed a fatally cumbersome NATO command chain, and also highlighted the inability of America's main allies, as they assumed a more prominent military role, to correctly master the fundamental principles of counterinsurgency (COIN) doctrine.[87] This chapter has shown that, in reality, such an analysis of the 2002–05 period is, at best, simplistic and self-serving, and at worst colossally delusional, and that it was in fact the near-lethal combination of blind optimism and neglect prevailing in 2002–05 (a cycle of optimism that has periodically recurred in Western decision-making councils regarding Afghanistan ever since) that laid the ground for the subsequent Taliban revival of 2006–07.

Both Barno and Ambassador Khalilzad were replaced in 2005, Barno on the military side by Lieutenant-General Karl Eikenberry, and Zalmay Khalilzad on the diplomatic side by Ambassador Ronald Neumann. Once in post, Neumann rapidly came to the personal conclusion that, in retrospect, the reports and briefings on progress in Afghanistan that he had heard or read back in Washington prior to his own posting were dangerously exaggerated.[88] While the sharp spike in violence that was to come can partly be attributed to coalition attempts from 2006 onwards to spread the remit of the Kabul government further into the Pashtun-dominated south of the country, clearly much on the ground had already gone wrong, and glaring underlying weaknesses had either been ignored or covered up, for the security situation after 2005 to suddenly deteriorate and spin so alarmingly out of control. Most American analysis was already ludicrously optimistic – to the point of delusion – about Afghanistan's progress and prospects in 2002–06.[89]

This continuity of over-optimism was also less than coincidental. The strategic narrative that Afghanistan had been generally heading along the 'right path' between 2003 and 2005 (a view also neatly encapsulated by this chapter's opening quote), with progress then only derailed by subsequent misguided changes in the administrative command structure, was also the later rationale behind US Senator (and 2008 Republican presidential candidate) John McCain's own vocal endorsement of a troop surge and a redoubled counterinsurgency 'strategy' in Afghanistan in early 2009.[90]

In June 2005, the Taliban carried out their single most sophisticated military attack to date, shooting down a US Chinook helicopter over Kunar province, killing all sixteen US Special Forces men on board, and then, for propaganda purposes, filming the captured laptop, field radio and GPS equipment that had fallen into their hands. Disturbing as such isolated incidents were, however, the full extent of the Taliban revival would not become completely apparent in the West until the British attempted to extend the remit of the Afghan government into Helmand province in 2006. The operation that followed both exposed the extent of coalition hubris regarding the progress made in Afghanistan up until that date, and also served as the opening act for several years of subsequent escalating violence and instability.

CHAPTER FIVE

RETURN TO THE 'FORGOTTEN WAR', 2006–08

After Colonel Knaggs had given his spiel about coming as friends and wanting to help the people of Helmand, the two women made speeches, to the shock of the men in this very conservative society. Several men jiggled worry beads noisily while they spoke and one cleaned his ear out with a cotton bud. Afterwards an old man in white got up and accused the women of being spies . . . The elders were then shown into another room where a projector had been set up. In a stunning indication of the chasm in thinking between London and the reality on the ground someone has come up with the idea of making a film to show locals which comprises five minutes of the underwater [television] BBC series Blue Planet, *followed by a message from the Governor of Helmand and the coalition forces, followed by five more minutes of the* Blue Planet. *The tribal leaders of Gereshk sat in utter bafflement, matched only by my own, as images of whales and dolphins were projected on the wall. 'Let's turn this off, shall we?' said Major Blair, looking embarrassed.*[1]

IF THE PERIOD 2002–05 saw incoherent international policy and strategy waste the opportunities that the overthrow of the Taliban and the scattering of Al Qaeda had presented, the year 2006 heralded the beginning of the period of consequences. The previous chapter illustrated the weaknesses and delusions in the thesis that claims Afghanistan had been on the 'right path' in this earlier stage, only to be derailed by greater NATO involvement later. Nevertheless, this critique does not imply that the manner in which NATO extended its remit, and the broader international approach from 2006 onwards, should be viewed positively. The strategic incoherence and lack of clarity that marked the intervention from the start was to continue unabated. This chapter will show that, while the coalition approach in 2006–08 did not *cause* the downward spiral in Afghanistan, it did nothing to arrest it, and in fact actually accelerated the pace.

NATO INCREASES ITS ROLE

As was discussed in the previous chapter, it is impossible to understand how and why NATO broadened its role in Afghanistan without grasping the complex and fraught intra-Alliance politics that preceded the move. To a large extent, NATO policy was driven more by concerns over what Afghanistan could do for NATO, than what NATO could do for Afghanistan. However, by 2006 cracks were already beginning to show in the coherence of the Alliance approach. The expansion of the remit to the west of Afghanistan had already become problematic. A combination of the Alliance principle that 'costs lie where they fall' (meaning simply that states cover their own costs for operations) and the embryonic recognition of a growing insurgency threat ensured that the perennial NATO problem of turning promises into forces on the ground asserted itself.[2] The Italians were finally inveigled into leading the expansion to the west.

Nevertheless, the general agreement that taking over ISAF and deploying to Afghanistan was vital if the Alliance was to be strengthened did not extend to agreement over the type of operations to be conducted. Many of the domestic populations of the European member states were ambivalent about the deployment and would be extremely hostile to full-scale combat operations. Indeed, for a number of states, participation in such operations would be politically impossible. From an early stage, therefore, NATO sought to differentiate the ISAF mission from the more robust counterterrorism mission being conducted mostly by American forces under Operation Enduring Freedom (OEF). Consequently, the ISAF mission was portrayed as post-conflict stabilization and reconstruction, rather than as counterterrorism or counterinsurgency.

Even the British, who had a recent history of conducting robust military operations, were keen to establish this distinction in the minds of the public. As late as April 2006, the UK secretary of defence at the time, John Reid, while on a trip to Kabul, was emphasizing the 'reconstruction' focus of the British mission. Indeed, it was on this excursion that he famously announced that 'we [the British] would be perfectly happy' to leave in three years (the projected length of the mission at that time) without a shot being fired.[3] When the number of bullets discharged by British forces in Afghanistan began to be counted in the millions, Reid was to claim that his statement had not been a prediction. Semantically this was true, but this subtle use of language was, as doubtless intended, rather lost on the British people in the run-up to the initial deployment.

The issue had been made even more sensitive by comments from Donald Rumsfeld in late 2005. As the security situation in Iraq rapidly deteriorated, it became clear that there was a growing Pentagon desire to replace some of the 20,000 American troops in Afghanistan with other NATO forces. Rumsfeld let it be known at a September meeting of NATO defence ministers in Berlin that it would be desirable for the Alliance to develop counterterrorism and counterinsurgency capabilities. The implications were clear, and a number of European ministers rushed out statements to the media rejecting a merging of the 'two missions' in Afghanistan.[4]

In December 2005, with spectacularly bad timing, Rumsfeld announced that American forces were to be reduced by 3,000 by the following spring.[5] It was a decision made against the strong advice of the US ambassador in Kabul.[6] The signal appeared unmistakable. Despite denials, it seemed that the US commitment was drawing down, and that US forces were to be replaced by those of other NATO members. As a morale booster for the Taliban and Al Qaeda, and an invitation to step up attacks on the new incoming forces, it would be hard to beat. This was compounded by the fact that the ISAF forces that had deployed since the well-received first rotation under General McColl in 2002 had not exactly impressed the Afghans with their martial spirit. Among Afghans, ISAF was beginning to acquire the nickname the 'International Shopping Assistance Force', on the grounds that its members were only visible when in Kabul, purchasing gifts at the end of their tours.[7] The frequency and intensity of violence increased steadily through 2006. However, it was to be the move south, led by the UK, that marked a new and deadly chapter in the conflict and that generated further questions about the strategic coherence with which the intervention was being conducted.

NATO CONTEMPLATES THE SOUTH

From early 2004 onwards, the British were aware that they were going to be in the vanguard of the move south. The Canadians were also committed, and the Dutch tentatively indicated that they would participate. Elements from other countries would also have a presence in what was to be called Regional Command (RC) South, but these three countries were to be at the heart of the deployment.[8] All three were initially motivated by their long attachments to NATO and concerns over the frostiness of transatlantic relations, but, as the agreed 2006 date approached, other considerations also entered into the British calculations. Their presence in southern Iraq was both increasingly unpopular domestically and onerous in terms of resources. As the Iraqi security situation began to deteriorate markedly through 2004 and 2005, a growing yearning became evident in London to reduce the British commitment. The problem was how to do this while maintaining the positive relationship with Washington that had been at the heart of the British decision to join the invasion of Iraq in the first place. Taking on some of the 'stabilization and reconstruction' burden in Afghanistan appeared to provide a neat solution.[9] UK forces could be presented not as 'going home' but rather as redeploying to the Afghan theatre.

In addition, the NATO expansion to the south was going to be initially run under the Allied Rapid Reaction Corps (ARRC). This is a British-led and dominated deployable headquarters that is viewed as something of a jewel in the crown of the UK's allied commitment – to quote General Sir David Richards, who was commander of the ARRC during its Afghan deployment and became head of the UK's armed forces in 2010: 'It [the ARRC] is a real prize that the UK possesses and needs looking after.'[10] A successful deployment under the ARRC would, therefore, not only enhance NATO generally, but would also solidify Britain's military reputation at a time when some elements of the US military were questioning Britain's reliability following the difficulties the British had faced in southern Iraq.

The notable absentee from all these debates and political currents surrounding NATO and its member states was, of course, any sense of profound thinking about developments in Afghanistan itself. The intervention still awaited a coherent strategy. At times, particularly in the NATO context, it appeared that the strategic goal was simply to deploy. The ends, ways and means calculations that could link the various strands of international activity in the country to a coherent and agreed political purpose seemed peripheral to the high politics being played out in Western capitals.

The almost casual way in which important decisions regarding the intervention were taken was further illustrated by the manner in which the southern provinces were divided up between Britain, Canada and the Netherlands. The two most challenging provinces were clearly going to be Kandahar and Helmand. Kandahar was, in essence, the spiritual home of the Taliban movement and a key focus for its activities. Helmand was less well known in NATO circles, but was home, as we shall see, to a highly complex array of tribal rivalries, drug gangs and armed groups. Many, including David Richards, assumed that the British would be based in Kandahar. It seemed logical, given the symbolic importance of Kandahar City and the fact that the British, it was further assumed, would be providing the strongest military force. However, at a meeting in Ottawa in early 2005, the Canadians asked to 'do' Kandahar and the British agreed.

The British agreement does not seem to have been based on a great deal of thought, and certainly not on consultation with the armed forces. When asked in 2010 why the decision had been taken, the head of the British army at the time, General Sir Mike Jackson, replied with a pithy 'Search me, guv!',[11] while Richards was rather more forthcoming when asked to give his views on the subject. His belief that Kandahar, not Helmand, was the key location led him to make inquiries about the rationale for the change; apparently to no avail, given his later comment that, 'I've never yet had a good reason given me why that decision was taken.'[12] Some superficial logic could be found in the fact that Helmand, in 2006, produced about 42 per cent of the poppy crop for the whole of Afghanistan, and the UK was, nominally at least, the 'lead nation' for counter-narcotics.[13] Yet nothing in the planning or execution of the UK mission suggests that this was at the heart of British thinking, and, as will be illustrated later in the chapter, the world still awaits a coherent rationale for where counter-narcotics fits into coalition intervention strategy.

It was an agreement the British would have some cause to regret. Detailed knowledge of the Helmand security landscape appeared to be in short supply in London. Those with an interest in military history could vaguely recall from their studies a great British defeat in the area at the battle of Maiwand in 1880, and the area's capacity to produce industrial quantities of opium had registered; but the overall intelligence picture was extremely limited.[14] Less forgivably, it appears that there were those in London who were relatively unconcerned about the lack of intelligence. Mark Etherington, a civilian contributor to the planning process, recalls the response of one official in late 2005 when doubts were expressed regarding the lack of an effective intelligence picture: 'We know what we need to know about Helmand.'[15] What that unnamed official clearly did not know was that the British were about to poke a very large hornets' nest with a very short stick.

ENDING 'UNGOVERNED SPACES': ONE MORE DELUSION

Before examining in detail NATO's, and particularly Britain's, deployment south, it is worth exploring one of the consistently debilitating obsessions of the international intervention. We are talking here about the belief that the most difficult areas of Afghanistan are those characterized as 'ungoverned spaces'. Furthermore, that a viable, sensible and enduring solution to the problems of Afghanistan, and the problems Afghanistan might cause, is to extend the range and effectiveness of central government control of these areas. Although an increasingly discredited analysis, this view has held remarkable sway over much of the thinking that has informed the intervention. Even the Bush administration, which had demonized 'state-building' in the period 2001–02, came to implicitly accept the logic of this position towards the end of its term in office. It represents, in a highly competitive field, perhaps the most overly simplistic of the analyses that have underpinned what has passed for strategy.

At its heart lies a series of linked assumptions about the relationship between liberal political and economic structures, security and stability, and the role of the state. Stripped to its essentials, the core belief is that the manner in which a state orders its internal social, political and economic relations is inextricably linked to the degree of threat likely to be posed by that state to the 'international community'. Thus, strong, authoritarian states are a threat because the behaviour of their leaders cannot be curbed by the naturally peaceable force of democratic checks and balances. However, weak, fragile and failed states are also a threat, because they cannot exert control over their territory and prevent malign forces from operating unchecked. Consequently, encouraging the development of 'effective' states, which can exercise control over their national territories, constrained by liberal social, political and economic structures, is not just a morally 'good' thing, but also a sensible, hard-headed strategy for the maintenance of international security.

This belief is deeply rooted in Western thinking, even in world views that may at first appear diametrically opposed. The Bush administration may have been initially vigorous in its opposition to American troops 'nation-building', but this was partly because it felt this to be unnecessary. By 'cutting the head off the snake' or 'regime-change', the natural desire of all peoples to organize themselves in a manner that resembles Western (or at least 'Western-lite') ways of life would inevitably win out. This deep ideological belief in the universality of American values littered the rhetoric of George Bush. In an exchange with Bob Woodward, he made this clear: 'I say that freedom is not America's gift to the world. Freedom is God's gift to everybody in the world.'[16] Others differ in their rhetorical emphases, but the sense of universal solutions to international problems is a common theme. The conditionalities applied by international organizations to aid provision, linked as they are to detailed notions of 'good governance', and the almost theological approach of Western development agencies also demonstrate this inclination.

Universal approaches, by definition, are the enemy of context and nuance. They also impede the careful balancing of ends, ways and means. When British Prime Minister Gordon Brown asserted in a speech on Afghanistan that 'there can be only one winner: democracy and a strong Afghan state', and elsewhere that 'a safer Britain requires a safer Afghanistan', we are entering a world of dizzyingly circular arguments.[17] The objective becomes indistinguishable from the means of achieving it. The goal of a democratic and strong Afghan state is not only inevitable but the only way by which terrorism can be defeated and the world made safe. However, terrorism must be beaten so that a strong and democratic Afghan state can emerge.

The twin beliefs that strong, democratic state institutions in Afghanistan are both achievable and the answer to all the security problems the intervention was designed to alleviate is deeply held. Ronald Neumann, US ambassador to Afghanistan between July 2005 and April 2007, recalls rejecting a particular Karzai initiative in mid-2006:

> In meetings in March and mid-May he [Karzai] repeatedly raised the ideas of rearming tribal forces to contest the Taliban and its allies operating in the east . . . We resisted this approach . . . as did all the ambassadors of allied states and the UN and EU chiefs . . . Even if militia forces backed-up by coalition troops and air strikes could win local victories, we would only be strengthening forces inimical to central government.[18]

Apart from the highly ironic aspect of rejecting an initiative from the democratically elected president of an ostensibly sovereign country on the grounds that it is 'inimical to central government', this passage shows the deeply ingrained belief, in 2006, that a centralized state would be able to resolve Afghanistan's security dilemmas. It also illustrates, of course, the fundamentally inconsistent approach of the US, given that arming and empowering militias appeared to be the centrepiece of American policy before and immediately after the fall of the Taliban.

Not to be outdone, the new British defence secretary, Des Browne, weighed in a few months later with his own take on the subject of 'governance'. When questioned before the House of

Commons Defence Committee on whether the UK was achieving its objectives, he expanded on the notion of extending the reach of Afghan government and on the difficulties in achieving this. Apparently, it was especially difficult in Pashtun-dominated areas. He asked the committee to realize that 'particularly in parts of the south and in the east, there was literally very little, or no, governance in the past, substantially these were ungoverned spaces . . . For *decades* [our emphasis] there was little or no governance in these areas.'[19]

Browne was clearly conflating the absence of central state control with the absence of 'governance' *per se*. The Pashtun lands of the south and east had rarely been under the control of Kabul. Indeed, attempts to exert such control had invariably provoked fierce, and successful, Pashtun resistance. However, traditionally, Pashtun tribal societies could lay claim to a history of being some of the most intricately 'governed' societies in the world.

Their form of governance is much less hierarchical than that seen in many tribal systems elsewhere in the world. *Khans* and *maliks* of clans or tribes may be highly respected, but they do not issue binding commands and orders in a traditional leadership sense. Similarly, the mullah may be the voice of the local religious establishment, but he does not dominate village decision-making. Major decisions are taken collectively, through the *jirga*, or tribal assembly of elders. More personalized informal clusters of *qawm* networks, discussed in Chapter One, also provide group identity.

Overlaying all this, and seeping into every aspect of Pashtun life, is the pre-Islamic tribal code of *Pashtunwali*. This combines collective mechanisms of social responsibility and justice with demands on individual conduct dominated by notions of honour, revenge, chivalry and freedom. Honour is at the heart of a Pashtun's notion of self. The loss of honour is an appalling fate that must be remedied, usually by revenge. In the early days of the intervention, Western soldiers would be puzzled by the extremely emotional reaction of families when even relatively low-key house-to-house searches were conducted. The reason was that the intrusion not only dishonoured the women present, but also – and far more importantly in this highly patriarchal society – humiliated the male members of the family charged under *Pashtunwali* with the protection of 'their' women's honour.

The traditionally delicate tribal balance has been progressively disrupted by the mass population movements and traumas caused by the Soviet invasion, civil wars and violent struggles for power and influence. The traditional form of Pashtun governance became fragmented, and the Taliban, suspicious of the solidarity and insularity of tribal mores, which they considered 'un-Islamic', took advantage by infiltrating mullahs trained in the Deobandi *madrasas* that proliferated over the border in Pakistan, and from which the Taliban were born.[20] It is through the mullahs that the Taliban partly reconstituted their influence after the rout of 2001. This subversion of Pashtun structures is a potential source of friction between Pashtuns in general and the Taliban. David Kilcullen quotes one Pashtun on the issue:

> The *mullah* is telling people in the *jirga* what to do, giving the prayers *and* giving the orders – but he is just a village schoolteacher, not a leader! *Pashtunwali* has been neglected, because of radicalization: they don't know our code of life because they only know the *madrassa* and how to make more *madrassas*.[21]

There is a huge conceptual and logical leap, however, from recognizing the disruption in Pashtun tribal structures to pontificating on ideas of 'ungoverned space'. *Pashtunwali* still governs the manner in which Pashtuns think about themselves and how they order their social relations. The notion that extension of central state control could be seen as a viable and legitimate alternative to Pashtun ways of governance is politically and historically illiterate. Johnson and Mason, in one of the best short expositions on the Pashtun way of life and the fatuity of the 'ungoverned spaces' thesis, conclude: 'With its own conflict resolution mechanisms, Pashtun hill society is one in which government and externally imposed order are not simply anathema but the antithesis of what is good.'[22] The failure to grasp this, typified by Des Browne's comments noted above, did not bode well for the success of the NATO mission in the south. It does, though, shed light on how the government he represented could come to the conclusion that it was reasonable to send brilliant, authoritative Western women, armed with slides of whales and dolphins, to lead the engagement with elders of one of the most male-dominated and conservative communities on the planet; and in a country that is land-locked.

POKING THE HORNETS' NEST

The NATO deployment south got off to a rocky start. The original plan called for it to begin in February 2006. However, a political storm in the Netherlands erupted when sections of the Dutch parliament, somewhat presciently, expressed concern that the security situation in the southern provinces was too volatile for meaningful 'stabilization and reconstruction' to be conducted.[23] The British let it be known that their preparations were on hold until the Dutch position became clear, and until the implications for force levels were apparent. The Dutch parliament finally gave its approval in early February, resulting in a two-month delay in

165

the overall deployment. The timing was significant, for it meant that troops would not begin arriving until April and would not be fully ready in theatre until July. The traditional 'fighting season' in the south begins in April and May, after the poppy harvest is gathered. Consequently, troops were in battle almost as soon as they arrived.

Relations with the Karzai government were also deteriorating. The British demanded that he remove the provincial governor of Helmand, Sher Mohammed Akhundzada, and the governor of Uruzgan, Jan Mohammed Khan, on the grounds that they were corrupt and deeply enmeshed in drug production and trafficking. The nine tonnes of opium discovered in the basement of Akhundzada's office rather supported the British claims.[24] Karzai, however, was reluctant to accede to British demands, partly because doing so might cast doubts over his independence from foreign influence, but also because the two men concerned were long-standing allies whom he had appointed on the grounds that they were powerful local tribal figures that could maintain a degree of influence, if not control, over the difficult provinces. From the perspective of Kabul in 2006, the main strategic problem was keeping together the rickety alliance of Tajiks, Uzbeks, Hazaras and Pashtuns that coexisted in uneasy proximity in the government. The fear of government collapse and civil war was never far from Karzai's thoughts.[25]

Installing powerful local figures and past associates like Akhundzada and Jan Mohammed Khan, brutal and corrupt as they were, was one of the few ways in which Karzai could exert even a modicum of influence over the violent and complex tribal politics of the south. Nevertheless, the British made their removal a precondition for deployment, and Karzai conceded. Akhundzada's replacement in the volatile Helmand province was Mohammed

Daoud, who took over in December 2005. Although Daoud had more connections, particularly around Gereshk, than most commentators gave him credit for, he was not anywhere near as powerful a figure in the region as Akhundzada had been.[26] Akhundzada was made an Afghan senator and his presence in Kabul would allow him to remain close to Karzai. His influence, as we shall see later in the chapter, would also continue to cast a long shadow over Helmand.

Karzai's irritation over British demands was magnified when news began to filter through to Kabul of the sort of force levels NATO was planning to send to the south. In particular, the news that only 3,300 additional British troops were slated to deploy left the government in Kabul incredulous. Incredulity would later turn to shock when it became clear that, given modern Western armies' long support and logistics tails, 3,300 actually equated to about a battalion, or around 600 combat troops. Following Britain's assertiveness over preconditions for deployment, the Afghans could be forgiven for wondering whether 'speak loudly and carry a small stick' had replaced Theodore Roosevelt's more famous dictum.

The likely results, viewed from Kabul, were obvious. The Taliban would see such a deployment, coupled with the announcement of the American reduction noted above, as a clear sign that ISAF and the West in general were not fully committed, thus opening the way for the Taliban to attack. The British would be forced, in the absence of 'mass' on the ground, to rely on air support as a force multiplier, causing inevitable civilian casualties and political fallout. The Karzai government was acutely aware that there was a virtually inexhaustible supply of cannon fodder in the *madrasas* across the border in Pakistan. Indeed, seeking to influence traditional mullahs to reassert their influence over the *madrasas*, and thus marginalize more radical religious leaders both in the border region and in Pashtun areas within Afghanistan, was a major focus for the government. Philip Wilkinson, who shared this basic analysis, was on the receiving end of Afghan frustration in the presidential palace. He confirms that he wrote a number of memos to the British embassy in Kabul, outlining the inevitable consequences if the deployment went ahead as planned.[27] It is not known whether his analysis reached London, or, if it did, whether it was even read. It was certainly not acted upon.

It is worth exploring in a little more depth what was awaiting the British in Helmand – partly because the province has seen some of the most consistently fierce fighting, but mainly because the complex interplay of tribal dynamics, drugs and Taliban activity gives a flavour of what such trite phrases as 'extending governance', 'stabilizing the country' and 'countering insurgency and terrorism' mean in the crucible of Afghanistan.

The main tribal groupings in the Helmand area are the Alizai, Alokozai, Baloch, Barakzai, Ishaqzai and Noorzai. In 2002, Karzai connected with those former influential tribal leaders, many of them warlords kicked out by the Taliban, who he felt would support him. In Helmand, that meant Akhundzada and Dad Mohammad Khan, known locally, but rarely affectionately, as Amir Dado. Akhundzada, of the Hassanzai branch of the Alizai, was made provincial governor, and Amir Dado, of the Alokozai, Helmand intelligence chief. From 2002 to 2005, a wearily familiar pattern asserted itself: initial hopes of improvement in the life of ordinary people were rapidly extinguished as the governor and intelligence chief ruthlessly favoured their individual and tribal networks, while excluding and preying upon rivals through use of their own personal militias.[28] The Ishaqzai, in particular, were systematically marginalized. To this already combustible mix was added the huge drug trade in the province and region more generally. The Ishaqzai and Noorzai were major players in the drugs trade, but Akhundzada and Amir Dado attempted to turn political influence into a bigger share of the pie in deals with the drug and transport mafias.

The growing Taliban presence in the province began to be swollen disproportionately by recruits from the marginalized tribes, particularly the Ishaqzai, who quickly became the leading Taliban-supporting tribe in the province. When Akhundzada was removed in late 2005, he would later claim that, no longer able to pay his people their full dues, he encouraged them to go over to the Taliban.[29] However, his brother, Amir Mohammed Akhundzada, was made Daoud's deputy, maintaining the family influence in provincial government. Taliban influence had increased steadily in Helmand through 2006. A brutal, but highly effective, commander, Mullah Dadullah Akhund, was at the forefront, and it was becoming clear that some sort of Taliban offensive was in the offing right across the south of the country.

The British were about to enter, therefore, a bewildering cauldron of overlapping conflict dynamics. Multiple connections between feuding tribes, drug mafias and local militias led, as Tom Coghlan notes, to 'endless factionalism'.[30] It was clear that the Taliban threat had been growing even under Akhundzada. However, the local militias, drug gangs, tribal politics and multiple loyalties formed a constraining environment for the Taliban as well, and they were obliged to do deals and make compromises. The removal of some of Akhundzada's influence created a gap that the British would be unable to fill. Broadly, the UK was faced with two basic choices: send a small force and recognize that, however unpalatable, it would be necessary to work with the power realities as they stood, including Akhundzada; or change those power realities, send a large force to fill the vacuum, and deal with the consequences. In keeping with the nature of the intervention in general, the option chosen combined the worst of both worlds.

British forces began to deploy in April, and on 1 May 2006 they officially took over control of the small American PRT in the provincial capital of Lashkar Gah. The plan, put together in late 2005, was for a 'development zone' to be established in the triangle between Lashkar Gah, the main military base at Camp Bastion to the north-west of the capital, and Gereshk. The military would establish security in this area, in order to create space for civilian agencies to begin their development work. It began to go wrong almost immediately.

The first issue concerned the confused and dysfunctional military command structure. NATO/ISAF was not due to take formal control in the south until 31 July, at which point the coalition's RC South headquarters in Kandahar, then under the command of a Canadian brigadier, David Frazer, would come under its remit. The British task force was actually deployed under OEF, which placed it, technically, under Combined Forces Command-Afghanistan (CFC-A), the US-led headquarters in Kabul. This American headquarters had a subordinate command, Combined Joint Task Force-76 (CJTF-76), led by US Major-General Benjamin Freakley, who would outrank the British brigadier in overall command of UK forces, Ed Butler. What this bewildering array of acronyms and lines of authority suggests, apart from the convoluted nature of the international military effort at the time, was that Brigadier Butler's only clear chain of command was back to the UK, not in theatre.[31] This might not have mattered if the force had simply been establishing itself and making preparations, as the NATO command structure would be in place three months later. However, the British were not afforded this luxury, and the dysfunctional command structure became a very significant issue.

In mid-May there was a serious upsurge in violence as Mullah Dadullah orchestrated attacks across four provinces, including Kandahar and Helmand.[32] As the security situation began to deteriorate rapidly, Butler came under pressure from Governor Daoud to deploy British troops to some of the main troublespots across the province. In a later interview, Daoud confirmed that utilizing his police force was not an option: 'Officially we had seventeen hundred policemen in Helmand, but actually we had two hundred and fifty ... the rest answered to warlords.'[33] 'Warlords' in this instance was probably code for the Akhundzada (including the deputy governor) and Amir Dado family networks.

In a move that was to prove highly controversial, Brigadier Butler deployed troops into small fortified bases that came to be called 'platoon houses', dotted around northern Helmand and the regionally vital Kajaki dam.[34] These deployments were well away from the original 'development zone' that the British plan had emphasized. Butler would later claim that he came under intense pressure from Daoud and the Afghan government in Kabul, which also got the Americans to exert pressure on the British government. Daoud's response was that the decisions were consensual. The truth probably lies somewhere in between. Certainly, Daoud was insistent, but the pressure to get to grips with the enemy was not wholly uncongenial to an SAS commander (which Butler had been) or to his battle group, which mostly comprised Parachute Regiment troops, some of the most robust in the British army.

The argument rapidly became overtaken by events, as small pockets of British forces in the platoon houses became fixed in a series of defensive positions that rapidly became the focus of major Taliban attention. The fighting was prolonged and very intense. Heavily outnumbered and at the end of long and precarious supply chains, the forces had no option but to call in heavy and frequent air strikes to prevent their positions from being overrun. The fighting played perfectly to Taliban propaganda, which had resurrected the ghosts of 'Maiwand' by emphasizing that the 'historical enemy', the British, had returned for revenge and, as counter-narcotics 'lead nation', were also determined to confiscate local people's poppy. For a population steeped in notions of slights and revenge, it was perfectly plausible. It showed that London's incomprehension of Pashtuns was mutual: the idea that the Blair government, which had gained a reputation as the epitome of liberal, metropolitan disdain for Britain's imperial past, would launch a punitive expedition to avenge the loss of a British force from the nineteenth century was risible.[35] However, it was a widely held view among local people.

The effects of the British 'platoon house' deployments were far-reaching. The plan to provide significant development assistance in an ever-growing area of stability was still-born. Formulaic references to 'winning hearts and minds' became embarrassing, given the destruction that was wreaked in the immediate vicinities of UK defensive positions. David Richards, the incoming ISAF commander, let it be known privately that he was appalled at the situation British forces had found themselves in. When questioned the following year by a parliamentary committee on whether there was a negative effect on local Afghan opinion, he replied with very heavy irony, 'clearly the immediate vicinities of the Platoon Houses became areas where the average civilian with any sense left and his home was destroyed, etc., so I am sure that they probably did have a negative influence on opinion . . . in terms of hearts and minds they [the platoon houses] probably are not very helpful'.[36]

The Taliban, emboldened, increased the tempo of their operations right across the south and east. The coalition response was to bring the full range of modern firepower to bear to compensate for relatively low levels of ground troops. Civilian casualties were inevitable, provoking fury among the population and ensuring a steady stream of local recruits for the Taliban. Increasingly, the Afghan government, and Karzai in particular, publicly criticized coalition tactics.[37]

Some of the British positions in Helmand were becoming very precarious. In Musa Qala, in particular, the situation was desperate. The only means of keeping the 'platoon house' resupplied were Chinook helicopters, and there was constant anxiety that one would be shot down as they ran the gauntlet of fire taking off and coming in to land. Brigadier Butler began to seriously consider abandoning Musa Qala. General Richards, by this time ensconced in Afghanistan as ISAF commander, was very much opposed to such a move, despite his belief that the original 'platoon house' approach was fatally flawed. His concern was that a precipitate withdrawal would cause significant domestic political fallout in the UK, and the collapse of British credibility with both the Afghans and the Americans.[38]

Salvation seem to be at hand when a tribal elder, Haji Shah Agha, supported by a fifteen-strong tribal *jirga* from the district, approached Governor Daoud with a proposal for a locally recruited police force, controlled by the *jirga*, to provide security in Musa Qala, on the basis that both ISAF forces and all other armed groups (including the Taliban) would withdraw to five kilometres from the district centre.[39] Negotiations in September 2006 between Daoud and Shah Agha produced a fourteen-point agreement, which also included a role for the *jirga* in provincial expenditure and revenue-collection plans for the district. It soon became obvious that the tribal leaders had also had contacts with the local Taliban to facilitate its agreement.[40] The British 'offered their support' to the process while attempting to conceal their glee at the prospect of a negotiated withdrawal.

The Taliban, clearly not fully aware of the parlous British situation, agreed, probably because of the losses and exhaustion it had suffered in the intense fighting. The deal was put into place in September and, in the main, respected until February of 2007. The implications of the accord were highly significant. It suggested an alternative 'governance' and conflict-resolution model, based on local tribal politics and Pashtun cultural mores. It was also, of course, the antithesis of the 'extending central government' approach that was at the heart of the coalition's rhetoric. Consequently, its importance went way beyond district or even provincial politics. It was immediately proclaimed by some as an exemplar of an alternative approach that could potentially ameliorate both Afghanistan's internal agonies and international security concerns. However, the implications also generated significant and influential opposition.[41]

The Americans, in particular, were deeply suspicious. The timing of the accord could not have been worse in terms of the US mood. On 5 September 2006, the Pakistan government had signed a peace deal with tribal groups in the North-West Frontier Province.[42] This solidified a belief in the American policy community that deals were being struck between Musharraf and Al Qaeda and Taliban-supporting tribal groups, hence reducing the pressure Pakistan was exerting on the militants on its side of the border, without reducing the level of cross-border militant activity.[43] Even a vague hint that such deal-making was developing within Afghanistan guaranteed American agitation.

However, there were also Afghan vested interests that viewed the Musa Qala accord with suspicion. The area around Musa Qala was a traditional power base for the Akhundzada family. Although it is a district dominated by the Alizai tribe, the behaviour of a number of Akhundzada associates had exacerbated intra-tribal feuding, and there was no guarantee (indeed probably the opposite) that increased tribal influence would benefit Akhundzada. Consequently, a whispering campaign began in Kabul, whereby the former governor's associates and elements of the National Directorate of Security (NDS), the Afghan intelligence service, raised doubts about the deal. The NDS motivation, at the time, was probably simply concern that it was being cut out of the decision-making process. The substance of the whispers suggested that the accord was, in reality, a British-inspired deal with the Taliban, one of a number allegedly being concocted.[44] In a country where conspiracy and rumour is ubiquitous, the inaccurate claim soon gained credibility.

Karzai had been aware of the developing accord and had given tacit consent. He was generally receptive to local deals, but quickly developed cold feet as the rumour mill fed his suspicions and the US opposition became clear. Daoud was sacked in December 2006, and the tribal leaders in Musa Qala were denied the direct support that could have strengthened their position locally. The final collapse came during the handover from Richards as COMISAF to American General Dan McNeill in late January and early February. An air strike killed the brother of the local Taliban leader, Mullah Ghafoor. He proclaimed this to be a breach of the agreement, even though the attack took place just outside the five-kilometre zone. Ghafoor re-entered Musa Qala at his second attempt (the first being repulsed by the local elders) and retook the town.[45] Musa Qala was, in turn, retaken by a combined ISAF and ANA force following intense fighting in December 2007, but the potential for the original accord to be a model with broader Afghan significance was ended.[46]

It is impossible to say whether the strike on Ghafoor's brother was a deliberately planned American attempt to scupper the accord. Certainly, the timing is suggestive. General McNeill had made his views forcibly known to Richards' staff, indicating that he saw the Musa Qala deal as 'a tactical defeat and a strategic disaster'.[47] During his first stint in command in Afghanistan, in 2002, McNeill had acquired a reputation for a robust operational approach, and it was not difficult to foresee the likely direction of ISAF under his command. The collapse of the Musa Qala deal, the hostility of the new ISAF commander and a general American aversion to the idea resulted in a presumption against such local accords. Ironically, by 2008, the NDS, which had done so much to undermine the Musa Qala elders' position, would support agreements between the government and local tribes as the key to stabilizing Afghanistan.[48] However, in 2007, with the Americans in the vanguard, spreading the reach of 'effective' central government and 'taking the fight to the enemy' was still the mantra. The only problem was that 'the project' was not going very well.

The security situation was deteriorating sharply, and 2007 saw the resurgent Taliban make a final breakthrough. Insurgent-initiated attacks rose a further 27 per cent compared to 2006 levels, and Helmand province saw a 60 per cent rise in violence between 2006 and 2007.[49] Rising violence was reflected not only in casualty figures, but also in an associated sharp increase in resource expenditure by both warring sides. British forces fighting in Helmand in 2006–07 expended 4 million bullets and 25,000 artillery rounds in fighting the Taliban, while the Taliban itself, during one 2006 battle around Kandahar alone (the NATO-led Operation Medusa) was subsequently calculated to have expended 400,000 bullets, 2,000 RPGs and 1,000 mortar rounds, while having also successfully stockpiled over a million rounds of additional ammunition.[50]

Such figures scarcely testified to an insurgency that had been 'defanged' by American military power.

AFGHANISTAN'S DOWNWARD SPIRAL

The international effort was hopelessly fragmented. The 'intervention' was, in reality, a series of multiple interventions. Dozens of states, international organizations, NGOs, private companies and interest groups had all initiated ongoing activity in Afghanistan with a bewildering array of often competing agendas. Even within ISAF, the campaign was balkanized. Individual states became obsessed with what was happening in 'their' province, fuelled by a domestic media voracious for signs of progress or failure, and hamstrung by an inability to effectively coordinate the activities of their own departments, let alone the international effort. Regional entities such as RC South could in theory have brought about a more strategic approach, but Alliance politics and domestic political considerations tended to trump the logic of a unified chain of command.

Various institutional attempts were made to bring some degree of order and logic to the international effort. Following the Afghan Compact of 2006, a Joint Coordination and Monitoring Board was established with the aim of providing some effective oversight and monitoring. However, as the US ambassador at the time sardonically noted: '[O]n two points all major nations had the same view: the board should be small and they should be on it.'[51] David Richards set up a Policy Action Group, which included a number of national ambassadors, ISAF and key Afghan ministries. It was generally considered to be a reasonably useful body, but the problems of coordination were simply too great to be solved by any particular committee structure.

These structural faultlines suffused every discrete area of policy. Counter-narcotics provided a classic example. All were agreed that drugs was a huge problem, fuelled corruption and created myriad complex connections between criminal gangs, insurgents, local tribes and government. Indeed, Afghanistan was, by this time, virtually a fully fledged narco-state. Yet it proved impossible to craft a counter-narcotics approach that was coherently situated within a broader policy framework. Without a coherent overall strategy, individual policy areas became disconnected from the whole.

The incoherence sometimes reached farcical levels. US Ambassador Neumann's account of his time in Afghanistan is replete with references to the huge pressure being exerted by Washington to conduct the forcible eradication of the poppy. Congress, in particular, appeared obsessed with the issue. At one stage, Neumann set a target – 10,000 hectares to be eradicated – that appeared to be almost entirely driven by the fear that, unless credible efforts were made, Congress might begin cutting budgets, including to the US Agency for International Development (USAID).[52] The drive to eradicate played into the hands of Taliban propaganda, which had proclaimed that only they could protect people's poppy. This was exacerbated by the fact that eradication was disproportionately concentrated in government-controlled areas. If this was not enough, corruption ensured that those marked by Afghan power brokers to have their fields eradicated were chosen on the grounds of local political rivalries.

Eradication appeared to be exacerbating, rather than ameliorating, the security situation.[53] Strong arguments for and against the utility of eradication in the overall intervention effort were rendered moot by artificial timelines and targets set to alleviate domestic political pressure in some Western capitals. Even agencies within the UN were divided on the issue, with the Food and Agricultural Organization against eradication and the UN Office of Drug Control for it. The pinnacle of farce was reached when it became clear that, to ameliorate the negative effects of eradication on local security, some ISAF forces in 2007 were handing out leaflets in the south (to a mostly illiterate population) stating, 'ISAF doesn't do eradication.'[54] Therefore, even as one element of the intervention was enthusiastically pursuing eradication, another was frantically disowning it.

A further strategy-free zone was the programme of targeted attacks on Taliban leaders, also known as 'decapitation'. It was clear through 2007 and 2008 that a significant toll was being taken on Taliban commanders through intelligence-led air strikes and Special Forces operations. The prioritizing of targets appeared to be related to available intelligence and the threat to coalition forces posed by various insurgent leaders. This made impeccable tactical sense, but was potentially problematic strategically. The 'Taliban' is an umbrella term for disparate groupings and motivations. Some 'Talibs' were disaffected local tribesmen alienated by rapacious and corrupt local officials, dishonoured by coalition military activity, seeking to avenge a relative's death or with myriad other personal gripes. Others were traditional 'Taliban' with an Afghan-centric focus. Still others were using the Taliban as a badge of convenience for entrepreneurial gain. However, a proportion were highly radicalized Islamists with agendas of global *jihad*, either 'foreign' fighters or products of the mosques and *madrasas* in Pakistan.[55] The proportions from each broad type varied across geographically distinct Taliban groupings.

Self-evidently, some of these Talibs posed a wider security threat to international interests than others. However, without a coherent overall strategy it is difficult to develop a targeting approach that achieves broader goals than simply providing tactical relief for coalition forces. Killing large numbers of the enemy may provide a temporary reduction in tactical pressure, but might also have the effect of removing reconcilable insurgents that could be part of a long-term political process. Hence it is a tactical not a strategic approach. The temptation is to target the most effective opposition fighters regardless of the broader political and strategic effects arising from their removal. Through 2007 and 2008, an aggressive approach designed to 'take the fight to the enemy', coupled with an overarching concern with extending the control of central government, led to an undifferentiated approach to insurgent leaders. 'Decapitation' was therefore both a symptom of, and a contributing factor to, ineffective and incoherent overarching strategy.

It was also (as was outlined in Chapter Three) open to manipulation. Intelligence passed by Afghans to the coalition was often slanted to further private feuds. There were also claims that the Taliban had manipulated the coalition forces. Supporters of Mullah Dadullah, the brutal but effective Taliban commander in Helmand, were adamant that the intelligence which led to his death by British Special Forces came from within the Taliban leadership, and that the capture of his brother, Mansur Dadullah, by the Pakistanis was the result of information from the same source.[56] The ISI had also shown itself to be a master of these Machiavellian arts. As the next chapter will show, press reports of high-profile arrests and captures in Pakistan should rarely be taken at face value. When the dust settled, it was often the case that the person arrested was seen as an impediment to some ISI scheme, or that the arrest followed a period of particularly intense US pressure or coincided with the arrival of a high-profile American visitor.

Through 2007 and into 2008, the security situation continued to deteriorate. ISAF officials admitted that between 2007 and 2008 there had been a one-third increase in attacks on international and Afghan forces. IED incidents alone went up by 27 per cent. Insurgents were also clearly focusing on Afghan government targets, attacks on which increased by a remarkable 119 per cent. The overall result was that deaths of Afghan civilians rose by over 40 per cent.[57] However, for the US, Afghanistan was still largely the 'forgotten war'. Iraq remained the priority, with Afghanistan an 'economy of force' mission. This was made explicit in testimony by Admiral Michael Mullen, chairman of the Joint Chiefs of Staff, to the House of Representatives Armed Services Committee in late 2007, when he confirmed, 'in Afghanistan we do what we can. In Iraq we do what we must.'[58]

Nevertheless, as the situation went from bad to worse in 2008, there were increasing calls for the US to refocus on Afghanistan. Relations between Karzai and the international community – particularly the Americans and British – were becoming poisonous. The president no doubt felt provoked. The complete inability of the international intervention to provide a clear, coherent approach was a source of despair to him. In addition, repeated Afghan government claims about the role of Pakistan in fuelling Taliban violence, while producing increasing diplomatic pressure on the Pakistanis from Washington behind the scenes, were not leading to a fundamental change of approach. One incident appears to have particularly infuriated Karzai: a British SAS operation against the Taliban in Helmand in 2007 had apparently resulted in the death of a Pakistani military officer, and, it was claimed, this had been kept quiet by the British so as not to jeopardize Anglo-Pakistani intelligence cooperation.[59]

The sense of growing crisis was exacerbated by the Taliban expanding their operations to provinces that had hitherto been relatively quiet. Along with a heightened level of attacks, the Taliban were increasingly putting themselves forward as an alternative source of local justice for people disillusioned with the often corrupt judicial decision-making dispensed by state officials. Taliban judges were beginning to appear in rural areas, presiding over cases at the invitation of local elders and meting out summary punishment to those found guilty. The families of some crime victims, angered by the not uncommon sight of criminals receiving ludicrously light sentences, either on the basis of their connections or in return for bribes, began to turn to the Taliban for redress.[60]

Kabul itself was the scene of a number of high-profile attacks that captured international media attention. The Serena hotel was attacked in January 2008, and in July the Indian embassy was subjected to a suicide-bomb attack that killed over forty people and led to a new round of recrimination as the Karzai government, with probable justification, accused the ISI of participation.[61] In April, an attempt was made on Karzai's life at a ceremonial event in the full glare of the international media. Responding to mounting evidence, Admiral Mullen appeared to revisit his earlier sentiments when he was quoted in September 2008 as saying: 'I'm not sure we're winning in Afghanistan.'[62] The Bush administration, clearly increasingly alarmed, stepped up the diplomatic pressure on Pakistan and, in a dramatic step, the president formally authorised US military operations on the Pakistan side of the border.[63] Responding with an unusual degree of public clarity for a NATO secretary general, Jaap de Hoop Scheffer answered with 'an unqualified no' to a question asking if the Alliance could be a part of such missions.[64]

General David McKiernan, who had taken over from Dan McNeill as COMISAF in June, responded to the deteriorating security situation by submitting a request for 30,000 additional US troops.[65] It was clear that, as the violence in Iraq continued to fall from its horrendous peak of early 2007, eyes in Washington were beginning to turn back to the 'forgotten war' in Afghanistan. By the end of 2008, it was difficult to find much reason for cheer. McKiernan's request for a major force uplift would become entangled with the approaching US presidential election and it would be left to the incoming Obama administration to take stock of where the intervention was heading.

North-West Frontier Province and Federally Administered Tribal Areas, Pakistan

CHAPTER SIX

THE PAKISTAN PROBLEM

The future of Afghanistan is inextricably linked to the future of its neighbor, Pakistan. In the nearly eight years since 9/11, al Qaeda and its extremist allies have moved across the border to the remote areas of the Pakistani frontier. This almost certainly includes al Qaeda's leadership: Osama bin Laden and Ayman al-Zawahiri. They have used this mountainous terrain as a safe haven to hide, to train terrorists, to communicate with followers, to plot attacks, and to send fighters to support the insurgency in Afghanistan. For the American people, this border region has become the most dangerous place in the world.
President Barack Obama, 27 March 2009[1]

THROUGHOUT THE INTERVENTION, the West has had inordinate difficulty in deciding whether Pakistan is an ally or an obstacle in the search for solutions to Western security concerns in Afghanistan. The US mood towards the country has oscillated sharply between warm words backed by fiscal largesse (in which

Pakistan is feted as the anti-terrorist 'anvil' in counterpoint to the NATO 'hammer') and outbursts of anger over the perceived duplicity of Pakistan's Afghan policy. There has been an additional and constant undercurrent of concern at Pakistan's own internal fragility. Western policymakers appear torn between treating Pakistan as an indispensable contributor to any lasting Afghanistan solution and as a major part of the problem. In addition, a growing number of voices have argued that the stability of Pakistan is of infinitely greater importance for Western security than that of Afghanistan itself, and that Western policy in Afghanistan should reflect this.[2]

The complexity of Pakistan's role in the intervention can be gauged from the fact that all these seemingly mutually exclusive Western judgements are plausible and persuasive. The paradox is rooted in the country's ambiguous and complex attitudes to Islamist militancy – attitudes which can only be understood in the context of remarkably consistent and deeply embedded beliefs regarding the nature of Pakistan's security interests. The country has two great fears: the first is internal fragmentation and, potentially, disintegration; the second is the looming presence of India – a fear not far short of paranoia. The combination of these factors is at the heart of Pakistan's policy towards Afghanistan and the militant groups in the border region that was the subject of such concern to President Obama in the quote above.

One of the few unambiguous conclusions that can be drawn from the Western intervention to date is that no lasting solution to the agonies of Afghanistan, or the security dilemmas it generates, is viable if it fails to recognize Pakistan's security calculations. Crafting an effective strategy for Afghanistan demands an understanding of the strategic vision across the border.

PAKISTANI GEOPOLITICS AND ISLAMIST EXTREMISM

On 13 December 2001, just a few weeks after the Taliban's final abandonment of Kandahar in the face of the combined American–Northern Alliance offensive in Afghanistan, India experienced its very own near-iconic terrorist attack live on national television, when five gunmen attacked the Indian parliament building in New Delhi. After slamming their vehicle into the car of the Indian vice president near the front entrance, the attackers, dressed in military fatigues, became involved in a deadly gun battle that played out for nearly an hour, during which time one terrorist exploded his suicide vest, whilst the other four were eventually gunned down by Indian security forces. During the fighting, six police officers were also killed and at least eighteen bystanders were wounded. In the wake of this shocking episode, the Indian government initially accused two of the best-known terrorist organizations on the subcontinent, Lashkar-e-Taiba (LeT) and Jaish-e Mohammad (JeM), of being involved in the planning and execution of the attack.

Both terrorist groups were noted for their ties to Pakistan, while LeT was also connected to Afghanistan, having been initially established there to help carry on the war against the Najibullah regime in Kabul after 1989. JeM, though almost exclusively Kashmir focused as a terrorist organization, shared with LeT a strong ideological affiliation to the Afghan Taliban: the major JeM leader until 2002, Hafiz Mohammad Saeed, fully endorsed the Taliban's own injunctions against music and photography as un-Islamic. Like the Taliban, both LeT and JeM enjoyed benign toleration from (and, most observers allege, intermittent collaboration with) the Pakistani ISI.

The 2001 attack on the Indian parliament building occurred against a background of longer-standing Indo-Pakistani tensions, the history of which also reflects Pakistan's self-image as a nation. Kashmir has been violently disputed territory between the two states since 1947, and the two countries have engaged in formal or informal hostilities with one another on the Kashmiri (and other) fronts in nearly every decade since independence. The Indo-Pakistani border wars of 1965 and 1971 (the latter entailing the secession of Bangladesh, formerly East Pakistan) marked individual peaks of tension against the backdrop of this longer-standing mutual antagonism. Pakistan's relationship with its immediate neighbourhood was accordingly always shaped by successive governments' 'zero-sum' view of regional geopolitics. Hence, as we have seen, the Pakistani ISI perceived Afghanistan as a potentially vital source of 'strategic depth' against India, if only a pro-Islamabad regime could be successfully assembled and entrenched in Kabul.

Pakistan's foreign policy has always reflected a deep sense of internal insecurity. The secession of Bangladesh inflicted a permanent psychological trauma on successive governments, both military and civilian, which have feared ever since that the entire Pakistani state might split asunder. Whilst the core of the state, Punjab, is home to more than 60 per cent of the country's population, the FATA and North-West Frontier Province (NWFP) zones bordering Afghanistan, with their distinctive legal status and predominantly Pashtun population, have, throughout Pakistan's history, represented both opportunity and potential threat (as a channel for political influence into Afghanistan, but also a source of bilateral dispute regarding their ultimate territorial allegiance – see Chapter One). The NWFP (renamed Khyber Pakhtunkhwa in 2010), with some 20 million inhabitants, and the FATA territories, with some 5.7 million people, remain underdeveloped, rugged and inaccessible, and the FATA is still legally governed, as late as 2010, by the draconian colonial-era 1901 Frontier Crimes Regulations first introduced by the British – regulations founded on the feudal concept of local political agents, serving as proxies of the central government, imposing collective punishment for individual wrongdoing.

Meanwhile, to the west, the vast desert province of Balochistan, which borders Iran, has a very low density of population, but is mineral and energy rich. Consequently, the Pakistani government has always been afraid that it might secede, or come under Iranian Shi'a influence (bearing in mind that Pakistan is predominantly Sunni). The local Baloch people for their part have borne resentment for years at the lack of benefit they derive from Islamabad's exploitation of local mineral, coal and gas reserves, and a separatist insurgency has consequently raised its head in the region in nearly every decade since independence, but most notably and violently in the 1970s, when some 5,000 Balochis and 3,500 Pakistani army personnel were killed.[3]

Persistent fears that India might seek to exploit these internal faultlines within the Pakistani state – either by funding Baloch insurgents, or by carving out its own countervailing sphere of Pashtun influence in Afghanistan – have helped to stoke and perpetuate decades of mutual Indo-Pakistani distrust.[4] After 2001 India built four regional consulates to accompany its embassy in Afghanistan, became one of that country's top six international aid donors with a $500 million support package, and also further assisted in key areas like strategic road-building near the Pakistani border – acts guaranteed to heighten Pakistani agitation.

The 2001 attack on the Indian parliament also occurred just a couple of years after the latest climax of a phase of near-traditional Indo-Pakistani tension, the 1999 Kargil conflict. During that confrontation, the Indian and Pakistani militaries had become locked in a dangerous stand-off along the official Line of Control between Indian-held Kashmir and Pakistan. At the height of this earlier crisis, Pakistan had begun field-deploying nuclear missiles, leading some observers to fear that a full-blown nuclear exchange was about to occur, before American diplomatic intervention then led to a rapid reduction in tension. Extremist irregulars fought alongside Pakistani regular forces on this occasion, underlining the fact that Pakistan saw Islamist insurgents as invaluable 'proxy forces'.[5] In the wake of the Indian parliament attack of December 2001, Indian and Pakistani conventional military forces were once again fully mobilized onto a near-war footing for ten months, while Pakistani President Musharraf continued to refuse to disband militant groups in Kashmir, even as he condemned the attack on parliament as an act of terrorism.[6] As a result of such tensions, the Pakistani ISI retained strong links to Islamist insurgent groups in Kashmir, which, as already noted, not only shared the same general world view, but were also often recruited from the same *madrasas*, or had passed through the same training camps, as Mullah Omar's Taliban.

These older tensions did not disappear after the outbreak of the 'war on terror'. While, as we have seen, Musharraf swiftly aligned himself with the American campaign in Afghanistan, the circumstances surrounding his own rise to power, together with the nature of Pakistani internal politics, forced him to manoeuvre constantly throughout his almost nine years in power (from October 1999 to August 2008). On the left, he had to neuter the disgruntled civilian political parties that were traditional opponents of military rule, of which the largest was ex-Prime Minister Benazir Bhutto's Pakistan People's Party (PPP), an ostensibly neo-socialist organization that had been run in practice since its inception in 1967 on a near-feudal basis by the Bhutto clan. On the right, meanwhile, he faced opposition from the recently deposed Nawaz Sharif's Pakistan Muslim League (N) – the PML(N) – and also had to contend with the 'official opposition' of the Muttahida Majlis-e Amal (MMA, United Action Council), an Islamist coalition of six religious parties with a significant power base in the FATA territories.

Keeping both Bhutto and Sharif physically exiled from Pakistan helped emasculate their respective parties' electoral prospects, but the main instrument of Musharraf's internal strategic balancing act after 2001 was his creation of the Pakistan Muslim League (Quaid-e Azam) – known as the PML(Q) – a coalition of veterans from the Zia ul-Haq and earlier Nawaz Sharif eras, which became known as the 'King's Party', on account of its unhesitating support for the Musharraf administration. Founded in 2002 to contest the parliamentary elections, which the Pakistan Supreme Court dictated must occur that year (elections which were advertised for external consumption as a 'return to democracy'), the PML(Q) went on to win the largest number of seats in parliament, with the PPP coming in second and the MMA third. However, the balance of power within this internal, artificially generated constituency was delicate, and over the course of the subsequent decade, Musharraf's strategic balancing act rapidly began to unravel.

MUSHARRAF'S BALANCING ACT: THE US, 'GOOD' *JIHADIS*, AND THE 'WAR ON TERROR'

From the very outset Pakistan's role in US-led Afghan strategy conveyed decidedly mixed messages. From late 2001 onwards Musharraf granted American OEF forces both overflight and landing rights in Pakistan, and additionally deployed regular army units, Special Service Group (Pakistan Special Forces), ISI and

Frontier Corps personnel along the Pakistan–Afghan border. In October 2001, he also replaced the then ISI chief, General Mahmood Ahmad, who was perceived as a pro-Taliban figure within Washington, with Lieutenant-General Ehsun ul Haq. From that time onwards, the ISI was headed by men who could outwardly simulate support for the US 'war on terror'. After serving the regulation three-year term, Haq was in turn replaced in October 2004 by Ashfaq Kayani, who went on, after Musharraf's own long-postponed military retirement in 2007, to become the Pakistani chief of the army staff. Over the course of the next few years Pakistan became a logistics hub for the United States, and by 2008 up to 80 per cent of the containerized cargo and approximately 40 per cent of all fuel used to support US and coalition forces operating in Afghanistan transited through Pakistan.[7]

In a televised address on 12 January 2002, Musharraf furthermore announced the banning of the most significant sectarian Islamist organizations operating within Pakistan, including JeM, Sipahe Sahaba Pakistan (SSP), Lashkar-e-Jhangvi (LeJ), Sipahe Mohammad (SM) and the aforementioned Lashkar-e-Taiba (LeT), as well as the FATA and NWFP-based Tehreek-e-Nifaze Shariate Mohammadi (TNSM) and the Kashmir-oriented Harkatul Mujahidin (HM). Shortly thereafter, the leaderships of these various organizations either went underground or were arrested. As a result, for the time being Washington appeared prepared to grant the seemingly moderate, even mildly secularist Musharraf (who proclaimed the modernizing Kemal Ataturk of Turkey to be his personal role model) the benefit of the doubt.

However, American forces on the ground in Afghanistan remained dissatisfied with the full extent of Pakistani cooperation at the time. In practice, most of the organizations Musharraf banned after January 2002 were permitted to reorganize and re-emerge some months later, with the majority adopting titles that implied less militaristic goals – JeM, for example, was rebranded as Tehreek-e Khudamul Islam (Movement of the Servants of Islam), HM became Jamiatul Ansar (Party of Hosts), and the SSP became Millat-e-Islamia (Islamic Fraternity). In the case of other organizations, the arrest and imprisonment of their leaders proved less than effective in terms of ending their activities. For example, the TNSM (which operated out of the NWFP's Malakand district and FATA's Bajaur agency, and which was historically closely affiliated with the Afghan Taliban), suffered the arrest and imprisonment of its leader and founder, Sufi Mohammad, for encouraging some 8,000 volunteers to go and fight the Americans in Afghanistan, but the leadership of the organization simply passed to his son-in-law, Maulana Fazlullah.[8] Similarly, Musharraf's proclamation in January 2002 that the proliferating private *madrasa* network in Pakistan would be subject to a tighter process of state registration and regulation proved short-lived, drifting into legislative quicksand as early as August 2002, in part as a consequence of the Islamist MMA faction holding the political balance of power within the Pakistani parliament.

Pakistani military operations against insurgents in the FATA and NWFP territories from May 2002 onwards meanwhile initially drew a clear distinction between 'foreign' insurgents (predominantly Uzbeks, Arabs and Chechens) and Taliban-aligned Pashtun fighters – the so-called 'good *jihadis*', who could still potentially serve Pakistan's strategic interests.[9] Consequently, over 200 of the more than 450 terrorists captured by Pakistani forces by late 2003 were Yemenis and Saudis.[10] This bias was made even easier by the proclivity of these same foreign fighters to openly distance themselves from, and periodically attack, Musharraf's government, with

Al Qaeda's deputy leader, Ayman al-Zawahari, issuing a *fatwa* calling for Musharraf's death as early as December 2003. Some Islamist organizations then attempted to assassinate Musharraf himself – most notably on 25 December 2003, when the presidential motorcade was rocked by two massive suicide car bomb explosions while leaving Rawalpindi, just two weeks after an earlier bombing attempt in the same area had been foiled by an electronic jamming device on Musharraf's vehicle.[11]

Pakistan also traded prominent foreign fighters to gain prestige with the United States in the global 'war on terror', with Abu Zubaydeh, the alleged head of Al Qaeda overseas operations, captured in Faisalabad in March 2002, and the even more high-profile Khalid Sheikh Mohammad (or KSM, one of the main planners of the 9/11 attacks on New York) captured by Pakistani security forces in Rawalpindi in March 2003 and handed over to the United States for the 'enhanced interrogation techniques' endorsed by the Bush administration. In his memoirs, Musharraf mentions the significant bounties, or prize money, paid out by the Americans for the handover of foreign fighters, and Abdul Zaeef, the Taliban ambassador to Pakistan prior to his arrest and dispatch to Guantanamo Bay in 2002, likewise makes bitter allusion to what appears to have been a fairly well-known policy.[12]

American financial and military support to Pakistan during this period was accordingly lavish, but also remained poorly focused towards what the Bush administration thought should be the real priority areas for the Pakistani armed forces. The US provided Pakistan in 2003 with a $1.5 billion loan write-off, then in 2005 lifted an arms embargo previously imposed as punishment for Pakistan's semi-covert nuclear programme. Overall, between 2002 and 2008, the United States supplied Pakistan with $6.6 billion in military aid to help fight extremists – over $1 billion a year. When taken alongside the rescheduling of about 90 per cent of Pakistan's debt obligations (a staggering 58 per cent of GDP in 1999), and official grants of nearly $2.5 billion across 2002 and 2003 combined, this new financial climate gave the early years of Musharraf's rule the patina of healthy economic growth. The IMF reported that foreign direct investment (FDI) inflows to Pakistan, excluding flows for privatization, rose 70 per cent between 2004 and 2006, encapsulating a period of (largely misguided) economic optimism.[13]

The Pakistani armed forces, however, spent most of this money on acquiring or upgrading various conventional weapons systems, including heavy artillery, a $200 million air defence radar system, F-16 fighter jets, air-to-air missiles and anti-ship missiles – the vast majority of them tools of more use in deterring India than in combating the Taliban or Al Qaeda. Later investigation uncovered the fact that over half of the total funds provided by the US (54.9 per cent) were spent on fighter aircraft and weapons; over a quarter (26.6 per cent) on support and other aircraft; and 10 per cent on advanced weapons systems. The lack of effective accountability for this US aid makes the international effort that was unfolding simultaneously across the border in Afghanistan seem transparent by comparison. Some $15 million was disbursed to Pakistan for constructing bunkers (whose actual existence remained inadequately documented); $30 million went on road-building projects (which also failed to materialize); and $55 million was spent on maintenance of the entire Pakistani national helicopter fleet (local engine failures suggested that this maintenance was not carried out).[14]

By contrast, in the critical border region where the Taliban insurgency was actually happening, one American investigator as late as 2007 uncovered men of the paramilitary Frontier Corps still deployed in First World War-era pith helmets, wearing sandals in the snow, and carrying barely functioning Kalashnikov assault rifles with just ten rounds apiece – and this against opponents armed with mortars, machine guns, satellite telephones, rocket launchers and RPGs. With over half of all funds also allegedly diverted from military spending to bolster the overall state budget, the conclusions of one later investigation into this era were damning: for many years, US officials had simply ignored clear evidence that the Pakistani military was not spending American funds to further US foreign policy objectives, despite the US effectively subsidising a quarter of Pakistan's military budget by 2007.[15] The Pakistani military establishment, meanwhile, continued to view warfare against such internal threats as 'low-intensity' operations, leaving them poorly positioned to carry out the type of population-centric counterinsurgency approaches that American think tanks had begun to emphasize as vital for restabilizing the region.[16]

'DEALING' WITH THE BORDER REGION

Between 2002 and 2006, therefore, Pakistani military operations allowed the Taliban to consolidate themselves in the FATA and NWFP territories, which in turn enabled them to re-establish their power across the border in southern Afghanistan. The first and most obvious symbol of Pakistani military ineffectiveness in the region was the signing, and subsequent collapse, of successive ceasefire agreements in the FATA territories, in the wake of military operations that cost the Pakistani army relatively heavy casualties.[17] Between April 2004 and February 2008, as the conventional Pakistani armed forces were deployed on a large scale into Waziristan for the first time in their history, some five different peace deals (the 2004 Shakai Accord, the Sararogha

Accord of 2005, the September 2006 Waziristan Accord, the
Bajaur Accord of 2007 and the Swat Accord of May 2008, this last
signed after Baitullah Mehsud had already declared a ceasefire that
February) were attempted with the local Taliban, each coming in
the wake of large-scale military sweeps that had failed to effectively subdue the territories concerned.

The Shakai Accord of 24 April 2004 in South Waziristan,
concluded in the aftermath of Pakistani army operations in
Kalosha that March, was representative of many of these initiatives. On this occasion, a fifty-member *jirga* was assembled with
the help of NWFP Governor Syed Iftikhar Hussain Shah, and
then presented with demands by the Pakistani government for the
unconditional surrender of foreign fighters, alongside the release
of Pakistani military personnel being held hostage. The deal that
was finally reached, however, featured several important tactical
concessions, including a ban on Pakistani army troops interfering
in internal tribal affairs and the payout of very substantial financial
compensation for damage incurred in recent operations, in return
for an oath that local insurgents would not attack government
personnel or infrastructure. Insurgents were permitted to keep
their arms, weapons being 'offered' to the military as a purely
token, ceremonial gesture, and perhaps unsurprisingly Nek
Mohammad, the leader of the Pakistani Taliban at the time, subsequently characterized the final deal as a climb-down by the army,
rather than as a reverse for the insurgents.[18]

At one level, this type of local horse-trading in fact characterized the traditional relationship between the Pakistani central
government and the FATA territories. When, for example, a bomb
blast in North Waziristan in September 2005 damaged the power
grid, the local political agent demanded the handover of those
responsible, threatening a collective fine of around $65,000 if they

were not turned in. Local tribes historically maintained a collective response fund for such eventualities, however, and a payout of around a fifth of the original demand was reportedly finally made.[19] On another level, though, the Taliban were now able to profit directly from this tradition, as well as from Pashtun traditions of hospitality and asylum (*melmastia* and *nanawatai*), to maintain and build up their own secure enclaves, even as they took measures that further entrenched their own power at the cost of the local tribal order.

Given that American commanders were aware of the need for an 'anvil' across the other side of the Afghan border, in order to give the 'hammer' of their own operations in southern Afghanistan any lasting effect, the timing of these various peace deals was poorly correlated with NATO efforts, particularly across 2006–07, provoking accusations that such accords actually strengthened the Afghan Taliban. The result was a downturn in relations between Islamabad and Kabul, a trend not helped by frequent exchanges of fire between Afghan and Pakistani forces near the border, alongside intermittent reports of Pakistani cross-border artillery support for Taliban operations in Afghanistan.[20] Pakistani proposals in 2006 to construct a massive security fence and minefield along the joint Afghan–Pakistan frontier were dismissed by many, not least in Kabul, as evidence of Islamabad's fundamental lack of seriousness when it came to combating cross-border terrorism, while President Musharraf was a prominent absentee from Karzai's (notably ineffectual) 2007 'Peace Jirga', which sought to bring together Pashtun tribal elders from southern Afghanistan and northern Pakistan to address the shared problem of Islamist extremism.[21]

The Taliban meanwhile systematically attacked both government infrastructure (such as schools and police stations) and traditional hierarchical structures within the FATA, as a means of creating a power vacuum, within which they then substantially increased their own authority. In 2005 and 2006 alone more than two hundred tribal elders in Pakistan's northern provinces were reportedly murdered by Taliban agents as 'spies' or 'collaborators', a pattern that the Afghan Taliban was to repeat in southern Afghanistan.[22]

Having been fought to a standstill in the field, by early 2006 Pakistani army garrisons in the region found themselves increasingly isolated and under attack as Taliban activity escalated. On 16 January 2006 a US drone strike unsuccessfully targeted Ayman al-Zawahiri in the village of Damadola in the Bajaur agency. Zawahiri himself escaped death, but the killing of civilians increased local resentment, while the strike may also have accelerated Al Qaeda's own plans to expand its influence in the region – an intention underlined by its announcement of the official foundation of the shadow-state 'Islamic Republic of Waziristan' the following month.[23]

By March of that year, during fighting over the town of Miranshah in Northern Waziristan between the Pakistani Taliban and government forces, a full-scale Taliban 'shadow government' was exposed. Locals who were fleeing the fighting into Afghanistan reported to journalists news on areas where Sharia law had been declared, where all local government employees or government supporters had been arrested and beheaded, and where the Taliban were now openly occupying government buildings. Pakistani forces retaliated by strafing buildings in Miranshah itself with gunfire from Cobra attack helicopters, mortars and artillery fire, eventually forcing a Taliban retreat that eradicated the direct threat to the town, but failed to tackle the wider encroaching cultural 'Talibanization' of the province.[24] Meanwhile, a suicide bomber successfully attacked and killed a US diplomat in Karachi in response to the Pakistani attacks.

This period of steady escalation culminated in the Pakistani army's bombing of a *madrasa* in Bajaur agency in October, killing seventy to eighty people, an act that led to a retaliatory suicide-bomb attack against the Pakistani paramilitary training ground in Dargai, 150km north-west of Islamabad, in November 2006. These tit-for-tat strikes overlapped yet another attempt by the Pakistani government to ease tensions via the latest peace deal, the 'Waziristan Accord', signed on 5 September 2006. However, Brigadier Mehmood Shah, a former secretary for security in FATA who had been involved in helping shape the previous two peace deals, acknowledged that the Waziristan Accord was even 'weaker' than the Shakai or Sararogha accords, with pledges given by the Taliban on this occasion being 'no more than a general statement that they will not do this and that'.[25]

The official truce soon ended, to be followed, amidst ongoing hostilities, by the birth and rapid ascendance of what became known as the TTP, an insurgent coalition under the leadership of Nek Mohammad's successor, Baitullah Mehsud. His organization's general offensive in the NWFP's Swat valley in 2007–08 was serious enough to help trigger Musharraf's declaration of a national emergency (although cynics suggest the president may also have been influenced by his increasingly bitter dispute with the Pakistani judiciary over his re-election). So severe did this military crisis in Swat become that according to some sources it nearly caused a serious rift between the Afghan Taliban under Mullah Omar and the Pakistani-based TTP, with the former allegedly concerned that the TTP's war with the Pakistani state risked not only becoming a serious distraction from the main conflict in Afghanistan, but also provoking government reprisals on a scale that would endanger the whole Taliban movement's traditional safe havens in north-western Pakistan.[26]

A further and highly significant trigger for the subsequent explosion in Islamist activity came as a result of events within Islamabad itself, in the shape of the so-called 'Red Mosque' (Lal Masjid) siege between January and July 2007. The Red Mosque, a large complex situated in the centre of Islamabad not far from ISI headquarters, was an openly pro-Taliban institution with long-running ties to Pakistani Islamist militancy more generally, including Maulana Masood Azhar, the founder and leader of JeM, the organization charged by India with co-organizing the parliament attack of 2001. In January 2007, the leadership and well-armed students of the mosque began to openly confront local government authority on the streets of Islamabad, harassing local shopkeepers, burning 'immoral' videotapes, and demanding the imposition of Sharia law.

Matters came to a head in June, with the kidnapping at a nearby massage parlour of seven Chinese nationals, whom the mosque students accused of being sex-shop workers. Following failed negotiations, Pakistani Special Forces, acting on Musharraf's orders and supported by intelligence provided by US Predator drones, successfully stormed the mosque. Over 150 people died in the fighting before the buildings were completely cleared. This struggle was almost immediately followed by calls from Al Qaeda deputy al-Zawahiri for Pakistanis to join in a *jihad* against Musharraf, and the operation as a whole then became a general rallying cry for Islamist hardliners across Pakistan. It also led directly to the final breakdown of both the 2006 Waziristan and the 2007 Bajaur accords, deals signed by the military with Baitullah Mehsud in Waziristan and with the TNSM in Bajaur agency, respectively; the fighting that followed in both these provinces was some of the most savage to date.

In early July 2007, Maulana Fazlullah's TNSM was already moving into Swat, and by September a total of five Pakistani army outposts had been overrun in South Waziristan. Commentators were particularly shocked by the surrender in that region of an estimated 280 soldiers, including a colonel and nine other officers, to a handful of Taliban at the very end of August.[27] ISI personnel were targeted by suicide-bomb attacks in Rawalpindi in September in a new form of escalation, while in North Waziristan, during the battle of Mir Ali (part of the Pakistan army's Operation Al Mizan) on 7–10 October, the military again used jet fighters and helicopter gunships to strafe suspected militant positions, leading to reports that over 50,000 civilians were fleeing the area.[28]

By the middle of October, the Pakistani government had admitted that it had lost control of Swat and deployed over 3,000 paramilitary forces to challenge the writ of Maulana Fazlullah there. This provoked savage fighting; quarter was neither asked nor given by either side, and captured Pakistani soldiers were often beheaded and dismembered. By November the TNSM remained in control of six out of eight townships in Swat, but airpower and artillery gradually helped the Pakistani army make a slow advance, and by December the military claimed that life was 'returning to normalcy'.[29] On 15 December, however, Baitullah Mehsud also announced the official formation of the TTP, unifying all Pakistani Taliban forces in Waziristan, and, after the breakdown of yet another ceasefire with Maulana Fazlullah, the latter half of 2008 was marked by the entire Swat valley falling under militant control, an era symbolized by what rapidly became famous footage of an accused adulteress being flogged on the ground in April 2009.[30]

After fighting in January 2009 had ended in another ineffective ceasefire, the worsening situation in Swat provoked a new (and large-scale) Pakistani military operation to clear Fazlullah's followers out in May. 'Operation Rah-e-Rast' involved the deployment of 15,000 troops with artillery and air support, in fighting which also displaced up to three million people. Fighting in May centred around the city of Mingora, normally home to a population of 200,000, in the course and aftermath of which the Pakistani army were subsequently accused in some quarters of having carried out as many as 249 extra-judicial executions.[31] The Pakistani armed forces during this period also used drone strikes to help target the TTP leadership, killing Baitullah Mehsud in August 2009, and targeting his successor, Hakimullah Mehsud, in a similar fashion in 2010, though apparently without success.[32]

THE ASSASSINATION OF BENAZIR BHUTTO AND THE FALL OF MUSHARRAF

Pakistan was now gripped by three simultaneous and overlapping internal crises of a political, economic and security-related nature. The country was sliding into a constitutional crisis, the internal insurgency was making rapid territorial gains, and the bubble economy – fed since 2001 by the strategic alliance with the United States – imploded. The trigger for the first crisis occurring was the growing constitutional conflict created by Musharraf's controversial suspension of Pakistani Supreme Court Justice Ifitikhar Mohammed Chaudhry in March 2007. Chaudhry was suspended for alleged misconduct, but ulterior motives were suspected (Chaudhry had politically embarrassed the sitting government on a number of occasions) and the Pakistani Supreme Court reinstated Chaudhry in July, helping to prompt Musharraf to declare a state of emergency that suspended both the constitution and parliament in November. The ex-prime minister Benazir Bhutto meanwhile, having cut a deal with an increasingly beleaguered Musharraf, herself made a dramatic return to Pakistani soil on

18 October 2007, in preparation for the Pakistani parliamentary elections, scheduled for the following year. Bhutto embarked almost immediately on a vocal political campaign in the public eye that, following government harassment and numerous death threats, ended in her assassination by a combined shooting and suicide-bomb attack in December 2007.

Sympathy for Bhutto's party, increased by her perceived martyrdom (Baitullah Mehsud, the TTP leader at the time, was charged with – but denied – masterminding the attack that killed her), was reflected in the elections that followed in February 2008. The PPP received more than 30 per cent of the vote, Musharraf's 'King's Party' (the PML(Q)) got less than 20 per cent, while the Islamist MMA also lost its dominance in the NWFP to a coalition led by the secular Pashtun Awami National Party (ANP). By 18 August 2008, under increasing threat of parliamentary impeachment from the two new Pakistani ruling parties, the PPP and the Pakistani Muslim League (N), and with the delicate political scaffolding that had maintained him in office for nearly a decade now collapsing underneath him, Musharraf resigned. After intense horse-trading between the PPP and Nawaz Sharif, leader of the PML(N), Benazir Bhutto's much disliked husband, Asif Ali Zardari, took over the presidency. Policy towards Afghanistan and Islamist extremism, however, continued to be heavily dominated by the ISI and the Pakistani military.[33]

By early 2009, as noted above, the TTP's renewed offensive had brought them within sixty miles of Islamabad, leading some within the international community to begin to fear that Pakistan might be on the verge of internal collapse on a scale that would completely shift the strategic paradigm in the region, or that Pakistani nuclear facilities might be in imminent danger of falling into Taliban hands.[34] This upsurge formed the second great general crisis of the period, culminating in the major military operations by the Pakistani armed forces in the Swat valley in 2008–09 outlined in the previous section. However, the third crisis that simultaneously unfolded across this period, less often commented upon, but forming a critical backdrop to these first two trends, was the implosion of the Pakistani economy.

Musharraf's decline and fall had occurred against a backdrop of rapidly falling foreign-exchange reserves, capital flight, and inflation that had risen to 25 per cent, accompanied by national power cuts, blackouts and angry street protests. This growing economic disaster partly reflected the wider crisis gripping the global economy from 2007 onwards, in particular the impact of high oil and associated food price shocks; but it was also a product of the missed opportunities, the inefficiencies, and the often blatant corruption attached to the attempted neoliberal restructuring of the Pakistani economy, together with the overconfidence concerning economic matters that characterized most of Musharraf's term in office.

Pakistan's general economic crisis, like that gripping many Western economies after 2007, resulted from the bursting of a credit bubble which had emerged without any underlying progress in raising productivity or conducting reinvestment into critical infrastructure.[35] In the case of Pakistan, much of the growth of the Musharraf years was based, as in the West, on cheap credit rather than on underlying economic fundamentals, but with the cheap credit itself generated by the higher liquidity enjoyed within the Pakistani banking system as a consequence of the larger external cash inflows into government coffers from the 'war on terror'.

The problem was further magnified by the fact that Pakistan's economic fundamentals were far less promising than those of most European states or North America. Even before the crisis fully struck, Pakistan's level of development in terms of infrastructure, education and R&D was grim. Basic literacy remained very low by international standards, at around 49 per cent, while 2.2 per cent annual population growth meant that there were also considerable demographic pressures. Gas and electricity consumption during the Musharraf years had shot up, but no new power stations had been built to meet increased demand, and exports had remained stagnant, while imports rocketed.

During his term in office, Musharraf had also failed to widen the fiscal tax base beyond the 1 per cent of the population already paying income tax, making Pakistan almost as ineffective a tax gatherer as Afghanistan. He also maintained the privileges and status quo of special-interest groups like the army. Government spending on health constituted only 0.6 per cent of GDP, while agriculture provided employment for 44 per cent of the population, but generated only 21 per cent of GDP. Pakistan consequently became a net importer of food after 2003, and by mid-2008 the World Food Programme estimated that nearly half the population was food insecure. Meanwhile, the UNDP Human Poverty Index for 2009 rated Pakistan 101st of the 135 countries reviewed (better than Afghanistan, which came last, but considerably behind India at 88 or Turkey at 40).[36] By mid-2008 the country was facing a balance of payments crisis, and was reduced to turning to the IMF for an $8 billion bailout package, which came with typically savage structural conditions.

AN ESCALATING SPIRAL OF VIOLENCE

As Pakistan span into constitutional and economic chaos on the back of an already worsening security situation, the US had become increasingly concerned that Pakistani military efforts were insufficiently effective in targeting the Taliban leadership. To compensate, Washington stepped up its policy of drone strikes in Pakistan. The use of the drone, or unmanned aerial vehicle (UAV), as a long-range weapons-delivery system was a recent innovation in American military practice. Early drones in the 1990s had purely been long-range spy systems, but from early 2001 onwards the Pentagon had begun experiments in 'weaponizing' UAVs with supersonic laser-guided Hellfire missiles – efforts that the CIA, in its desire to eliminate Osama bin Laden, further encouraged. Remotely controlled by joystick from bases as far away as Tampa, Florida, the first weaponized drone system, the MQ-1 Predator, began combat flights in Afghanistan on 7 October 2001. Before long it was supplemented by its larger and more powerful cousin, the MQ-9 Reaper, a hunter-killer, long-endurance UAV capable of carrying up to fourteen Hellfire missiles, or four missiles and two 500 lb Paveway laser-guided bombs.

The combination of high altitude and precision-guided supersonic ordnance gave US drones unique, and highly lethal, operational advantages. No area was now too remote to escape a drone overflight, drones could both watch and 'loiter' over a potential target for longer periods of time than any conventional fighter jet, and the drones themselves were practically inaudible from the ground, making the explosion of a missile generally the first signal any of their victims received that there was even a drone in the area.

Drone strikes in the FATA territories of Pakistan began in earnest in 2004, with one strike that year, and between two and five strikes in the following couple of years. The number of officially recorded annual strikes then escalated to thirty-five in 2008 and ninety-nine by 2010.[37] Though consistently praised by the US military as an ideal means of decapitating the senior Al Qaeda and Taliban leadership in the region, the escalating use of drone strikes also provoked protests in Pakistan, as well as questions in other quarters about their true efficacy, particularly given that hard and accurate intelligence was often lacking. In 2009, the Brookings Institution, a Washington-based think tank, issued a report estimating that ten civilians were killed for every militant who died in a drone attack.[38]

Pakistani public opinion polling in 2010 revealed a surprisingly limited awareness of the American drone strike campaign – just over one respondent in three was aware of the issue – but of those polled who *were* aware, 93 per cent were violently opposed. The same poll revealed that 59 per cent of Pakistanis viewed the United States as an enemy and that similar numbers opposed the US war on terror and the NATO presence in Afghanistan, although 63 per cent also wanted better relations with Washington. Such polls support the theory that American policy towards the region since 2001 has, if anything, only fuelled latent anti-Americanism among the general Pakistani public.[39]

When considering the overall effectiveness of joint US and Pakistani efforts to combat terrorism since 2001, one must also bear in mind that one of the biggest side effects has been the number of internally displaced persons (IDPs) generated by Pakistani army operations. Many such IDPs have been herded into poorly resourced tent cities that serve as potential breeding grounds for further radicalization. Operations in 2008–09 alone resulted in the internal displacement of at least 2.2 million, and probably (by UN estimates) closer to 6 million persons from the FATA and NWFP territories, the majority of whom were condemned to a tenuous hand-to-mouth existence in cramped, disease-ridden and squalid refugee camps. Though the vast majority have been able to return to their homes, the antagonism generated by such operations has left the door open to ongoing radicalization among the affected population.[40]

By the end of 2009, a total of 2,810 security forces personnel and some 7,354 civilians had also been killed in operations against extremists, in suicide attacks or as a result of collateral damage. The 3,300 civilian deaths that occurred in Pakistan in 2009 alone outnumbered the 2,412 killed in Afghanistan that same year, and led the International Institute of Strategic Studies to dub the former state the official epicentre of global *jihadism*.[41] Suicide bomb attacks, previously little known in Pakistan, also witnessed a striking increase. In 2006 there were six suicide bomb attacks within Pakistan; in 2007 there were fifty-six; in 2008 at least sixty-one; and in 2009 no fewer than eighty-seven.[42] A visitor to Islamabad in November 2009 found the city physically and psychologically transformed from the one she had experienced just four years before by roadblocks, sandbag obstacles, evening curfews, intrusive body searches, and an overwhelming climate of fear.[43] Further north, the TTP were now being repressed by government-sponsored village militias, an initiative which brought with it its own problems, but the group continued to raise their international profile by claiming credit for the failed Times Square bombing in New York in May 2010, and also to some extent rebounded locally across both North and South Waziristan by the end of the year, prompting calls for yet another full-scale Pakistani military offensive in North Waziristan. Al Qaeda were meanwhile rumoured to have pledged over $23 million for a renewed TTP offensive in Swat during 2011.[44]

Unsurprisingly, the upsurge in suicide bombings and Islamist violence, combined with the worrying longer-term economic, demographic and environmental trends, triggered a reassessment of American foreign policy towards Pakistan.[45] President Obama, on coming into office in January 2009, undertook a rhetorical shift of direction by beginning to refer to the 'AfPak' theatre of operations, a signal that stability within Pakistan was now coming to be recognized as a goal just as vital as stability in Afghanistan. In the words of Obama's national security adviser, the United States would continue to treat Afghanistan and Pakistan as two separate countries, but also as 'one challenge in one region ... focus[ing] more intently on Pakistan than in the past'.[46]

The Obama strategy announced in 2009 recognized the fact that governance, security and economic crises in Pakistan were now converging in a manner that was, in many ways, even more alarming than comparable trends in Afghanistan. The root of the problem remained, as in Afghanistan, the ineffectiveness of military operations to produce the desired strategic results. At least at one level, the relative ineffectiveness of the Pakistani military in combating the Taliban in FATA and the NWFP during this period mirrored the comparable failure of Western coalition efforts in southern Afghanistan, and indeed earlier Soviet efforts. The issue for conventional militaries in all these scenarios remained not whether they could defeat the insurgents in battle – with overwhelmingly superior firepower and air support, they could invariably do so – but what happened afterwards. Western COIN doctrine urged the militaries to 'clear, hold and build': an area is 'cleared' of insurgents before being 'held' and secured as population confidence increases as a prelude to 'building' economic and governance capacity. However, the complete lack of follow-through aid or support, and of any credible and non-corrupt government infrastructure capable of delivering it, rendered this approach rather hollow. The gap between military theory and reality was even more striking in the case of Pakistan than in Afghanistan.[47]

By the end of the decade, insurgents on both sides of the border had mastered the art of avoiding battle and preserving their strength, in readiness for moving back into the governance vacuum that conventional military offensives invariably left in their wake. The Pakistani army offensive in South Waziristan launched in October 2009, for example, though highly praised in some quarters as evidence of a Pakistani counterinsurgency 'learning curve', was in reality a strikingly cumbersome operation. After weeks of bombardment by artillery and aircraft, 30,000 troops moved forward, successfully seizing known militant strongholds, but engaging in very little heavy fighting, and capturing relatively few prisoners. Though the Pakistani military subsequently claimed to have killed 589 Taliban foot soldiers, literally thousands of fighters, along with all the top leadership, were able to scatter into neighbouring territories to regroup.[18]

The natural consequence of such phenomena, on both sides of the border, was the dispiriting process that the British in Helmand termed 'mowing the lawn' – conducting an offensive to clear individual villages of Taliban insurgents or representatives, only to find a few weeks later that the Taliban had returned and the whole process had to be repeated all over again. The Pakistanis experienced a similar phenomenon in Bajaur agency, where Pakistani army offensives repeatedly ended in declarations that the area had been cleared of militants. The first of these operations began in August 2008 and lasted six months; but the clear failure of this effort then led to a second attempt, which ended in the third week of April 2010 with the army claiming to have killed over 1,800 militants and again confidently declaring Bajaur agency a 'conflict-free zone'. These claims were undermined by Taliban attacks as early as May, and by August it was already clear that Bajaur agency remained just as troubled by Islamist violence as it had ever been.[49]

The Pakistani case was further complicated, of course, by the ambiguous relationship between the Pakistani military in general (and the ISI in particular) and the Taliban, and the more general reluctance of Pakistani officers and ordinary soldiers alike to kill their fellow countrymen. This attitude, reflecting the still prevalent view that India remained Pakistan's main enemy, was evident in December 2008 when, negotiating yet another ceasefire in the FATA, and in the wake of the brutal LeT attack on Mumbai which again heightened Indian–Pakistani tensions, a Pakistani military official emphasized that TTP leaders Baitullah Mehsud and Maulana Fazlullah were 'patriots', and that fighting between their organizations and the Pakistani military was not due to any 'big issues' between the government and the militants, but only because of some 'misunderstandings'.[50]

External and Pakistani commentators alike have speculated as to whether particular outrages may have served as a final tipping point in persuading the Pakistani establishment that Islamist militancy represented the main existential threat to the state. Popular candidates for such a tipping point include the Red Mosque siege of 2007 and its aftermath, or the deadly attack on Islamabad's Marriott hotel in September 2008, which killed more than sixty people. In 2010, the well-informed Pakistani journalist Imtiaz Gul claimed that a fundamental paradigm shift had occurred early in 2007 within the Pakistani military and the governmental establishment, in terms of increased cooperation with the US and stepping up their own efforts to combat internal militancy.[51]

However, the available evidence could also be read another way – that the Pakistani military remained more than content to target TTP leaders like Baitullah Mehsud or his successor Hakimullah Mehsud, who gave clear evidence of having become 'rogue elements', even to the extent of killing them in US drone strikes, but that it remained much more reluctant to move against the entire Islamist movement in the northern territories, including

Mullah Omar and the Quetta Shura. In the view of another analyst at the start of 2010, Pakistani officers continued to view the US presence in Afghanistan as essentially destabilizing, welcomed discussion of a US withdrawal, and retained their fundamental affection for home-grown Islamist militants as proxy fighters against India and for use in the *jihad* in Kashmir.[52]

Meanwhile, some argued that ISI support for the Taliban remained as clear as 'the sun in the sky', with Taliban members claiming, off the record, that three to seven ISI members regularly sat within the Quetta Shura as observers. One interviewee reported, 'the reality is that the ISI controls the leadership. Mullar Omar has [the] strong support of Pakistan; he has to listen to them and do what they say.' Other respondents confirmed to the same Western investigator that the ISI remained absolutely critical to the Taliban war effort in terms of funding, recruitment and training, right down to the paying of monthly salaries.[53] ISI involvement was generally suspected to lie behind both the Taliban bombings of the Indian embassy in Kabul in July 2008 and October 2009; and some also saw its hand in the 2008 Mumbai attack by LeT.[54]

Explanations for this relationship have again varied, with some blaming rogue elements or retired ex-ISI officers like Hamid Gul, others speculating on the existence of multiple internal splinter factions, and yet others accusing the ISI of playing an elaborate double game. Supporters of the last position would point out, for example, that the ISI's capture of Abdul Ghani Baradar, Mullah Omar's second-in-command, in January 2010 may in fact have been a covert disciplinary measure by Islamabad to warn the Taliban against engaging in independent peace talks with Kabul. In the words of one Pakistani official speaking off the record, the purpose of the Baradar arrest was not so much to further the broader cause of anti-terrorism, as to send a warning to the Quetta Shura, that '[w]e protect the Taliban. They are dependent on us. We are not going to allow them to make a deal with Karzai and the Indians.'[55] The ongoing utility for Islamabad of contacts with militants as leverage in any strategic discussions was further underlined in 2010, when Pakistani officials offered to act as interlocutors between the Kabul government and the Jalaluddin Haqqani network.[56]

The situation in Pakistan at the end of nearly a decade of Western intervention in Afghanistan therefore embodied a strategic paradox. By any objective measure, Pakistan itself had internally become less, rather than more, stable; but the Pakistan government, regardless of who was in charge, retained a strategic outlook which had changed remarkably little since at least 1975. From this perspective, Afghanistan remained a proxy in a wider regional struggle with India, and the challenges that Islamist extremists posed to Pakistan's stability were counterbalanced by the geopolitical advantages that they brought. Internal Taliban fronts like the TTP could be disciplined militarily if they got out of hand, while providing a recruitment pool for the Afghan Taliban, which could likewise be intimidated and constrained sufficiently to be a tool of political influence in Afghanistan itself.

As for Pakistan's own increasing internal challenges, there were plenty of Western (and some internal Pakistani) suggestions as to how Islamabad could better improve stability within its borders in future – by, for example, addressing the issue of government corruption head on, improving the rule of law, abolishing the arcane Frontier Crimes Regulation, or instituting development programmes such as land reform within the FATA.[57] Unfortunately, the majority of these projects remained as removed from reality as similar projects for 'community engagement' in

Afghanistan, given the lack of capacity within the Pakistan government to execute any of them – a point underlined when proposed reforms in the FATA became deadlocked in 2010 under the pressure of dealing with Pakistan's wider humanitarian crisis.[58] This left Pakistan to fall back on the one basic strategy that it had always possessed – to act as a regional spoiler, thus posing significant obstacles to the proposed 2009 'regional grand bargain' that President Obama was offering in the latest iteration of Western strategy in Afghanistan.

Meanwhile, the Americans were now openly looking for an exit strategy from Afghanistan, an agenda guaranteed to re-energize Pakistan's traditional geopolitical game plan as well as re-emphasize the leverage to be gained from sheltering and controlling the Taliban. NATO's decade of strategic engagement in the region had, paradoxically, become notable not only for reinforcing Pakistan's traditional strategic mindset, but also for escalating violence and instability.

CHAPTER SEVEN

SILVER BULLETS AND THE SEARCH FOR AN EXIT, 2009–11

Shevardnadze [Soviet foreign minister]: Right now we are reaping the fruit of un-thought-out decisions of the past. Recently, much has been done to settle the situation in Afghanistan and around it. Najib has taken up leadership. He needs practical support, otherwise we will bear the political costs. It is necessary to state precisely the period of withdrawal of Soviet troops from Afghanistan. You, Mikhail Sergeevich [Gorbachev], said it correctly – two years. But neither our, nor Afghan comrades have mastered the questions of the functioning of the government without our troops.

Dobrynin [head of international department of the Communist Party's Central Committee]: We must give liberty to Najib. Two questions arise here. First – the idea of national reconciliation, and second – the political settlement of the situation around Afghanistan.

Minutes of a meeting of the Soviet Politburo,
13 November 1986[1]

By 1986, SOVIET personnel in Afghanistan, after over six years of near-fruitless efforts to stabilize the country, had begun to realize that the government they were supporting in Kabul was corrupt, ineffective and unrepresentative.[2] The Soviet Politburo consequently began to implement an exit strategy, which it hoped the newly elected Afghan leader, Najibullah, would facilitate. Earlier Soviet hopes for an ordered exit, some form of local reconciliation of the fighting factions, a more benign general regional environment, and, above all, their doubts concerning the capacity of the Kabul government itself, would echo loudly in 2009–10. The international community was by now itself contemplating switching course (and possibly even preferred local leader) in Afghanistan, and planning to reduce their own force levels, with a corresponding transfer of greater responsibility to the Afghan armed forces and government.

Officially, NATO policy favoured continued robust commitment to Afghanistan for another decade or more. Unofficially, growing political and practical constraints meant that it would be increasingly difficult to maintain the international effort at the tempo of 2006–07. Repeated complaints by Washington that other NATO members were not pulling their weight had limited effect, with the number of allied combat battalions increasing from fourteen to twenty, while US battalions in the country surged from eight to twenty-three between January 2008 and September 2009.[3] Several countries also announced publicly that they intended to reduce their combat forces in Afghanistan. In September 2008 the Canadian government committed itself to withdrawing the majority of its combat troops by 2011; in April 2009, despite American pressure, President Sarkozy of France ruled out sending any more troops to Afghanistan to bolster the 3,750 personnel already there; and the Dutch government at the very start of 2010 witnessed haemorrhaging domestic support, and then finally lost office, over an attempt to extend the remit of its mission in Afghanistan beyond December of that year.[4]

Since 2006, the NATO and US missions had integrated more and more until, by August 2009, the ISAF commander (COMISAF) was a four-star general 'double-hatted' as commander of both ISAF and the American forces still operating under OEF. Politically, this meant that COMISAF had to be an American. In a *quid pro quo* for allowing this merging of missions, NATO member states had extracted a bewildering array of national caveats, limiting the range of tasks that national contingents could perform. At one end of the spectrum lay Germany, which had so many restrictions that its mission was not far short of a non-combat role; at the other end were Britain, Canada, Australia, Denmark, the Netherlands and the US, which had no, or very few, formal caveats. The forty or so other countries that had some role within ISAF lay at various points in between.[5]

This not only added to the complexity for operational planners but created significant political problems. The perception that some countries were paying a blood price while others were not exacerbated tension both within NATO and within member states themselves. Public hectoring directed towards states with major caveats, however, proved counterproductive. Overwhelmingly, caveats reflected domestic political realities. Even if German politicians (for example) wanted to abandon them completely, they could not do so without precipitating a political crisis and immediate withdrawal.[6] Those nations that did not have caveats, such as the British, were already operating at the limits of their practical capability. Consequently, any major increase in combat troops could only come from the US. The result was that, by the middle of 2009, the intervention had come full circle, and the conflict in Afghanistan was, once again, overwhelmingly an 'American war'.

A NEW STRATEGY FOR AFGHANISTAN

During his 2008 election campaign, Barack Obama had committed himself to a revived US-led coalition effort in Afghanistan – a tactic that helped to offset what might otherwise have been potentially damaging Republican criticism of his intention to withdraw all US combat troops from Iraq by mid-2010 (a commitment that he eventually fulfilled, albeit at a slower pace than originally proposed).[7] Now in office, the administration sought to bring some strategic order to an effort widely perceived to have lost its way. Initial pronouncements emanating from the White House seemed to suggest a shift towards a clearer, more pragmatic approach to Afghanistan and the region. However, the pattern of internally incoherent strategy that had become the hallmark of the intervention soon manifested itself once again.

Even the very first announcement regarding the new strategy reflected the ongoing disconnect between stated US ends and the ways and means of getting there. In March 2009 President Obama narrowed the stated core US objective in Afghanistan down to 'disrupt, dismantle and defeat Al Qaeda in Pakistan and Afghanistan, and to prevent its return to either country in the future'. However, the administration's key policy brief then went on to list, as the means towards achieving this goal, an almost impossibly broad series of necessary steps. These included creating a 'capable, accountable and effective government in Afghanistan', tackling corruption, carrying out a 'civilian surge' to address the challenges facing rural Afghanistan, breaking the link between narcotics and the insurgency, ensuring civilian control of government and a 'vibrant economy' in

Pakistan, bringing the entire international community on board, and encouraging an 'important leadership role' for the UN.[8]

Hence this ostensibly focused programme reverted to an impossibly complex web of intermeshed factors, spanning development to security-sector reform to state-building, all of which NATO and the international development community had already spent years trying and failing to resolve, and which implied decades of further effort. If the aim was simply to prevent Al Qaeda acquiring a safe haven, this looked like an extraordinarily expensive way to go about it. In an era of growing financial austerity and shrinking domestic support, it seemed incongruous that a more cost-effective way could not be found to deter a few hundred terrorists (the core leadership group of Al Qaeda), particularly when those self-same terrorists could potentially find alternative sanctuaries such as Yemen or Somalia.

The Obama administration therefore appeared to be slipping seamlessly back into the pattern of strategic incoherence that had characterized the intervention from its inception. Another recurring pattern was soon to reappear: the subordination of policy and strategy to fashionable operational and tactical military concepts. Whereas in the early days of the intervention this had been the Bush administration's desire to 'redefine war on our terms', through the 'transformation agenda', in 2009 and 2010 it was to be the application of counterinsurgency theory. The effects of this will be examined later in the chapter; meanwhile, 2009 also marked a number of developments in internal Afghan politics, few of them positive.

THE 'KARZAI PROBLEM' AND THE 2009 ELECTION

2009 in Afghanistan was dominated by the Afghan presidential elections, at which Hamid Karzai sought re-election after his almost uncontested 2004 victory. At the 2004 elections numerous voting irregularities had largely slipped under the Western media radar; the 2009 election, however, was destined from the outset to be highly controversial.

The declining security situation in the country had increasingly focused Western attention on the corruption and inefficiency of Karzai's government, and on Karzai's own apparent limitations. Even before voting began, Afghan politicians were predicting a corrupt election, with reports that voter registration cards were being counterfeited on a massive scale.[9] Karzai retained his reputation as a political conciliator, but the consensus of international opinion had shifted towards the view that this trait represented a weakness rather than an asset. James Dobbins, the former US ambassador to the Bonn conference, remarked in comments to this book's authors in 2010:

> He [Karzai] was originally chosen for his ability to unite a wide range of factions and interests, and has since been criticized for failing to provide strong leadership and discard support from former warlords and those accused of corruption. The criticisms are largely valid, but reflect in large measure the characteristics which made him attractive in the first place.[10]

A British Foreign Office official, who wished to remain anonymous, articulated a widely shared view when he summed up Karzai as 'a great king but a poor chief executive' on account of his tendency towards excessive personal micro-management. According to Gerard Russell, a member of the British embassy in 2007–08, the main issue was that the Afghan people lacked confidence in Karzai's staying power, a perception scarcely helped by rumours that Karzai's family was stockpiling future retirement funds in Dubai. Indeed, open-source revelations in 2010 revealed that, over the previous three and a half years, over $3 billion had been flown out of Kabul airport in boxes and suitcases.[11]

Dr Abdullah Abdullah and Ashraf Ghani, both of whom had been ministers in previous Karzai administrations and both of whom ran against Karzai in 2009, were even more vitriolic in their condemnation. Ghani labelled Karzai's choice of running mates in the campaign a 'declaration of war against the Afghan people', and also blamed the president personally for the fact that Afghanistan was now officially ranked the fifth most corrupt country on earth. This enmity reflected a wider culture clash between the Western-trained technocrats in the Kabul government and the indigenous warlords. The latter described the technocrats as 'dog washers', a phrase implying that they had lived abroad for decades, performing menial tasks, before returning when things were safe to profit from US reconstruction contracts. By 2005 the warlords had for the most part pushed the technocrats out, having success-fully utilized the preceding parliamentary elections to entrench their positions in the Afghan state.

A reporter who visited Karzai in 2009 found the president visibly strained by these tensions. He appeared paranoid about his representation in the Western media, trapped by the increasingly elaborate web of corruption reportedly spun by his various brothers (one of whom, Ahmed Wali Karzai, had by the end of 2009 been alleged to be not only a narcotics kingpin but a CIA asset, allegations he vigorously denies), and exhausted by the effort of balancing the internal factions within his own government and the broader competing demands of the international community.[12] The arrival of new American representatives, in the shape of Ambassador Karl Eikenberry and General Stanley McChrystal, further complicated the situation. According to many insiders, Karzai attempted to play McChrystal off against Eikenberry, even as the two Americans themselves tried to 'manage' the Afghan president via a 'good cop, bad cop' routine. The appointment of Richard Holbrooke as President Obama's 'special adviser' on Afghanistan and Pakistan added yet a third dimension to the equation, with Karzai and Holbrooke reportedly swiftly falling out.[13] The ensuing tensions soon bubbled over into a spate of cross-briefings to the global media.

The August 2009 election was marked not only – as predicted – by massive vote fraud, but by the extraordinarily virulent and public open dissent that erupted between Kai Eide, the Norwegian head of the United Nations Assistance Mission in Afghanistan (UNAMA), and his deputy, the American diplomat Peter Galbraith, who in late September was formally fired by Ban Ki-Moon, the UN secretary-general. Galbraith later alleged that he had been fired for opposing the official UN line, which played down the level of electoral fraud. Eide and his supporters, by contrast, claimed that Galbraith had suggested persuading Washington to force Karzai to resign, so that the US could then impose a new government led by Ashraf Ghani or Ali Jalali. Galbraith had reportedly raised these proposals with the deputy US ambassador in Kabul, with no success; but rumours regarding the scheme had allegedly also reached Karzai, and in Kai Eide's account this minor scandal then played a significant role in Galbraith's dismissal.[14]

The election itself, the first not to be policed by the UN but by a Karzai-created Afghan electoral commission, was marked by widespread fraud, including 'ghost' polling stations, intimidation, and the complete breakdown of all the statutory regulatory procedures. Election monitors themselves participated in multiple voting, while it became apparent within hours of the polls opening that the 'indelible' ink used in the electoral registration process was easily washed off, that voter turnout in many provinces was extremely low, and that extensive armed coercion, ballot box stuffing and vote tampering had also occurred. To take just one instance, 600 ballots were cast at one polling station, but President Karzai ended up with 996 votes in the final tally.

Voter turnout in general was around 33 per cent nationwide, but less than 10 per cent in some districts of Helmand and Kandahar. In the Babaji district of Helmand province, where the British had launched an offensive just weeks before polling began with the aim of clearing and securing ground from the Taliban specifically to facil-itate elections, around 150 people voted out of a population of 55,000.[15] That August, the election month, was also the deadliest month for US troops killed in Afghanistan since 2001, with at least fifty-one deaths, contributing to a toll for the year that was also the single deadliest for foreign forces as a whole to date – 521 fatalities.[16]

Although the initial count gave President Karzai a crushing majority, the sheer number of ballots discounted as fraudulent during subsequent post-election investigations reduced both Karzai's and Abdullah Abdullah's shares of the vote to below the requisite 50 per cent mandated by the French-style electoral laws, necessitating a run-off vote.

The US, UK and other Western powers tried to force Abdullah Abdullah and Karzai into talks, in order to force through a compromise and avoid the need for a fresh round of voting, but Karzai rejected any power-sharing formula. On 1 November, however, as preparations for the run-off were under way, Abdullah Abdullah pulled out of the contest, declaring that a transparent election was not possible without dismissing and reorganizing the electoral commission, and leaving Karzai to be re-elected by default. With Karzai now guaranteed to remain in office until 2014, American strategists were left to devise a new policy towards Afghanistan in cooperation with a partner who was now regarded by many in the international community as hopelessly compromised, inept and corrupt.

THINKING ABOUT GRAND STRATEGY? OBAMA'S REVIEW PROCESS

The Obama administration set up a three-month internal review of Afghan policy in the autumn of 2009, but received criticism from many commentators for its length. In reality, the whole process probably took the minimum time necessary – there were, to paraphrase Soviet Foreign Minister Shevardnadze, quite literally years of 'un-thought-out past decisions' to sift through and mull over. On the other hand, the final outcomes of the review were rather underwhelming, being focused narrowly and almost entirely on military operations.

The first casualty of the policy pruning process was a much-touted diplomatic offensive. At the outset of the debate, both Richard Holbrooke and one of his key advisers, the American scholar Barnett Rubin, had repeatedly (and correctly) underlined the need for a new regional 'grand bargain'.[17] This would involve co-opting the regional neighbours – Pakistan, India, China, Iran, Russia and the Central Asian states – by persuading them of the benefits of a stable Afghanistan.

However, organizing such a coalition proved elusive, and this approach seems to have been rapidly abandoned as a coherent policy objective even before being struck the further blow of Holbrooke's untimely death in December 2010. While still in post,

Holbrooke was not given diplomatic leeway to offer Pakistan any assurances over Kashmir, and Pakistan, in turn, made it clear that it would only help the US if Afghanistan was then encouraged to be a 'friendly' neighbour within Pakistan's sphere of influence, and with India strictly excluded from any strategic role.[18] Meanwhile, US relations with Iran during 2009 if anything worsened as a result of the nuclear issue and the Iranian crackdown on domestic dissidents. China, for its part, had already expressed interest in Afghanistan as a significant investment opportunity, successfully placing a $3.4 billion bid for exclusive exploitation rights to Afghanistan's largest copper mine in 2007; but though willing, via this commercial partnership, to build related infrastructure such as railways, roads, and even schools, Beijing consistently rebuffed requests to contribute security forces.[19]

Obama had meanwhile promised Moscow a 're-set' in US–Russian relations in the wake of the 2008 Georgian conflict, and as a result Russia allowed NATO to transport lethal weapons along Russian and Central Asian railways, an overland supply route known as the 'Northern Distribution Network'. However, in 2010 traffic along this route was still dogged by heavy delays and disruption, while Russian and American military bases continued to jostle for influence in Central Asia, and Russian criticism of the ineffectiveness of NATO counter-narcotics operations grew louder.[20] Overall, therefore, one of the few aspects of the review process that genuinely merited the term 'strategic' was stalled almost before it began, largely because it would have involved conducting a genuine dialogue with governments which Washington traditionally found both politically uncongenial and insufficiently subservient to American interests.

It soon became clear that a review that was ostensibly about strategy was rapidly devolving down to the operational and tactical levels of war – a pattern, as we have seen, that had been repeated, with depressing regularity, throughout the intervention. A further casualty of this process was the squashing of the possibility, again raised by some in the early stages of the review, and even mentioned by President Obama himself, of initiating behind-the-scenes negotiations and a reconciliation and reintegration process with the Taliban and their backers.

Since at least mid-2008, UK military officers and statesmen had articulated the need to pursue a political solution to the conflict, with the UK ambassador to Kabul, Sir Sherard Cowper-Coles, and Labour Foreign Secretary David Miliband both advocating a dual-track approach to divide the Taliban. A highly selective reading of UK counterinsurgency experiences during decolonization and in Northern Ireland had led to a degree of British over-confidence early on in both Iraq and Afghanistan. Nevertheless, one of the relevant lessons the UK drew from these earlier conflicts was that pressure by the military and intelligence services could only contain an insurgent problem, and a political back channel of dialogue with one's declared enemies was required for true progress to be made.[21]

However, US officials and advisers proved psychologically unwilling to engage in serious negotiations, largely perhaps because the US war-fighting tradition was one of pursuing all-out victory (*pace* Vietnam or the 'Sunni Awakening' in Iraq), and had therefore never fully inculcated the need to talk to one's enemies. American analysts therefore generally preferred to emphasize the fairly simplistic notion that wars end 'when someone wins', and that talking to the Taliban was inherently unthinkable anyway, since they remained 'misogynous, intolerant, ruthless' and 'barbaric'.[22] Against this moralistic backdrop, the advice of the distinguished American historian Edward Luttwak to consider the example of the Byzantine

Empire, which had successfully sustained itself for over 800 years at least in part because it never hesitated to hold talks with 'barbarians', was never likely to gain traction.[23]

Therefore, despite UK, German and Saudi attempts to initiate covert roundtable talks with the Taliban at a neutral overseas location, the American approach towards wider strategic talks with the Taliban leadership remained lukewarm. Richard Holbrooke and General McChrystal did endorse a policy of encouraging the defection and reintegration of lower-ranking Taliban foot soldiers, and significant funds – $250 million – were allocated to this initiative. However, this policy of attempting to fragment the Taliban from the ground up, rather than from the top down, was perhaps the least promising approach. The problems that had blighted past efforts in this direction – broken promises regarding food aid, housing, or protection for defectors, together with a lack of credible financial incentives given the parlous state of the Afghan economy – remained seemingly insuperable obstacles. Internal bickering also delayed the Afghan government's creation of an executive committee to oversee the programme or establish a coherent approach.[24] By the latter half of 2010 the initiative was widely acknowledged to have stalled, with the US having expended only $200,000, and other donors little or nothing at all, while the number of Taliban fighters who had actually defected stood at a few hundred at most.

BACK TO THE COMFORT ZONE: OPERATIONAL AND TACTICAL MILITARY DEBATES

Given the difficulties encountered in initiating 'strategic' initiatives, it is perhaps unsurprising that the review ended up promoting an altogether narrower approach. It was an approach whose particular slant, however, was also perhaps inevitable, given the main military appointment made by the Obama administration in the early days of the Afghanistan policy-review process: General Stanley McChrystal.

McChrystal came to the job of NATO commander in Afghanistan as the former head of the Joint Special Operations Command (JSOC), which was associated with high-intensity covert operations against Al Qaeda-affiliated insurgents in Iraq from 2006 onwards. There, over the course of two years, US and UK Special Forces had launched nightly raids aimed at sheer attrition of the insurgency, in a covert, intelligence-led campaign that inflicted upwards of 3,000 deaths.[25] Strikingly, McChrystal's accession in Afghanistan occurred not through normal turnover, but after American Defence Secretary Robert Gates explicitly requested the resignation of General McKiernan, McChrystal's immediate predecessor in Kabul, who had another twelve months of his formal term to run. Gates justified this step by emphasizing the urgency of bringing to bear in Afghanistan McChrystal's own 'unique skill set in counterinsurgency', an indication that the new administration was already beginning to look to recent developments in Iraq as a template for curing America's Afghanistan ills.[26]

With many of the genuinely strategic aspects of the review ruled out or shelved, the Obama review in practice then spent almost three months discussing the best way to employ American military power at the operational and tactical level in Afghanistan. Vice President Joe Biden was, within the administration, the best-known advocate of a so-called 'counterterrorism' option, which, broadly defined, envisioned a policing action using roughly the same troop numbers present in Afghanistan before McChrystal first arrived. Emphasis here would fall on accelerated training, to hand over responsibility to Afghan forces sooner rather than later, and on hunting Al Qaeda via an intensified drone campaign across the Afghan–Pakistani borderlands.

This proposal was heavily criticized by the counterinsurgency lobby in the US media, on two main grounds: that a 'light footprint' had already been tried in Afghanistan in the past and found wanting, and that, without a significant ground presence, it would be impossible to acquire the detailed intelligence necessary for guiding the drone strike campaign.[27] An extraordinary amount of vitriol and animus was expressed both online and in the press against Vice President Biden personally, with the subtext that such matters should be left to the military, whose self-anointed new intellectual elite (of whom McChrystal was most certainly one), allegedly now understood counterinsurgency, 'the graduate school of warfare', better than at any other time in their history. Typical of US coverage were the on-air remarks in October 2009 of Lara Logan, the CBS foreign affairs correspondent, who publicly dismissed the Biden proposals for a counterterrorism approach in Afghanistan as 'just ludicrous', and plaintively asked, 'So I don't understand why no one would listen to the man [General McChrystal] you put your faith in and said, "He is the guy who is going to do this for us."'[28]

There was, in fact, more merit to the Biden proposals than many were willing to acknowledge at the time. In the first place, they focused attention on what a longer-term sustainable end-state might look like – one with significantly fewer US resources on the ground, but sufficient force available to prevent the Taliban from massing to storm Afghan cities or Al Qaeda from establishing formal training camps once more. The Biden approach actually addressed President Obama's stated aim of targeting Al Qaeda better than did the plans of the counterinsurgency lobby, who now unashamedly embraced the need for a massively expensive state-building project in Afghanistan. Secondly, Biden was one of the few commentators to emphasize that a violently destabilized Pakistan was the most worrying scenario, and that Pakistan itself might therefore merit a greater allocation of resources.[29]

In November 2009 US Ambassador Eikenberry also waded into the debate. In two widely leaked cables, he warned that increasing troop levels as McChrystal was proposing would merely deepen Afghan dependence on external actors, that this would be a military approach to a problem without a military solution, and that President Karzai himself was 'not an adequate strategic partner'. Pointing to Afghanistan's pervasive corruption, ongoing lack of an effective political class, and limited revenue base, Eikenberry also warned of the dangers of overrating the capacity of the Afghan security forces, and of the deepening strategic dependency that a narrow operationally focused COIN approach would foster.[30] Partly in response, advocates of COIN began to publicize economic 'silver bullets' (such as a story about Afghanistan's reportedly vast mineral reserves), with the aim of providing a context in which the McChrystal strategy would seem more credible.[31]

These 'Washington Beltway' disputes were far more important than normal internal wrangles, since the result would set the direction of the international intervention for at least the medium term. Initially the clear winners were the advocates of a COIN approach for Afghanistan that was modelled (unconvincing denials aside) on the post-2007 US approach to Iraq. In short, once again, an operational and tactical military approach was driving intervention strategy.

THE ILLUSION OF A COIN 'STRATEGY' FOR AFGHANISTAN

Calls for more troops in Afghanistan had already begun to be made in 2008, with both General McKiernan and General Sir David

Richards specifying the need for an additional 30,000 troops.,
However, General McKiernan at this stage had also deliberately
avoided the use of the word 'surge', emphasizing that he foresaw
such heightened troop levels needing to be maintained for up to
four years.[32]

The emerging consensus on the need for greater troop numbers
and strategic patience in Afghanistan related to studies that had been
conducted by the US-based RAND (Research and Development)
Institute, which, during 2006–08, had carried out quantitative studies
which concluded that successful counterinsurgency campaigns
historically took fourteen years, and that effective stabilization
demanded an extremely high per-capita security presence (as
opposed to the 'light footprint' approach used in Afghanistan up to
2006). By a circuitous (and mathematically questionable) route, the
RAND calculations suggested that Afghanistan, given the size of its
population, required security forces (international and indigenous
combined) of 200,000, meaning that, as of 2006, a dangerous
security 'gap' existed of at least 80,000 'missing' police and soldiers.[33]

The conclusions of these RAND studies were debatable, not
least because the quantitative techniques used took no account of
variations in the methods, ability and motivation of the insurgent
groups analysed, which ranged from the Viet Cong to the Kenyan
Mau Mau and the Shining Path in Peru. They also underplayed
differences between the approaches employed by counterinsur-
gents, and the difficulties of defining what counted as 'victory'.
Nonetheless, they fed into the new US army 2006 counterinsurgency doctrine, which shaped operations in Iraq from 2007
onwards and which became known, famously and universally, by
its issue number acronym – FM 3-24. Among the conclusions
drawn by the manual was the ruling that successful counterinsurgency generally required around twenty to twenty-five police or

soldiers for every thousand citizens.[34] In Afghanistan, this at face value implied a figure of between 580,000 and 750,000 security personnel, a level that was simply impossible to achieve.

Imbibing perceived 'lessons' from the writings of previous generations of counterinsurgency writers like David Galula, a veteran of France's disastrous campaign to retain hold of Algeria, the new doctrine manual also emphasized 'population-centric counter-insurgency' – essentially, area control, or what the French had earlier termed *quadrillage*. This involved the establishment of regular security foot patrols, bunkers, block posts, finely tuned intelligence operations (including knowledge of a neighbourhood right down to its social, ethnographic and cultural hierarchies) and more effective local governance. Enemy-dominated neighbourhoods were to be cleared of insurgent forces, then held against insurgent re-infiltration until local governance and reconstruction could take place ('clear, hold and build').

This was an example of 'systems thinking' *par excellence*. Applied on a block-by-block basis to an urban environment such as Baghdad, it brought about an unquestionable downturn in violence, though it was less than effective in addressing underlying social, economic and political tensions. However, applying it to a predominantly rural context such as Afghanistan – a country that is far larger and more populous than Iraq, with much more impenetrable terrain – struck many observers as distinctly more problematic, not least because the counterinsurgency manual itself stressed, as necessary factors for eventual success, such conditions as border security, a reliable and capable host government, and honest, impartial and self-sustaining host-nation security forces – conditions that were unlikely ever to be fully achieved in Afghanistan.[35]

The first and most obvious challenge was generating the force levels that the RAND studies suggested were needed. Since

NATO force levels (apart from, temporarily, the US's) were on their way down rather than up, the only option was to focus manically on local recruitment. Hence, shortly after arriving in post, General McChrystal called for a dramatic ramping up of the Afghan National Army (ANA) and Afghan National Police (ANP). On 30 August 2009, in a report that was quickly leaked, McChrystal emphasized that his proposed new strategy involved a 'target ceiling' of 240,000 ANA and 160,000 ANP troops to complement his request in September for 40,000 additional US forces, some of whom were destined to become trainers partnered with the Afghan army.[36] The latter request for more US troops quickly caused widespread apprehension in Washington, and was subsequently moderated down to 30,000 reinforcements, but ultimately passed largely because US Defense Secretary Robert Gates had, in the interim, also been persuaded to change his earlier reluctance to endorse a sharp rise in the foreign troop presence in Afghanistan.

As a CIA eyewitness to the earlier Soviet failure in Afghanistan (which he had actively helped to accelerate), Gates nurtured well-founded concerns that a dramatic rise in US force levels would lead to the Afghans increasingly seeing the US presence as an imperial occupation. However, over the course of 2009, a barrage of articles and opinion pieces by a well-organized and choreographed group of academics working within the Washington Beltway – among them Max Boot, Frederick Kagan and Stephen Biddle, all of whom were more or less closely aligned to McChrystal, Petraeus and the new 'counterinsurgency' lobby within the US army – helped persuade Gates to support a rapid escalation in the US ground presence in Afghanistan.[37] By November, President Obama had signed off on the troop increase, and in December he announced the dispatch of an extra 30,000 troops over the following six months, but with the caveat that US troops would begin to withdraw from Afghanistan by July 2011.

Simultaneously announcing the planned date of a future draw-down and implementing a troop increase was a controversial step, one that was quickly criticized by conservative groups in the US as evidence of the president's alleged lack of resolve. Some also worried that it offered succour to the enemy. However, Obama was determined to avoid what threatened to become an intractable quagmire, and wanted to ensure that the Afghan government did not expect an open-ended US commitment. Although Washington soon clarified that the drawdown would be 'conditions based', rather than rigidly time-lined, the withdrawal date itself remained in force.[38]

In the wake of the announcement, the new Conservative govern-ment in the UK declared that UK troops would be withdrawn from combat operations in Afghanistan by 2015, regardless of whether the Afghan government had put its own house in order.[39] Germany, the third biggest NATO troop contributor, committed itself to begin a troop drawdown in 2011, and Poland likewise began to discuss withdrawing its 2,600 troops from Afghanistan by 2012, further emphasizing that the endgame over international involvement in Afghanistan was approaching.[40]

GROWING PROBLEMS WITH THE COIN APPROACH

Despite the increase in troop numbers, McChrystal would still lack the force ratios that, according to the new field manual, were necessary to 'defend the population' in the south. Defenders of the counterinsurgency approach argued that this should not be a problem, since northern and western Afghanistan was relatively peaceful – '70 per cent of the violence occurs in 20 per cent of the country'.[41] This in itself was a questionable assumption, however. By 2009, the Taliban revival had begun to affect the entire country. In the north of the country, the most obvious example of a growing Taliban presence was in Kunduz and Faryab provinces, where the German PRT found itself suddenly struggling to cope with a sharp escalation in ambushes and roadside bombings. Chahrdara district became a veritable Taliban stronghold in 2009, to the point where Taliban forces had established their own governmental structures and taxation system, and by spring 2010 all the administrative subunits of Faryab province in the north-west of the country were affected by insurgent violence to a greater or lesser degree. Furthermore, it appeared that, when military pressure in the south became particularly intense, trained Taliban fighters were shifted to what were becoming safe havens in the north-west of the country, where non-Pashtuns were also being recruited by Taliban forces. The decision to concentrate US forces therefore now risked being overtaken by events, given the Taliban's demonstrated capacity to withdraw and regroup at a later date, as they did in Pakistan. There has been much speculation meanwhile as to whether this political and cultural penetration of north-west Afghanistan represents a conscious Taliban strategy, but at the very least it places a serious question mark over some of the planning assumptions of the US counterinsurgency lobby.[42]

The spreading footprint of the Taliban within Afghanistan aside, McChrystal's plan relied on two further assumptions – that it was not necessary to defend every village, but merely the largest population centres; and that most of the Taliban resistance was also based on local grievances, so that securing the border need not be a priority.[43] The latter assumption might charitably be viewed as an attempt to ignore the safe havens in Pakistan enjoyed by the Taliban, whose presence might otherwise suggest that an effective counterinsurgency approach was simply unfeasible. The consequent focus on securing Kabul, Kandahar, Kunduz, Jalalabad and other cities though, while certainly 'population-centric', resembled the former Soviet policy of controlling the roads and cities. Its relevance in tackling a rural insurgency remained questionable, particularly when the redeployment of forces from remoter outposts might allow the Taliban to seize ground and achieve easy propaganda victories. The policy also suggested that much of the US operational template relied on recent, but rather different, experience in Iraq.

Perhaps the most striking assumption of the new counterinsurgency approach, however, was that the Afghan government, at both the central and the local level, would suddenly somehow 'come good' and be in a position to benefit from the increased troop presence. Quite apart from the escalating insurgency, few underlying trends in Afghan governance and state performance gave grounds for increased optimism. Opium cultivation in Afghanistan was certainly affected by a sharp drop in farm-gate prices in 2008 (from $1 billion to $730 million), and, by the winter of 2009, twenty out of the thirty-four provinces in Afghanistan were essentially poppy free.[44] However, this reduction in opium cultivation seemed to be essentially market driven, a function of oversupply at source then compounded by a crop blight epidemic in 2010 which cut opium production by 48 per cent compared to 2009, and lowered market penetration in Europe. Military operations to target the crop remained merely an irritation by comparison, with Afghan and NATO forces in the first half of 2009 for example destroying only around 90 tonnes of precursor chemicals, 50 tonnes of opium and 7 tonnes of morphine, alongside 27 laboratories. The 2009 UNODC Afghan Opium Survey identified a longer-term trend of emerging organized narco-cartels, while efforts to ban trafficking through the FATA region in Pakistan remained non-existent.[45] UN investigators in December 2010 subsequently reported that Afghan opium prices were 'skyrocketing' towards a six-year high, prompting widespread fears that whatever shallow gains had been made in reducing opium cultivation since the record crop of 2007 now stood on the verge of being dramatically reversed.[46]

Despite post-election promises by President Karzai, corruption was now also increasingly looking like a crippling problem in rural Afghanistan, and a major source of discontent and continuing Taliban mobilization. By 2010, Afghanistan was, according to Transparency International, the second most corrupt country in the world (after Somalia). A UNODC report in January 2010 recorded that 52 per cent of adult Afghans reported having to pay at least one bribe to a public official in the past twelve months. In 2009, Afghan citizens had to pay the equivalent of 23 per cent of the country's entire GDP in bribes, while drugs and bribery together constituted the two largest income generators in Afghanistan, at about half the country's (licit) GDP. The institutions most affected by bribe paying were the courts, police and customs, while the prevalence of bribe paying was also recorded as higher in rural areas (56 per cent) than in towns (46 per cent). Ineffective and overwhelmingly corrupt rural governance constituted a ripe recruiting ground for what remained predominantly a rural insurgency.[47]

In 2010, however, reports on the sheer scale of institutional government corruption also triggered a run on the Kabul bank, which fulfils a central role in payments for Afghan schoolteachers, soldiers and police. Though its cash holdings were tiny by international standards, the near collapse of the bank threatened, for a few days, to drive the country back to an entirely informal economy, thereby emphasizing – as the elections had done the previous year – the sheer shallowness and fragility of much of the Western institution-building project in Afghanistan.[48]

The issues of local capacity and troop numbers aside, the overarching criticism that could be made of the counterinsurgency approach was that it showed little evidence of working in practice. The scheduled sharp increase in ANA and ANP numbers, in a country without an effective identity card system, left the way open to widespread Taliban infiltration of the security forces, and 2009–10 was marked by small-scale but persistent instances of Afghan soldiers or police shooting their Western advisers before defecting to the Taliban.

A broader problem was that, for any military organization, a swift increase in manpower very rarely translates into an equivalent increase in real capacity or professionalism. In June 2010, a US government audit stated that the US military had consistently overstated or failed to adequately measure the capabilities of Afghan security forces in the past; personnel readiness for example was routinely overstated by recording the number of personnel assigned to each unit, rather than the number actually present for duty. As of March 2010, only 74 per cent of personnel assigned for duty were present in ANA-fielded combat units, with whole battalions on occasion reportedly being at only company strength on the ground. The ANA had an AWOL rate of 12 per cent, while within the ANP comparable attrition rates ran at 17 per cent. Poor logistical support, lack of fixed infrastructure (including even basic housing), widespread drug abuse (17 per cent of police tested positive for drug use in one unit), illiteracy and corruption were other issues raised in the report, which concluded by recommending a complete overhaul of assessment procedures.[49]

McChrystal's plan to ramp up ANA and ANP numbers also called for 2,325 foreign trainers, but NATO countries persistently failed to deliver on these commitments, imposing further complications for an extraordinarily accelerated build-up and handover process. Against this backdrop, meeting the basic benchmark recruitment goals – which the ANA in August 2010 did, with 134,000 troops in the ranks a whole two months ahead of schedule – threatened to prove meaningless in the medium to longer term, despite the introduction in 2010 of compulsory literacy courses, and an improvement in the most basic performance requirements like live firing exercises. As if to emphasize the longer-term overarching problems, in December 2009 President Karzai also estimated that it would be another fifteen years before the Afghan government could meet the operating expenses of its own army and police.[50]

'Clear, hold and build', the essence of General McChrystal's much-vaunted counterinsurgency approach, also bore ambiguous results across much of 2010. This threatened to become a serious issue, given that the Obama administration was committed to reviewing progress in December 2010, and even McChrystal's own defenders had confidently prophesied that 'if the new strategy is successful, we will see clear evidence of that by late 2010 or 2011'.[51] McChrystal had heavily advertised his new approach of having 'government in a box, ready to roll in' to deliver a local police presence, vital services and development in a town as soon as hostilities were over. A showpiece offensive by 15,000 NATO and Afghan troops on the town of Marjah in Helmand province in February 2010 resulted in tougher and more prolonged fighting than anticipated, but offered a perfect opportunity to demonstrate this approach.[52] By July, however, the newly installed Afghan governor in the town had already been fired, the population remained intimidated by the Taliban on a daily basis, the US marines regularly came under Taliban sniper fire, and the entire operation had come to be labelled by McChrystal a 'bleeding ulcer'.[53]

The outcome of the Marjah offensive cast doubt over the next stage of the advertised approach – a major campaign (Operation Hamkari) to secure the symbolically important town of Kandahar, an operation which McChrystal now presented as aiming to bring about a 'slow, rising tide of security' rather than engaging in any kind of frontal assault.[54] On 23 June, however, McChrystal was abruptly fired by President Obama, in the wake of remarks to *Rolling Stone* magazine that were widely seen as insubordinate and disrespectful, but that also reflected the well-known internal divisions within the US administration that had emerged the previous year over the correct policy to adopt towards Afghanistan. McChrystal's sudden forced retiral both underlined the frictions occurring within the Washington Beltway and placed President Obama in the difficult position of having now very publicly recalled two generals from Afghanistan before their term in office was complete. This left the president little political breathing room to recall or publicly disagree with McChrystal's successor, especially after the emergence of a traditionally pro-military Republican-dominated Congress after the November 2010 elections.

McChrystal's replacement, General Petraeus, was the founding father of the US army's current counterinsurgency doctrine, but had little specialized knowledge of Afghanistan. At the time when Petraeus was appointed, there was also no clear 'plan B' if population-centric counterinsurgency failed. Insiders confessed that the Kandahar offensive was seen as a 'go for broke' operation, involving 10,000 US troops and 80 per cent of USAID's budget for Afghanistan, but that success was also to be measured by 'atmospherics', such as public opinion polling and levels of street commerce. Given all this, some commentators inevitably speculated that the operation would have to be presented as a success by December, even if the reality on the ground by then remained far more ambiguous.[55]

By August, General Petraeus was in practice emphasizing success in halting Taliban momentum via the types of special operation that had already been practised in Iraq, pointing out that NATO Special Forces in the course of ninety days had already captured or killed 365 insurgent leaders, detained 1,335 foot soldiers and killed a further 1,031 Taliban fighters on top of that.[56] This revived enthusiasm for enemy 'kills' as a metric of success sat ill with a narrative that had been proclaiming the importance of population-centric security, and was a shift back towards the 2006–08 drive to 'take the fight to the enemy'. However, such operations undoubtedly bought a degree of political breathing space, though they left unanswered the wider problem of when Afghanistan might become a fully functioning state, how the open border with Pakistan would be addressed, or how the radically expanded Afghan security forces could be transformed into a self-sufficient, stable and reliable force.

By December 2010, Operation Hamkari in Kandahar province, intended to be the centrepiece of 'non-kinetic' COIN activity with a rising tide of governance and population security, had cleared away significant quantities of Taliban infrastructure, notably their IED factories, but continued to illustrate these wider strategic problems. As late as November 2010, the security ring established around Kandahar city was still failing to significantly inhibit Taliban movement in and out of the city. The quality of ANA forces engaged in the operation remained extremely uneven, the governor of Kandahar city was a Karzai appointee who continued to lack local legitimacy, and the sheer quantity of US aid money being thrown at the problem fostered further corruption amongst the local contracting mafias, to the extent that eight out of eleven successful local candidates in the 2010 elections had demonstrably made personal fortunes from such contracts. These increasingly entrenched semi-criminal networks, which fed on delivering goods and services funded by international aid, also conducted political vendettas that contributed to continuing instability; for example, in June 2010 Abdul Jabar, the Arghandab district governor, was assassinated by a local mafia that felt it was not receiving a sufficient cut of the US development assistance channelled through his office.[57]

US official reports by the beginning of 2011 emphasized progress, circulating overblown statistical claims regarding Afghan civilian access to healthcare, whilst also confirming that a gradual drawdown in US troop numbers could indeed begin in July 2011. International aid agencies in Afghanistan by contrast painted a consistently bleaker picture of worsening human security, as Taliban forces redeployed to the north to evade contact with US forces, and humanitarian aid budgets as a whole remained unmet (the 2010 annual appeal was fulfilled by only 66 per cent).[58] The alleged strategic panacea of counterinsurgency was rapidly wearing thin in the face of actual Afghan conditions; accordingly, midway through 2010, supporters of the war effort grasped at one last thread that could potentially make the entire campaign look credible and sustainable.

ONE FINAL SILVER BULLET: AFGHANISTAN'S UNTAPPED BILLIONS

By this time it was clear that COIN was facing severe challenges, and this filtered through to wider strategic assessments of the situation in Afghanistan. In September 2010, the widely respected London-based International Institute for Strategic Studies committed the heresy of pointing out that the West's effort in Afghanistan had ballooned out of all proportion to the stated goals of the mission, and that containment and deterrence potentially represented a better way forward – the revival, in all but name, of Vice President Joe Biden's previously much-reviled counterterrorism approach.[59] That same month, the New America Foundation in the United States presented its own 'plan B', advocating an alternative fast-tracked peace and reconciliation process, a reduced US military footprint in Afghanistan, a revived regional 'grand bargain' and a greater strategic emphasis on Al Qaeda and homeland security.[60] Few of these ideas were new, but the very fact that they resurfaced so quickly bore eloquent testimony to the rapid waning of belief in counterinsurgency doctrine.

For advocates of continued large-scale engagement, however, the question of how the projected 305,600 personnel of the Afghan security forces could ever become economically sustainable over the long term had long posed a central conundrum, given that, despite years of privatized reconstruction efforts, Afghanistan remained among the poorest countries on earth. The question of how to achieve sustainable government revenues of sufficient size was particularly acute for a country with a growing desertification problem, where droughts occurred on average every four years, and which correspondingly remained heavily dependent on foreign aid. After 2007 Afghan growth rates had slowed from around 10 per cent to 3.4 per cent per annum. Such low levels of annual growth are sustainable without the risk of a social crisis only if a country is essentially already rich, with large quantities of long-term fixed infrastructure assets already in place. By no stretch of the imagination was Afghanistan in this category.

For evangelists of the COIN-based approach, however, there appeared to be one silver bullet on the horizon – Afghanistan's abundant mineral resources. In 2010, the Afghanistan country director of the Asian Development Bank remarked, 'I think the [Afghan] mining sector is this magic bullet that everyone is looking for to sustain things without [foreign donors] having to cover costs until kingdom come.'[61]

The 'discovery' of Afghan mineral wealth was scarcely a new story, but the timing of the announcement was significant. In June 2010 it was announced that US surveys begun in 2006 had disclosed an alleged $1 trillion worth of untapped mineral deposits in Afghanistan (later estimates revised the figure down to $908 billion), including huge veins of cobalt, copper, iron, gold and lithium, this last a key raw material in the manufacture of laptops and smartphones. General Petraeus immediately made reference to the 'stunning potential' that the survey had disclosed, encouraging dissemination of a 'good news story' that suggested Afghanistan's decades-old developmental crisis suddenly had a natural solution.[62]

The truth, as is so often the case with such stories, was rather more prosaic. Soviet geologists had identified potentially rich seams of mineral wealth in Afghanistan as far back as the 1960s, but Afghanistan had very few of the materials, or the technical or cultural expertise necessary, to benefit from such discoveries. The same conditions that had prevented the country's mineral wealth from being fully exploited in previous decades – lack of stability, infrastructure and government capacity – remained just as entrenched in 2010 as they ever had been. Moreover, it seemed entirely probable that the potential large flows of money might simply increase already endemic corruption and instability in Afghanistan, as had happened in other countries – such as the

Democratic Republic of the Congo or Sierra Leone – that had suffered what has been termed the 'resource curse' of extraordinary mineral wealth.

In addition, the development timeline in the mineral extractive industry is traditionally longer than in the oil or gas industries, with extensive and very expensive field work required to determine whether commercially viable quantities of ore can be extracted – even a huge deposit of gold, for example, may be completely worthless if the grade is low and it contains large quantities of carbon, which would obstruct gold recovery. Typical physical start-up costs for major mine works in Afghanistan were estimated to run to $5 billion apiece. To take another not entirely facetious parallel, even the North Sea contains an estimated $207 billion of gold, but once start-up and extraction costs are taken into the equation, they render it a clearly uneconomic mining prospect.[63] The degree of benefit in mineral extraction is also usually shorter term than in the oil or natural gas industries. Large-scale mine workings typically encounter the law of diminishing returns within a matter of a decade. Above all, the Western commitment to a sizeable security presence lasted only up to 2015 at the very latest, whereas the infrastructure and development timeline for Afghanistan's mineral wealth required between ten and fifteen years of investment – up to 2025.

The mineral wealth story was a typical example of the hazy quick fixes and loose linkages that had characterized Western interest and activity in Afghanistan since 2001. Far from representing a genuine breakthrough, it marked merely the latest in a long line of supposed 'turning points' in the Western narrative regarding the country: from the Bonn process, to the 2004 elections, to a redoubled emphasis on doctrinally pure population-centric counterinsurgency after 2008. These repeated cycles of optimism and subsequent disappointment were, in fact, wholly characteristic of a broader syndrome, which entailed the West never being able to correlate ways, ends and means in Afghanistan into a balance that looked either plausible or genuinely long term. After ten years of intervention in Afghanistan, the only real conclusion that could be drawn regarding the whole effort was that the West had truly lost its way.

CONCLUSION

Without the controlling principle that the nation must maintain its objectives and its power in equilibrium, its purposes within its means and its means equal to its purposes, its commitments related to its resources and its resources adequate to its commitments, it is impossible to think at all about foreign affairs . . . An agreement has eventually to be reached when men admit that they must pay for what they want and that they must want only what they are willing to pay for.[1]

Walter Lippmann, 1943

IT IS SAFE to assume that Walter Lippmann would not have been particularly impressed by the manner in which those shaping the bloody ten years of international intervention in Afghanistan have balanced the 'ends, ways and means' calculations that are at the heart of strategy. Just about every conceivable approach, in a variety of combinations, has, at some point in the ten years, been attempted. There have only been two consistent themes. The first has been the mismatch between the dominant policy fashions pursued at particular points in time and the cycle of events in Afghanistan itself. The second has been the flawed execution of the policies, suggesting that, even if there had been a closer alignment of approach with conditions on the ground, 'success' would have been elusive.

This book has outlined the myriad reasons why Afghanistan is unlikely to develop into a state that bears some resemblance to Western notions of modernity and stability. It has no historical experience of the sort of central government–periphery relationships that are a distinguishing feature of modern states. The ethnic, tribal, clan and *qawm* networks that are at the heart of the society are inimical to central government and ensure that national politics, if it resonates at all, does so almost inevitably as a winner-takes-all arena, whereby one group's gain is automatically perceived as another's fundamental loss. In particular the Pashtuns, the ethnic group of most concern to Western security calculations, traditionally view external interference of any sort as anathema, and the notion of deferring to an outside, central authority as a source of dishonour.

Onto this unpromising landscape has been grafted a particularly dysfunctional Western approach to 'development', 'governance' and 'capacity building'. Aid and development funds have been funnelled through a bewildering complex of NGOs, private companies and international organizations that have bypassed and marginalized the fledgling state structures they are supposedly intended to buttress. Notions of 'capacity building' look plausible from the vantage point of ministries and conferences in Western capitals, but are utterly divorced from Afghan realities. In 2005–06, the current mid-point of the intervention, only 8 per cent of estimated income in the Afghan state budget was derived from taxation – the very epitome of a 'rentier state'. The development of 'human capital' can be gauged from the fact that, again in 2005, the education minister in Uruzgan province was illiterate.

None of this suggests that the international community should withdraw aid and development support to Afghanistan. Apart from the moral responsibility to help the people of this ravaged country, much good can be done in terms of infrastructure, public health and education. However, these projects must respond to the needs and grain of Afghan society and be decoupled from grandiose and essentially unachievable dreams of modern state-building and central governance.

Ironically, the one time in Afghanistan's history when Western state-building schemes had even a glimmer of a chance of making progress was in the period immediately following the overthrow of the Taliban. After decades of civil war and conflict, the Afghan people were as receptive as they have ever been to the prospect of international assistance, support and the idea of effective government. However, at this point, and almost inevitably given the overall conduct of the intervention, little was done in this regard.

Instead, the US empowered a network of thugs and minor warlords to pursue a counterterrorist approach that itself fell victim to confused strategy, competing agendas and inflexible decision-making, to the extent that Osama bin Laden himself was allowed to escape. Then, when the brief window of opportunity had closed, the intervening powers increasingly turned to a traditional state-building agenda as a panacea for a rapidly deteriorating security situation, while the US directed its main gaze and efforts to the unfolding drama in Iraq. The result was a reconstituted Taliban, supported by the remnants of Al Qaeda, stabilizing itself in the sanctuaries of the border areas and coaxed back to life by a Pakistani security bureaucracy walking a tightrope between its traditional strategic approach to Afghanistan and a Western coalition still fearful of an international terrorist threat.

By 2005, it was clear to those who cared to look that Afghanistan was in a downward spiral. To all intents and purposes it was a narco-state, in which powerful criminal gangs both cooperated and competed with corrupt national and local power brokers, overlaid with what looked uncomfortably like a full-blown insurgency. It was past time for a fundamental reconsideration of the basic questions of strategy articulated in the introduction to this book: what was considered to be at stake in Afghanistan? What were realistically achievable goals? How much blood and treasure was the West willing to expend to bring about its preferred outcomes?

Instead, the response was an inchoate fusion of state-building with an increasingly aggressive military response designed to 'take the fight to the enemy'. Individual policy areas became disconnected from any sense of a coordinated whole. Each had its own internal dynamics, controversies, differences of emphases and debates. Counter-narcotics, security sector reform, reconciliation, anti-corruption, counterinsurgency and regional engagement were all pursued to a greater or lesser extent, but in an uncoordinated manner that produced often contradictory and mutually exclusive initiatives.

By the end of the Bush administration there was a general consensus that the security situation in Afghanistan was out of control. The incoming Obama administration initially appeared to be asking some of the fundamental strategic questions that the intervention had been crying out for from the start. However, although it apparently narrowed the political objectives down to a much more manageable focus on Al Qaeda in Pakistan and Afghanistan, its proposed plan of action involved the broadest and most ambitious of approaches. This still involved building an accountable and effective government in Afghanistan, self-reliant Afghan security forces at numerical levels previously seen as totally disproportionate and unsustainable and, if this were not enough, a stable Pakistan with a dynamic economy. It also seemingly required a prolonged counterinsurgency effort against the Taliban, even though many of the latter's members had no links with Al Qaeda. The result was a policy framework that, once again, provided little guidance on how to differentiate the vital from the peripheral; the essential from the desirable; or the threatening from the simply problematic. To quote the former British diplomat and shrewd observer of the Afghan scene Rory Stewart, in testimony to the US Senate Foreign Relations Committee:

> This policy is rooted in the pre-set categories of counter-terrorism, counter-insurgency, state-building and economic development. These categories are so closely linked that policy-makers appear to put them in almost any sequence or combination. You need to defeat the Taliban to build a state and you need to build a state to defeat the Taliban. There cannot be security without development, or development without security. If you have the Taliban you have terrorists, if you don't have development you have terrorists, and as Obama informed the *New Yorker*, 'If you have ungoverned spaces, they become havens for terrorists.' These connections are global: in Obama's words, 'our security and prosperity depend on the security and prosperity of others.' Indeed, at times it seems that all these activities – building a state, defeating the Taliban, defeating al-Qaida and eliminating poverty – are the same activity.[2]

However, a strange and protracted dialogue began, in which strategic questions from Washington were met with operational and tactical answers from theatre. General McChrystal, the US commander, was an evangelist, but his creed was counterinsurgency, and specifically the 'rediscovered' and 'rearticulated' approach put into effect by General Petraeus in Iraq. Therefore, as the Obama administration was seeking to get to grips with fundamental questions of strategy, the leader of the coalition military effort in Afghanistan was demanding the force uplift that would allow him to put in place what was, essentially, a tactical doctrine. Faced with increasingly strident requests from the commander that he had only recently appointed, and amid growing political heckling that the delay reflected indecision, President Obama agreed to most of the force uplift.

Thus the penultimate 'silver bullet' of the ten years of intervention was in play: counterinsurgency doctrine. Its advocates saw the COIN approach used in Iraq as a template for how the US should think about the future of its military, and believed that its application to Afghanistan promised not only success in that conflict, but victory in a domestic wrangle between theorists about how the US military should henceforth be configured. The only problem was that COIN, as articulated by its most fervent supporters, is a deeply flawed approach to remedying the strategic incoherence of the coalition intervention in Afghanistan.

The first problem relates to Iraq. COIN's supporters strongly refute any suggestions that they see what happened in Iraq as an undifferentiated template for Afghanistan, but it is never long before the debate returns to the 'proof' offered by the Iraq experience. This is clearly illustrated by a response from Major General Flynn, a key associate of McChrystal, when questioned on the likely success of a COIN approach in Afghanistan: 'We know what success tastes like from Iraq; we're a team that has won national championships.'[3] This (by no means isolated) triumphalism is eloquent testimony to the domination of operational and tactical military concerns over broader geopolitical vision. 'Success' in Iraq has witnessed civilian casualties measured in six figures; Iranian influence burgeoning not only in Iraq, but in the region more widely; Saudi Arabia looking nervously and balefully at its Shi'a minority; a cost to the US alone of well above $1 trillion, even by the most conservative estimates; severe diplomatic tension between Western allies; a rejuvenated Al Qaeda; and nearly five thousand coalition military deaths. Despite all this the future of Iraq, with its consequences for Western security, is still highly uncertain. It's hard to imagine the people of Afghanistan feeling much enthusiasm for 'success' of this type.

Even when Iraq is viewed purely from an operational COIN perspective, caution is required when assessing claims about what was achieved and its applicability elsewhere. The Petraeus approach in Iraq largely took advantage, albeit skilfully, of dynamics already in train. The 'Sunni Awakening', as it is often called, involved a local reaction against the horrific excesses and atrocities of foreign Al Qaeda elements that had created local revulsion. The dynamics are totally different from those in Afghanistan. In addition, what was achieved in Iraq was a dampening down and arresting of a violent downward spiral. While this was hugely welcome, it did not deliver strategic objectives. As noted above, the future of Iraq, and its relationship to US broader policy, is still in great doubt, with a number of uncomfortable current indicators.

This latter point is vitally important. Despite its prevalence in the media, the term 'COIN strategy' is a false construct. 'COIN' can never be a 'strategy'. It can be part of an understanding of 'ways', but tells you very little about 'ends' and 'means', and nothing about how they should be kept in balance. Many of its advocates reduce the concept still further to the construct 'clear, hold and build'. These are essentially activity descriptors that can provide a useful tactical framework, but shed virtually no light on strategic questions.

The approach, as it has manifested itself in Afghanistan, is also incoherent, in terms of both its own theoretical underpinnings and the manner in which it has been executed. COIN theory demands a legitimate and credible local partner that can be supported and ultimately can 'transition' to taking full control. The Karzai government is a very long way from being such a partner, and time is not on the coalition's side, which presents a further theoretical problem. COIN is unanimously recognized as a very long-term approach to conflict resolution. Yet, apparently, 'proper' COIN has only been practised in Afghanistan since 2009. The full force uplift did not take effect until the fall of 2010, with the analysis of its effects to come within a year. This is the COIN equivalent of putting a DVD into a player and fast-forwarding the movie at thirty times its normal rate.

Doubters are directed towards a series of quantitative studies designed to 'prove' the utility of 'population-centric' COIN. One of the most currently ubiquitous assertions, a staple of writings and utterances by the COIN lobby, is that, historically, '70 per cent of the counterinsurgencies that focused on population security have been effective'.[4] Obvious questions such as how one can provide timeless and objective definitions for terms like 'population security' or 'effectiveness', let alone why Afghanistan should be in the 70 per cent (rather than the remaining 30 per cent), even if such definitions could be provided, are left unanswered; and, even more disturbingly, the questions are usually unasked.

All this comes, in its most egregious manifestations, with generally facile understandings of the way that populations in general, and Afghans in particular, think about their situation. Miraculous properties are associated with local consent-building efforts. A freshwater well dug here, or a road built there: these are meant to persuade local people to weigh up their options in a rational, utility-maximizing sense and transfer support to the good guys. All experience points, by contrast, towards people behaving in accordance with local power realities and threat perceptions – which the Taliban have consistently shown greater capability to influence than the coalition. In addition, cultural literacy is meant to provide a roadmap to local people's 'hearts and minds'. A crash course in Pashto or Dari, and a quick immersion in tribal cultural folklore are deemed sufficient to provide an entry ticket to the game of identity and tribal manipulation. Finally, feelers are put out to the Taliban that the West is ready to 'reconcile', despite no known example of Pashtuns, in particular, 'negotiating' from what they perceive to be a position of strength.

The suspicion is that the new goal is simply to provide a cover for withdrawal. A concerted military attempt to pressure the Taliban might get them to negotiate. Couple this with meeting essentially arbitrary, and unsustainable, levels of ANA and ANP recruitment and a window of opportunity could be created that will allow the West to withdraw its forces in something that resembles good order. The central problem of this 'exit strategy' is that many of its assumptions are dubious at best. For example, great store is set by the ability of the Afghan National Security Forces (ANSF) to gradually shoulder the counterinsurgency burden. However, the timelines articulated by the West and the Karzai government do not seem to mesh with Karzai talking about fifteen years before such a handover can safely be accomplished.

Such a timeframe would seem to present major problems. Yet there is evidence, in US official documentation itself, that even the problematic Karzai prediction may be optimistic. A recent report by the US government's own accountability office includes the startling forecast that by 2024 ANSF costs are still likely to be 154 per cent of Afghanistan's entire domestic revenues.[5] Given such figures, it is clear why such unquestioning excitement was on show when the most recent 'silver bullet' of the intervention – hitherto untapped mineral reserves – was presented to an unsuspecting world. However, even if the ANSF could, miraculously, be funded at anything like the level that the 'exit strategy' implicitly assumes, it is highly questionable whether such forces would take up the challenge of robustly countering those groups allegedly most threatening to Western interests in the south and east of the country. In the ANA, for example, Tajiks are still significantly over-represented in relation to their numbers in the Afghan population as a whole; providing a rather obvious problem if the ultimate goal is to conduct COIN operations in Pashtun areas. A former British ambassador to Kabul, Sir Sherard Cowper-Coles, recounted, in an interview with one of the authors of this book, an anecdote regarding an exchange between then British Foreign Secretary David Miliband and an Afghan counterpart. The foreign secretary asked how long Afghan authorities would remain in the south of the country after Western forces left – expecting, reasonably, a reply in the order of 'three years'. He was told 'twenty-four hours'.[6]

Despite the poor record for successful predictions in Afghanistan, it is possible to venture some reasonable assumptions. The Karzai government will never be capable of exerting anything that resembles control of the country, and Afghanistan is doomed to remain an essentially 'rentier state' for the foreseeable future. A clear-cut 'victory' over insurgents in the south and east of the country is unattainable. Pakistan will never fully control the lawless tribal areas that border Afghanistan, yet no long-term solution can be viable that does not recognize and genuinely take into account Pakistan's strategic concerns. Elements of the Taliban will eventually be brought into some sort of political settlement on terms that the West may find uncomfortable.

The important strategic question that must be addressed, even ten years too late, is to what degree all this matters. Most answers focus on two broad problems. The first is the possibility that groups with an international terrorist agenda might find the sort of safe havens in Afghanistan and the border regions that were so helpful to them previously. The second is that Pakistan itself, with its nuclear capability, could succumb to the complex forces threatening it and collapse into state failure.

The first problem is a lesser-order threat. Al Qaeda is no more capable of turning the clock back than is the coalition. Al Qaeda achieved success on 9/11 partly because competing priorities and perspectives in the US, in particular, meant that successive administrations had previously had insufficient incentive to take the political risk associated with decisively dealing with the Al Qaeda threat. That is not the case today or likely to be in the future. In addition, the value of fixed safe havens is dubious in the contemporary environment. They make very tempting and attractive targets for a US military no longer hamstrung by concerns over diplomatic fallout or legal minutiae when it comes to Islamist terrorists, particularly in Afghanistan. The related threat of a Taliban takeover of the whole of Afghanistan is also relatively low risk. The US can prevent such an occurrence even more easily than it overthrew the Taliban in the first place; any Taliban force attempting to march on Kabul would face the same fate at the hands of US air power as it did in 2001. Tajiks, Uzbeks and Hazaras would also react ferociously to such a prospect, and could be mobilized once more as a robust anti-Taliban ground force.

The US cannot, however, expunge Taliban influence from the Pashtun lands of the south and the east.

The second problem, Pakistan, is more troubling. However, it is simply not in the West's gift to fully control events. Al Qaeda finds Pakistan more congenial than Afghanistan precisely because the West cannot operate there with impunity, and they have established a complex network of relationships within a bewildering array of radical groups. Only a broad regional approach can provide the beginnings of a coherent strategy – an approach in which competing security concerns are genuinely addressed, rather than lip-service merely paid.

This is one of several lessons that the West's experience in Afghanistan has brought home – most of which should not have required ten years of bloody intervention to register. A number of these lessons arise from the pricking of some simplistic and ideo-logically driven bubbles. Perhaps most glaring is the idea that all peoples universally crave some approximation of Western social, political and economic life and will rise up to create the necessary structures if only the malevolent elites holding them down can be removed. This belief has been tested to destruction in Afghanistan and Iraq, and regime change as a blanket solution to the West's security dilemmas has lost whatever intellectual vitality it may once have possessed. Similarly, the conventional wisdom of state-building, based on the assumption that strengthening central government should be the basis for supporting all fragile and failed states, has been undermined by events in Afghanistan. While the rhetoric still lingers, based more on the demands of the West's exit strategy than the realities of contemporary Afghanistan, most new thinking is based on developing local political settlements and solutions rather than investing all hope in shaping the structure, behaviour and effectiveness of the government in Kabul.

The West has also learned some valuable lessons about the complexity of power. Turning military dominance into strategic and political success is not nearly as straightforward as initial hubris seemed to suggest, particularly in the context of Afghanistan and the broader search for security against the threat of terror. For NATO, the institutionalized manifestation of Western military dominance, the lesson is to avoid picking challenges on the basis of what a crisis can do for NATO rather than what the Alliance can do to ameliorate the crisis. Perhaps the most basic lesson of all is to think long and hard before embarking on attempting to reshape states and societies to make them conform to our whims. These are usually generation-long projects that often end up sapping the will and vitality of those that attempt them. To paraphrase Walter Lippmann, be sure that you know the cost of what you want before finally deciding that you want it.

None of this bodes particularly well for the people of the region. However, ten years of dysfunctional strategy and failed policy removes good options. There is plenty of blame to go round, but Washington must bear the lion's share. This might seem harsh, given that this book has documented the failings of a range of international, regional and local actors. Key allies of the US, such as Britain, have displayed just as much, if not more strategic clumsiness. NATO blundered into Afghanistan obsessed by its own problems of internal crisis. The UN was also unable to provide any coherence to the international effort. Aid agencies and NGOs too often pursued their own ideological agenda. Corruption and graft has been rife throughout the Afghan institutions themselves and regional states have invariably pursued a cynical and blinkered approach. However, harsh judgements regarding America's culpability are part of the price of power. Strategic vacuity costs less when it is conducted by the weak. It costs considerably more when it is conducted by the powerful. At key points in the depressing story of the intervention in Afghanistan, only one actor had the capability to bring genuine coherence to the ends, ways and means calculations that should have informed the international effort. That actor was the US, and it failed to do so.

NOTES

CHAPTER 1: THE GREAT ENIGMA: AFGHANISTAN IN HISTORICAL CONTEXT

1. Sir Olaf Caroe, *The Pathans, With an Epilogue on Russia*, Oxford University Press, Karachi, 1983/2001, p. xv.
2. Jeffrey J. Roberts, *The Origins of Conflict in Afghanistan*, Praeger Publishers, Westport, 2003, p. 32.
3. David B. Edwards, *Heroes of the Age: Moral Fault Lines on the Afghan Frontier*, University of California Press, California, 1996, p. 111.
4. Mahnaz Z. Ispahani, *Roads and Rivals: The Politics of Access in the Borderlands of Asia*, I.B. Tauris, London, 1989, pp. 100–1.
5. Thomas Barfield, *Afghanistan: A Cultural and Political History*, Princeton University Press, Princeton, 2010, pp. 160–9.
6. Richard Tapper, 'Ethnicity, order, and meaning in the anthropology of Iran and Afghanistan' in J.P. Digard (ed.), *Le Fait Ethnique en Iran et en Afghanistan*, Editions du CNRS, Paris, 1988, p. 27; Armando Geller and Scott Moss, 'The Afghan nexus: Anomie, neo-patrimonialism and the emergence of small-world networks', Centre for Policy Modelling Report 07-179, July 2007, available at: http://cfpm.org/pub/papers/Geller&Moss_TheAfghanNexus.pdf
7. Thomas H. Johnson and M. Chris Mason, 'Understanding the Taliban insurgency in Afghanistan', *Orbis* (Winter 2007), p. 78.
8. Olivier Roy, *Islam and Resistance in Afghanistan*, second edition, Cambridge University Press, Cambridge, 1990, p. 17.
9. https://www.cia.gov/library/publications/the-world-factbook/geos/af.html. Pro-Pashtun accounts by contrast are inclined to stress censuses, which emphasize Pashtuns as an absolute ethnic majority – see, for example, the account of Nabi Misdaq, which places the percentages at 62.73 per cent Pashtun, 12.38 per cent Tajik, 9 per cent Hazara, 6.10 per cent Uzbek, 2.69 per cent Turkmen and

2.68 per cent Aimaq: Nabi Misdaq, *Afghanistan: Political Frailty and Foreign Interference*, Routledge, London, 2006, p. 7.

10. Barnett R. Rubin, *The Fragmentation of Afghanistan: State Formation and Collapse in the International System*, Yale University Press, Yale, 2002, pp. 62–5.
11. A. Rasanayagam, *Afghanistan: A Modern History*, I.B. Tauris, London, 2005, p. 281.
12. These factors are worth considering in depth, because, as this book will argue, the same cycle of log-jammed development and social implosion risks being repeated today. Between 1957 and 1967, the number of Afghan children receiving school education rose from 126,000 to 540,000 – dramatic figures, but ones which are nonetheless eclipsed by the steep rise in Afghan children receiving education since 2001. Traditionally tough environmental conditions have nonetheless also worsened in recent years as a result of substantial war damage and neglect, imperilling the future inheritance of this younger and better-educated generation.
13. Gilles Dorronsoro, *Revolution Unending: Afghanistan, 1979 to the Present*, Hurst & Company, London, 2005, pp. 64–5.
14. The Soviet government on 25 April 1978, two days before the Khalq coup in Kabul, continued to emphasize to the PDPA the need to reach an accommodation with Daoud: Odd Arne Westad, *The Global Cold War*, CUP, Cambridge, 2005, p. 302.
15. David N. Gibbs, 'Reassessing Soviet motives for invading Afghanistan', *Critical Asian Studies*, 38:2 (2006), pp. 250–51.
16. Westad, *The Global Cold War*, p. 316.
17. Evgenii Nikitenko, *Afganistan: Ot voiny 80-kh do prognoza novykh voin*, AST, Moscow, 2004, p. 271.
18. David N. Gibbs, 'Afghanistan: The Soviet invasion in retrospect', *International Politics*, 37 (June 2000), pp. 241–2.
19. Rubin, *The Fragmentation of Afghanistan*, pp. 196–7.
20. Alex Marshall, 'Managing withdrawal: Afghanistan as the forgotten example in attempting conflict resolution and state reconstruction', *Small Wars & Insurgencies*, 18:1 (March 2007), p. 80.
21. Caroe, *The Pathans*, pp. 44–5; Frank L. Holt, *Into the Land of Bones: Alexander the Great in Afghanistan*, University of California Press, London, 2005, pp. 128–44.
22. Andrew Hartman, ' "The Red Template": US policy in Soviet-occupied Afghanistan', *Third World Quarterly*, 23:3 (2002), pp. 467–89.
23. R.A. Medvedev, 'Pod kontrolem naroda', *Voenno-Istoricheskii Zhurnal*, 2 (1999), p. 64. For a full summary of 'what we now know' regarding Soviet decision making towards Afghanistan in 1979, see Gibbs, 'Reassessing Soviet motives for invading Afghanistan', pp. 239–63.
24. See, for example, the writings of Professor Stephen Blank on Central Asia more generally: 'It does not suffice to be able to deploy and sustain long-range strike forces in the theatre; the theatre itself must be cooperatively reordered by the US, its other partners, and host governments, working together to stabilize it and legitimize US presence and a political order that has a genuine chance to evolve in a liberal, democratic direction enjoying popular support. America must also develop an appropriate long-term and multi-dimensional strategy for retaining permanent access to the area.' In 'After two wars: Reflections on the American strategic revolution in Central Asia', Conflict Studies Research Centre, Central Asian Series 05/14, April 2005, frontispiece.
25. Alex Marshall, 'Managing withdrawal'; Lester W. Grau, 'Breaking contact without leaving chaos: The Soviet withdrawal from Afghanistan', *Journal of Slavic Military Studies*, 20:2 (April–June 2007), pp. 235–61.

26. M.A. Gareev, *Afganskaia Strada (s Sovetskimi voiskami i bez nikh)*, 'INSAN', Moscow, 1999, p. 163. NATO planning in 2009 envisaged an Afghan National Army (ANA) of 260,000 by 2016, but this also represented army growth on an 'industrial scale', more than doubling the existing force size. The ANA in 2009 (at a point since the initial intervention that was chronologically directly comparable to the Soviet-era ANA in 1988–89) still possessed only around 80,000 officers and men, with no air power or significant artillery resources. Robert D. Kaplan, 'Saving Afghanistan', *The Atlantic*, 24 March 2009, available at: www.theatlantic.com/doc/200903u/saving-afghanistan

27. Dr Anton Minkov and Dr Gregory Smolynec, *3D Soviet Style: A Presentation on Lessons Learned from the Soviet Experience in Afghanistan*, Defence R&D Canada, October 2007.

28. For a breakdown of the parties, see Robert Canfield, 'Afghanistan: The trajectory of internal alignments', *Middle East Journal*, 43:4 (Autumn 1989), pp. 635–48.

29. The four best known of these groups after 1985 were Burhannudin Rabbani's Jama'at-i Islami-yi Afghanistan (JIA), Gulbuddin Hikmatyar's Hizb-i Islami-yi Afghanistan (HIH, where second H signifies Hikmatyar), Mawlawi Khalis's splinter group Hizb-i Islami-yi Afghanistan (Khalis) (HIK), and the Saudi favourite Abd al-Rabb al-Rasul Sayyaf's Ittihad-i Islami bara-yi Azadi-yi Afghanistan (ITT). The leaders of most of these groups had already drawn the attention of the Afghan government authorities to their activities prior to the 1978 coup, all having been, to a greater or lesser extent, graduates of the increasingly violent underground student politics which had emerged at Kabul University during the 1960s and early 1970s. Rabbani had served on faculty there as a junior professor after visiting Egypt between 1966 and 1968, where he, like Khalis, had translated and brought back the writings of Sayyid Qutb; both men were likewise also inspired while abroad by the organizational model offered by the Egyptian Muslim Brotherhood. Sayyaf himself was a lecturer in Kabul University's *shari'a* faculty.

30. Mohammad Yousaf and Mark Adkin, *Afghanistan – The Bear Trap: The Defeat of a Superpower*, Leo Cooper, Barnsley, 1992, p. 29.

31. *ibid.*, p. 81.

32. Rizwan Hussein, *Pakistan and the Emergence of Islamic Militancy in Afghanistan*, Ashgate Publishing Limited, Aldershot, 2005, p. 123; Ahmed Rashid, *Taliban: Islam, Oil and the New Great Game in Central Asia*, I.B. Tauris, London/New York, 2000, p. 186.

33. Neamatollah Nojumi, 'The rise and fall of the Taliban' in Robert D. Crews and Amin Tarzi (eds), *The Taliban and the Crisis of Afghanistan*, Harvard University Press, Cambridge, MA, 2008, pp. 96–8.

34. Yousaf and Adkin, *Afghanistan – The Bear Trap*, p. 40.

35. Abdulkader H. Sinno, *Organizations at War in Afghanistan and Beyond*, Cornell University Press, Ithaca & London, 2008, pp. 131, 235–6.

36. Neamatollah Nojumi, *The Rise of the Taliban in Afghanistan: Mass Mobilization, Civil War, and the Future of the Region*, Palgrave, New York, 2002, p. 85.

37. Steve Coll, *Ghost Wars: The Secret History of the CIA, Afghanistan and Bin Laden, from the Soviet Invasion to September 10, 2001*, Penguin Books, London, 2005, p. 12.

38. Ali A. Jalali, 'Afghanistan: Regaining momentum', *Parameters* (Winter 2007–08), p. 12.

39. Coll, *Ghost Wars*, pp. 218–19.

40. Rubin, *The Fragmentation of Afghanistan*, pp. 270–3.

41. Coll, *Ghost Wars*, p. 172.

42. Nojumi, *The Rise of the Taliban in Afghanistan*, chapter nine.

43. *ibid.*, p. 112.
44. *ibid.*, p. 114.
45. William McCoy, *The Politics of Heroin: CIA Complicity in the Global Drug Trade, Afghanistan, Southeast Asia, Central America, Columbia*, revised edition, Lawrence Hill Books, Chicago, 2003, pp. 506–11.
46. Ikramul Haq, 'Pak-Afghan drug trade in historical perspective', *Asian Affairs*, XXXVI:10 (October 1996), p. 954.
47. *ibid.*, pp. 954, 957–8.
48. Rashid, *Taliban: Islam, Oil and the New Great Game in Central Asia*, pp. 189–93; I.V. Zhmuida, 'Rol' tenevoi ekonomiki i korruptsii v Pakistane' in V.Ia. Belokorenitskii and A.Z. Egorin (eds), *Musul'manskie strany u granits SNG*, IVRAN-Kraft, Moscow, 2002, p. 259.
49. Rashid, *Taliban: Islam, Oil and the New Great Game in Central Asia*, pp. 184–5.
50. Anthony Davis, 'How the Taliban became a military force' in William Maley (ed.), *Fundamentalism Reborn? Afghanistan and the Taliban*, Hurst & Company, London, 1998/2001, pp. 52–3.
51. Hussein, *Pakistan and the Emergence of Islamic Militancy in Afghanistan*, pp. 139–40.
52. Abdul Salam Zaeef, *My Life with the Taliban*, Hurst & Company, London, 2010, pp. 62–5, quote from p. 65.
53. Davis, 'How the Taliban became a military force', p. 50.
54. *ibid.*, p. 28.
55. Nojumi, 'The rise and fall of the Taliban', p. 102.
56. Kamal Matinuddin, *The Taliban Phenomenon. Afghanistan 1994–1997, With an Afterword covering Major Events since 1997*, OUP, Oxford, 1999, p. 167.
57. Sinno, *Organizations at War in Afghanistan and Beyond*, p. 233.
58. A *lashkar* is a traditional ad hoc tribal gathering together of forces, often in response to a *cheghar* or 'call' to confront a defined enemy. It is, therefore, different from a standing army or formation.
59. Davis, 'How the Taliban became a military force', pp. 48–9.
60. *ibid.*, p. 53–4.
61. *ibid.*, pp. 61–2.
62. Nojumi, *The Rise of the Taliban*, p. 148.
63. *ibid.*, pp. 137–9.
64. Rashid, *Taliban*, pp. 119, 191.
65. Anthony Davis, 'Foreign fighters step up activity in Afghan civil war', *Jane's Intelligence Review* 13:8 (August 2001), p. 14.

CHAPTER 2: 9/11 AND THE RESPONSE, 11–25 SEPTEMBER 2001

1. Steven Metz drily notes that this analysis privileges 'possibility rather than plausibility'. Metz, *Iraq and the Evolution of American Strategy*, Potomac Books, Dulles, VA, 2008, p. 87.
2. See Bob Woodward, *Bush at War*, Pocket Books, London, 2003, p. 282.
3. See Michael Gordon and Bernard Trainor, *Cobra II*, Atlantic Books, London, 2006, p. 14.
4. Speech by George W. Bush entitled 'A Period of Consequences', at The Citadel, Military College of South Carolina, 23 September 1999.
5. For good overviews of 'transformation', see Gordon and Trainor, *Cobra II*; Metz, *Iraq and the Evolution of American Strategy*; and Thomas Adams, *The Army After Next*, Stanford University Press, Stanford, 2008.
6. See http://www.newamericancentury.org/statementofprinciples.htm

7. See Jack Matlock, *Superpower Illusions*, Yale University Press, New Haven, 2010, particularly pp. 213–36.
8. Timeline provided by National Commission on Terrorist Attacks upon the United States, *The 9/11 Commission Report* (Final Report), 22 July 2004, available at: http://govinfo.library.unt.edu/911/report/911Report.pdf[0] and the BBC News website.
9. DEFCON 5 is normal peacetime readiness. DEFCON 3 refers to an increased state of military readiness.
10. Text of the speech is available at http://edition.cnn.com
11. See George Tenet, *At the Center of the Storm: My Years at the CIA*, HarperCollins, New York, 2007; and Richard A. Clarke, *Against All Enemies*, Simon & Schuster, New York, 2004.
12. Clarke claims that the earlier 1993 attack on the World Trade Center and failed plans to attack New York landmarks and US airliners were also Al Qaeda operations. See *Against All Enemies*, p. 134.
13. Woodward, *Bush at War*, p. 271.
14. Christopher Meyer, *DC Confidential*, Phoenix, London, 2006, p. 234.
15. *9/11 Commission Report*, p. 330.
16. This exchange is recorded in Woodward, *Bush at War*, p. 43.
17. President Bush's address to a joint session of Congress, 20 September 2001.
18. Woodward, *Bush at War*, p. 45.
19. This exchange is recorded in Clarke, *Against All Enemies*, p. 32.
20. Gordon and Trainor, *Cobra II*, p. 15.
21. *9/11 Commission Report*, p. 479, footnote 2.
22. Casualty figures from www.cnn.com
23. Tenet, *At the Center of the Storm*, pp. 116–17.
24. See Clarke, *Against All Enemies*, for a frustrated account of these plans.
25. Tenet, *At the Center of the Storm*, p. 116.
26. Gordon and Trainor, *Cobra II*, p. 14.
27. *9/11 Commission Report*, p. 207.
28. The Principals Committee was normally chaired by Assistant to the President for National Security Affairs Condoleezza Rice, and attended by Vice President Dick Cheney; Secretary of State Colin Powell; Secretary of Defence Donald Rumsfeld; CIA Director George Tenet; Chairman of the Joint Chiefs of Staff General Henry Shelton; and White House Chief of Staff Andrew Card.
29. This became NSPD-9, and was signed by the president on 25 October 2001. See www.fas.org/irp/offdocs/nspd/nspd-9.htm
30. As its name implies, this committee is mostly made up of the deputies to the principals.
31. *9/11 Commission Report*, p. 206.
32. On the meeting with the CIA director, see Tenet, *At the Center of the Storm*, p. 141. On seeing the smoke from the Pentagon, see *ibid.* p. 162.
33. For the verbatim list of the seven demands see the *9/11 Commission Report*, p. 331.
34. For an account of this meeting, see Ahmed Rashid, *Descent into Chaos: How the War against Islamic Extremism is Being Lost in Pakistan, Afghanistan and Central Asia*, Allen Lane, London, 2008, pp. 28–30. The idea that Pakistan could also be at risk of attack was aired at the Principals Committee meeting on 13 September. See the *9/11 Commission Report*, p. 331.
35. For a detailed account of the complex relationships between religion and the military in Pakistan, see Husain Haqqani, *Pakistan: Between Mosque and Military*, Carnegie Endowment for International Peace, Washington, DC, 2005.
36. In attendance were the president; Dick Cheney; Colin Powell; Donald Rumsfeld; Condoleezza Rice; George Tenet; Deputy Director of the CIA John

McLaughlin; Deputy Secretary of Defence Paul Wolfowitz; Attorney General John Ashcroft; Deputy Assistant to the President for National Security Affairs Stephen Hadley; Director of the Federal Bureau of Investigation Robert Mueller; Director of the Counterterrorism Center Cofer Black; and Chairman of the Joint Chiefs of Staff Henry Shelton (Shelton would be replaced two weeks later by General Richard Myers).

37. See *9/11 Commission Report*, p. 335.
38. *ibid.*, p. 332.
39. The most comprehensive account of these meetings can be found in Woodward, *Bush at War*, pp. 74–92.
40. There was also a smattering of small Pashtun tribal groups included at various times in the NA ranks.
41. Woodward, *Bush at War*, p. 97.
42. *ibid.*, p. 115.
43. The most complete overview of these complex relationships can be found in James Mann, *Rise of the Vulcans: The History of Bush's War Cabinet*, Penguin Books, New York, 2004.
44. Colin Powell, *My American Journey*, Ballantine Books, New York, 1995.
45. For an account of this see James Dobbins, *After the Taliban*, Potomac Books, Dulles, VA, 2008, p. 15.
46. For an account of the main planning and operational concerns, see General Tommy Franks, *American Soldier*, HarperCollins, New York, 2004.
47. Putin had a number of motivations for this counter-intuitive stance. First, he suspected that Central Asian leaders might be bought off by the Americans anyway; second, removing the Taliban and undermining extremist Islamist groups was as much a national interest for the Russians as for the West; third, by linking Russian counterinsurgency efforts in Chechnya with a 'Global War on Terror' he could inhibit Western criticism of Russian human rights abuses in Chechnya.
48. See 'US and Uzbekistan agree pact', http://news.bbc.co.uk/1/hi/world/asia-pacific/1596654.stm, 13 October 2001.

CHAPTER 3: 'BOOTS ON THE GROUND': FROM THE ARRIVAL OF THE CIA TO THE EMERGENCY LOYA JIRGA, 26 SEPTEMBER 2001–JUNE 2002

1. Gary Schroen, *First In*, Presidio Press, New York, 2007, p. 40.
2. The most complete accounts of the CIA and Special Forces activities in Afghanistan in the initial intervention can be found in Schroen, *First In* and Gary Berntsen, *Jawbreaker: The Attack on bin Laden and Al Qaeda*, Three Rivers Press, New York, 2005. Bernsten would relieve Schroen as the commander on the ground of the Jawbreaker teams.
3. See Henry Crumpton, 'Intelligence and war: Afghanistan, 2001–2002', in Jennifer Sims and Burton Gerber (eds), *Transforming US Intelligence*, Georgetown University Press, Washington DC, 2005, p. 163.
4. Schroen, *First In*, p. 96.
5. Berntsen, *Jawbreaker*, p. 136.
6. Rashid, *Descent into Chaos*, p. 64.
7. See Abdul Salam Zaeef, *My Life With the Taliban*, Hurst, London, 2010, p. 147.
8. *ibid.*, p. 153.
9. Although Zaeef does not reveal the date, it is probable that this meeting took place in mid- to late October.
10. Numbers are imprecise. However, Ali Jalali estimates that, prior to 9/11, specifically Al Qaeda fighters, organized into what was called Brigade 055, numbered

about 600 at any one time, although the number of 'foreign fighters' present in Afghanistan in general would have been in the low thousands. See Ali Jalali, 'Afghanistan: The anatomy of an ongoing crisis', *Parameters* (Spring 2001), pp. 85–98.

11. Christina Lamb, *Small Wars Permitting: Dispatches from Foreign Lands*, HarperPress, London, 2008, pp. 227–8.
12. See Schroen, *First In*, p. 163.
13. This piece of kit weighs about 12 lbs and looks like a small slide projector. The user trains it onto a target from a distance of up to 20,000 metres (although the units used in 2001 would have had a much shorter range) and it electronically 'lights up' the target, thus identifying it to incoming aircraft.
14. Michael O'Hanlon, 'A flawed masterpiece', *Foreign Affairs*, 81:3 (May/June 2002), p. 51.
15. See Stephen Biddle, 'Afghanistan and the future of warfare: Implications for army and defense policy', US Army Strategic Studies Institute, November 2002, p. 14.
16. For NA estimates, see Franks, *American Soldier*, p. 261.
17. For an account of this action, see Berntsen, *Jawbreaker*, pp. 136–8.
18. Rashid, *Descent into Chaos*, pp. 77–8.
19. See Woodward, *Bush at War*.
20. For a detailed account, see Rashid, *Descent into Chaos*, pp. 90–3.
21. See *ibid.*, p. 92; Berntsen, *Jawbreaker*, p. 241; and Seymour Hersh, 'The getaway', *New Yorker*, 28 January 2002.
22. Rashid, *Descent into Chaos*, pp. 3–4.
23. Tenet, *At the Center of the Storm*, p. 219.
24. These differing accounts can be found in Tenet, *At the Center of the Storm*, pp. 219–20; and Rashid, *Descent into Chaos*, p. 85.
25. See Berntsen, *Jawbreaker*, p. 202.
26. For an account of the battle, see Berntsen, *Jawbreaker*, pp. 215–6.
27. For an account of the battles for Kandahar, see John Carland, 'The campaign against Kandahar', US Army Center of Military History Information Paper, Washington, DC, March 2002, pp. 2–5.
28. See Sarah Chayes, *The Punishment of Virtue: Inside Afghanistan after the Taliban*, Penguin Books, New York, 2006.
29. William Maley, *Rescuing Afghanistan*, Hurst & Co., London, 2006, pp. 39–40.
30. This aphorism is most notably ascribed to Tom Lehrer, the American satirist, on being told the news that Henry Kissinger had won the 1973 Nobel Peace Prize.
31. Tenet, *At the Center of the Storm*, p. 218.
32. Maley, *Rescuing Afghanistan*, p. 23.
33. This incident is recalled in Berntsen, *Jawbreaker*, p. 298. When discussing the 'Eastern Alliance' leaders Berntsen habitually refers to Haji Zahir, the nephew of Abdul Haq; 'Babrak'; and 'Nuruddin'. It is clear from other accounts, however, that 'Babrak' is Hazrat Ali, and 'Nuruddin' is Haji Zaman. For confirmation of this, see Peter Krause, 'The last good chance: A reassessment of US operations at Tora Bora', *Security Studies*, 17:4 (2008); and Philip Smucker, *Al Qaeda's Great Escape: The Military and the Media on Terror's Trail*, Brassey's, Washington, DC, 2004.
34. Committee on Foreign Relations United States Senate Report, *Tora Bora Revisited: How We Failed to Get bin Laden and Why it Matters Today*, Washington, DC, 30 November 2009, p. 4.
35. Berntsen, *Jawbreaker*, p. 215.
36. Committee on Foreign Relations, *Tora Bora Revisited*, p. 4.
37. For an account of his experiences, see 'Dalton Fury', *Kill bin Laden: A Delta Force Commander's Account of the Hunt for the World's Most Wanted Man*, St Martin's Press, New York, 2008.

38. For a good overview of what such an operation would entail in the conditions of Tora Bora, see Krause, 'The last good chance'.
39. To gauge Berntsen's increasing frustration, see Berntsen, *Jawbreaker*, p. 289.
40. Committee on Foreign Relations, *Tora Bora Revisited*, p. 17.
41. *ibid.*, p. 13.
42. See Franks, *American Soldier*, p. 324.
43. Sean Naylor, *Not a Good Day to Die: The Untold Story of Operation Anaconda*, Penguin Books, London, 2006, pp. 23–5.
44. See, for example, Committee on Foreign Relations, *Tora Bora Revisited*, p. 14; Michael Sherry, *The Course of Operation Enduring Freedom in Southern and Eastern Afghanistan*, US Army Center of Military History Information Paper, Washington, DC, 15 March 2002, p. 3; Rashid, *Descent into Chaos*, pp. 98–9.
45. Franks, *American Soldier*, p. 315.
46. Woodward, *Bush at War*, p. 310.
47. See www.un.org/Docs/sc/search2001
48. Rashid, *Descent into Chaos*, p. 103.
49. Dobbins, *After the Taliban*, p. 46.
50. *ibid.*, p. 89. It is doubtful, of course, whether Abdullah Abdullah 'lobbied' Pakistan in the traditional sense. Presumably Pakistan came to its own conclusion that Karzai was the 'least bad' option.
51. Berntsen, *Jawbreaker*, p. 288.
52. For a detailed account of these manoeuvres see Dobbins, *After the Taliban*, pp. 92–6.
53. *ibid.* p. 121.
54. For a full account of this incident, see Tenet, *At the Center of the Storm*, pp. 311–13.
55. For the terms of the Bonn agreement, see www.afghangovernment.com/AfghanAgreementBonn.htm
56. For details of the attack, see Dobbins, *After the Taliban*, p. 114; and Rashid, *Descent into Chaos*, p. 106.
57. Dobbins, *After the Taliban*, p. 120.
58. Alan Sipress, 'Peacekeepers won't go beyond Kabul, Cheney says', *Washington Post*, 20 March 2002.
59. Author interview with General Sir John McColl, Deputy Supreme Allied Commander Europe (DSACEUR), July 2010.
60. For a detailed analysis of Operation Anaconda, see Sean Naylor, *Not a Good Day to Die*; and Paul Hastert, 'Operation Anaconda: Perception meets reality in the hills of Afghanistan', *Studies in Conflict and Terrorism*, 28:1 (January/February 2005), pp. 11–20.
61. http://news.bbc.co.uk/1/hi/world/south_asia/2032169.stm
62. For a good overview of the Loya Jirga, see Rashid, *Descent into Chaos*, pp. 138–42.
63. Antonio Giustiozzi, ' "Good" state vs "bad" warlords? A critique of state-building strategies in Afghanistan,' London School of Economics Crisis States Programme Working Paper No. 51, October 2004, p. 2.
64. Woodward, *Bush at War*, p. 321.
65. *ibid.*, p. 224.
66. Donald Rumsfeld, 'Transforming the military', *Foreign Affairs*, 81:3 (May/June 2002), p. 22.
67. The danger of fighting wars by committee was highlighted in a Rumsfeld speech at the National Defense University on 31 January 2002. See also David H. Dunn, 'Innovation and precedent in the Kosovo War: The impact of Operation Allied Force on US foreign policy', *International Affairs*, 85:3 (May 2009), p. 543.

CHAPTER 4: 'TAKING THE EYE OFF THE BALL?' THE ROOTS OF TALIBAN REVIVAL IN AFGHANISTAN, 2002–05

1. Ann Marlowe, 'Lurching toward disaster in Afghanistan,' *Wall Street Journal*, 3 February 2010, available at http://online.wsj.com/article/SB10001424052748703389004575033222236113024.html
2. On 'liberal peace theory', see: Oliver P. Richmond, 'A post-liberal peace: Eirenism and the everyday', *Review of International Studies*, 35 (2009), pp. 557–80; Mark Duffield, *Development, Security and Unending War: Governing the World of Peoples*, Polity, Cambridge, 2007; David Chandler, *Empire in Denial: The Politics of State-building*, Pluto Press, London, 2006; Raymond Paris, *At War's End: Building Peace after Civil Conflict*, Cambridge University Press, Cambridge, 2004; Michael Doyle, 'Kant, liberal legacies, and foreign affairs', *Philosophy and Public Affairs*, 12:3 (Summer 1983), pp. 205–35; and Michael Doyle, 'Kant's perpetual peace', *American Political Science Review*, 80:4 (1986), pp. 1115–69.
3. Dobbins, *After the Taliban*, pp. 120–1.
4. Donald P. Wright, James R. Bird, Steven E. Clay, Peter W. Connors, Lt. Col. Scott C. Farquhar, Lynn Chandler Garcia, Dennis Van Wey, 'A different kind of war. The United States Army in Operation Enduring Freedom (OEF) October 2001–September 2005', Combat Studies Institute, Fort Leavenworth, Kansas, 2010, p.198, available at: http://documents.nytimes.com/a-different-kind-of-war#p=1
5. Antonio Giustozzi, 'Military reform in Afghanistan' in M. Sedra (ed.), *Confronting Afghanistan's Security Dilemma: Reforming the Security Sector*, Brief 28, BICC, Bonn, September 2003, p. 26; Seth Jones, *In the Graveyard of Empires: America's War in Afghanistan*, W.W. Norton & Company, London/New York, 2009, pp. 113–14, 178.
6. See chapter one, note 27, and Thom Shanker and Eric Schmitt, 'U.S. plans vastly expanded Afghan Security Force', *New York Times*, 18 March 2009, available at: www.nytimes.com/2009/03/19/us/politics/19military.html
7. For a detailed examination of the Bush administration's deliberations in the run-up to the invasion of Iraq in 2003, see Bob Woodward, *Plan of Attack*, Pocket Books, London, 2004.
8. See Toby Helm and Ben Fenton, 'Germany and France warn Bush on Iraq', *Daily Telegraph*, 19 February 2002; and Steven Weisman, 'US set to demand that allies agree Iraq is defying UN', *New York Times*, 23 January 2003.
9. Craig Smith, 'Europeans try and stem anti-US anger', *New York Times*, 2 January 2003.
10. Phrases included (but were by no means restricted to) 'cheese-eating surrender-monkeys' and the 'axis of weasels'. For an indication of how all this was viewed in France, see Nicole Mowbray, 'Cheese-eating monkeys and Gallic merde', *Observer*, 16 February 2003.
11. See Toby Helm and Toby Harnden, 'American fury as German justice minister compares Bush to Hitler', *Daily Telegraph*, 20 September 2002.
12. For a good overview of the effects on NATO and the wider intra-Alliance issues, see Terry Terriff, 'Fear and loathing in NATO: The Atlantic Alliance after the crisis over Iraq', *Perspectives on European Politics and Society*, 5:3 (September 2004), pp. 419–46.
13. For detailed overviews of the political machinations, see Philip Gordon and Jeremy Shapiro, *Allies at War: America, Europe and the Crisis over Iraq*, McGraw-Hill, New York, 2004; and Elizabeth Pond, *Friendly Fire: The Near Death of the Transatlantic Alliance*, Brookings/EUSA, Washington, DC, 2003.
14. Under a UN resolution (UNSCR 1546) the Alliance set up a NATO Training Mission in Iraq (NTM-I) in 2004 to provide training assistance to Iraqi security

forces. It has been a relatively low-level mission and, since 2007, has largely concentrated on gendarmerie-type training to the Iraqi federal police.

15. See Michael Gordon, 'NATO chief says Alliance needs role in Afghanistan', *New York Times*, 21 February 2003.

16. Terriff, 'Fear and loathing in NATO', p. 432.

17. Paris, *At War's End*, p. 118.

18. Shahrbanou Tadjbakhsh and Michael Schoiswohl, 'Playing with fire? The international community's democratization experiment in Afghanistan', *International Peacekeeping*, 1:2 (April 2008), p. 265, footnote five.

19. Emma Sky, 'The lead nation approach: The case of Afghanistan', *RUSI Journal*, 151:6 (December 2006), 22–6.

20. Toby Poston, 'The battle to rebuild Afghanistan', BBC News, 26 February 2006, available at: http://news.bbc.co.uk/1/hi/business/4714116.stm; Griff Witte, 'In Kabul, a stark gulf between wealthy few and the poor', *Washington Post*, 9 December 2005, available at: www.washingtonpost.com/wp-dyn/content/article/2005/12/08/AR2005120801881.html

21. Antonio Giustozzi, 'Auxiliary force or national army? Afghanistan's "ANA" and the counter-insurgency effort, 2002–2006', *Small Wars & Insurgencies*, 18:1 (March 2007), pp. 48–56.

22. 'Afghan soldiers pick up US weapons', *The Nation*, 4 January 2009, available at: www.nation.com.pk/pakistan-news-newspaper-daily-english-online/International/14-Jan-2009/Afghan-soldiers-pick-up-US-weapons

23. Tonita Murray, 'Police-building in Afghanistan: A case study of civil security reform', *International Peacekeeping*, 12:1 (January 2007), p. 113.

24. Rashid, *Descent into Chaos*, p. 205.

25. United States Government Accountability Office, *Afghanistan Security. Efforts to Establish Army and Police Have Made Progress, but Future Plans Need to be Better Defined*, GAO-05-575, June 2005, p. 23, available at: www.gao.gov/new.items/d05575.pdf

26. C.J. Chivers, 'Suppliers under scrutiny on arms for Afghans', *New York Times*, 27 March 2008.

27. Vanda Felbab-Brown, 'Peacekeepers among poppies: Afghanistan, illicit economies, and intervention', *International Peacekeeping*, 16:1 (February 2009), p.106.

28. For a useful chart, see Barnett Rubin, *Road to Ruin: Afghanistan's Booming Opium Industry*, Center on International Cooperation, New York, 7 October 2004, p. 3, available at: www.cic.nyu.edu/archive/pdf/RoadtoRuin.pdf. The 2007 figure comes from Pierre-Arnaud Chouvy, *Opium: Uncovering the Politics of Poppy*, I.B. Tauris, London, 2009, pp. xiii, 37–8. Total global opium production in 2006 was 6,610 tonnes.

29. Chris Johnson and Jolyon Leslie, *Afghanistan: The Mirage of Peace*, Zed Books, London, 2004, p. 112.

30. Felbab-Brown, 'Peacekeepers among poppies', pp. 106–7.

31. UN Office on Drugs and Crime, *Afghanistan: Opium Survey 2005*, November 2005, p. 8, available at: www.unodc.org/pdf/afg/afg_survey_2005.pdf

32. Rashid, *Descent into Chaos*, pp. 134–5.

33. Antonio Giustozzi, *Empires of Mud: War and Warlords in Afghanistan*, Hurst & Company, London, 2009, pp. 233–4.

34. Sonali Kolhatkar and James Ingalls, *Bleeding Afghanistan: Washington, Warlords, and the Propaganda of Silence*, Seven Stories Press, New York, 2006, p. 140.

35. Drug sales were repeatedly marked up in transit, so that, for example, smuggled opiates worth $2.23 billion in Central Asia then acquired an estimated street worth of $11 billion in Russia.

36. Joanna Wright, 'Afghanistan's opiate economy and terrorist financing', *Jane's Intelligence Review*, 18:3 (March 2006), p. 37.
37. Jonathan Goodhand, 'Corrupting or Consolidating the Peace? The Drugs Economy and Post-Conflict Peacebuilding in Afghanistan', *International Peacekeeping* 15:3 (June 2008), p.415.
38. Felbab-Brown, 'Peacekeepers among poppies', pp. 107–8.
39. Marc W. Herold, 'Pulling the rug out: Pseudo-development in Karzai's Afghanistan', 7 March 2006, available at: http://cursor.org/stories/emptyspace2.html
40. Jonathan Goodhand, 'From war economy to peace economy? Reconstruction and state building in Afghanistan', *Journal of International Affairs*, 58:1 (Fall 2004), p. 160.
41. Sayed Yaqub Ibrahimi, 'Afghan disarmament a never-ending process', Institute for War & Peace Reporting *ARR*, 215 (12 May 2006); Antonio Giustozzi, 'Bureaucratic façade and political realities of disarmament and demobilisation in Afghanistan', *Conflict, Security and Development*, 8:2 (June 2008), pp. 187, 190.
42. Jones, *In the Graveyard of Empires*, pp.175–6; Ahmed Rashid, 'Afghanistan and its future', Eurasianet website, 26 June 2006, available at: www.eurasianet.org/departments/insight/articles/eav062606.shtml
43. Barnett R. Rubin, '(Re)Building Afghanistan: The folly of stateless democracy', *Current History* (April 2004), pp. 166–7.
44. Mark Sedra and Peter Middlebrook, 'Beyond Bonn: Revisioning the international compact for Afghanistan', Foreign Policy in Focus brief, November 2005, p. 17.
45. For an effective summary of the historical blindness inherent in much Western development theory, see Ha-Joon Chang, *Kicking Away the Ladder: Development Strategy in Historical Perspective*, Anthem Press, London, 2003.
46. Roland Paris, 'Peacebuilding and the limits of liberal internationalism', *International Security*, 22:2 (Fall 1997), pp. 54–89.
47. The authors wish to thank Dr Peter Middlebrook of Cranfield University, who worked closely with the World Bank on helping to develop the Afghan Compact, for his personal insights here.
48. Carl Robichaud, 'Remember Afghanistan? A glass half full, on the Titanic', *World Policy Journal*, 23:1 (Spring 2006), p. 21.
49. Author interview with Peter Middlebrook.
50. Robichaud, 'Remember Afghanistan?', p. 19; also Matt Waldman, *Falling Short: Aid Effectiveness in Afghanistan*, Kabul, ACBAR, March 2008, p. 1, available at: www.oxfam.org.uk/resources/policy/debt_aid/downloads/aid_effectiveness_afghanistan.pdf
51. Ronald E. Neumann, *The Other War: Winning and Losing in Afghanistan*, Potomac Books Inc., Washington, DC, 2009, pp. 39–50.
52. Ann Jones, 'How US dollars disappear in Afghanistan: Quickly and thoroughly', *San Francisco Chronicle*, 5 September 2006.
53. *ibid.*
54. Joe Stephens and David B. Ottaway, 'A rebuilding plan full of cracks', *Washington Post*, 20 November 2005.
55. Peter Marsden, *Afghanistan: Aid, Armies and Empires*, I.B. Tauris & Co. Ltd., London, 2009, pp. 133–4.
56. Barnett Rubin, 'Making aid to Afghanistan effective', testimony before the House Committee on International Relations, Subcommittee on Oversight, 9 March 2006, pp. 8–9.
57. Michael J. McNerney, 'Stabilization and reconstruction in Afghanistan: Are PRTs a model or a muddle?' *Parameters* (Winter 2005–06), p. 32; Antonio Giustozzi, *War, Politics and Society in Afghanistan 1978–1992*, Hurst & Company, London, 2000, pp. 40–5.

58. Paul Burton, 'Developing disorder: Divergent PRT models in Afghanistan', *Jane's Intelligence Review*, 20:10 (October 2008), pp. 31–2.

59. Touko Piiparinen, 'A clash of mindsets? An insider's account of provincial reconstruction teams', *International Peacekeeping*, 14:1 (January 2007), pp. 151–3.

60. McNerney, 'Stabilization and reconstruction in Afghanistan', pp. 43–4, and see the influential work of Lewis Sorley on Vietnam: *A Better War: The Unexamined Victories and Final Tragedy of America's Last Years in Vietnam*, Mariner Books, New York, 2007.

61. Peter Runge, *The Provisional Reconstruction Teams in Afghanistan: Role Model for Civil-Military Relations?* Occasional Paper IV, Bonn International Center for Conversion (BICC), October 2009, pp. 21–4, available at: www.bicc.de/uploads/pdf/publications/papers/occ_paper_04/occasional_paper_IV_11_09.pdf. For an example of such criticisms at a very early stage in the process, see Save the Children Fund, *Provincial Reconstruction Teams and Humanitarian-Military Relations in Afghanistan*, 2004, available at: www.rusi.org/downloads/assets/Save_the_Children_UK_-_PRTs_and_Humanitarian-Military_Relations_in_Afghanistan_2004_09.pdf

62. Jones, *In the Graveyard of Empires*, p. 140.

63. Kolhatkar and Ingalls, *Bleeding Afghanistan*, p. 142.

64. Anthony H. Cordesman, 'The Afghan elections: Another Milestone on the Road to Nowhere?' 21 September 2010, available at: http://csis.org/publication/afghan-elections-another-milestone-road-nowhere; Barnett Rubin, 'Making aid to Afghanistan effective', testimony before the House Committee on International Relations Subcommittee on Oversight 9 March 2006, available at: http://www.internationalrelations.house.gov/archives/109/rub030906.pdf

65. Daniel Markey, 'Don't waste the Afghan election crisis', *Foreign Policy*, 15 September 2009.

66. For preliminary attempts in this direction, see Seth Jones, 'The rise of Afghanistan's insurgency: State failure and jihad', *International Security*, 32:4 (2008), pp. 7–40; Wilton Park Conference, 'Winning "Hearts and Minds" in Afghanistan: Assessing the effectiveness of development aid in COIN operations', 11–14 March 2010, final report available at: http://kingsofwar.org.uk/wp-content/uploads/2010/04/WP1022-Final-Report.pdf

67. Anthony Davis, 'Afghan security deteriorates as Taliban regroup', *Jane's Intelligence Review*, 15:5 (May 2003), pp. 11–12.

68. Thomas Ruttig, 'The other side: Dimensions of the Afghan insurgency: Causes, actors, and approaches to "talks" ', Afghan Analysts Network, July 2009, pp. 1–2, available at: http://aan-afghanistan.com/uploads/200907%20AAN%20Report%20Ruttig%20-%20The%20Other%20Side.PDF

69. Giustozzi, *Koran, Kalashnikov and Laptop*, p. 35; 'US: Taliban has grown fourfold', 9 October 2009, available http://english.aljazeera.net/news/americas/2009/10/20091091814483962.html

70. Giustozzi, *Koran, Kalashnikov and Laptop*, pp. 81–2, 90.

71. Bill Roggio, 'The Afghan Taliban's top leaders', *Long War Journal*, 23 February 2010, available at: www.longwarjournal.org/archives/2010/02/the_talibans_top_lea.php

72. Hassan Abbas, 'A profile of Tehrik-i-Taliban Pakistan', *CTC Sentinel*, 1:2 (January 2008), pp. 1–4; Claudio Franco, 'The Tehrik-i-Taliban Pakistan' in A. Giustozzi (ed.), *Decoding the New Taliban: Insights from the Afghan Field*, Hurst & Company, London, 2009, pp. 271–84.

73. Richard Tomkins, 'Afghan, Pakistani Taliban diverge on goals.' *The Washington Times*, 18 November 2009, available at: http://www.washingtontimes.com/news/2009/nov/18/afghan-pakistani-taliban-diverge-on-goals/

74. Davis, 'Afghan security deteriorates as Taliban regroup', p. 13; Muhammad Tahir, 'Gulbuddin Hekmatyar's return to the Afghan insurgency', *Terrorism Monitor*, 6:11 (29 May 2008), available at: http://www.jamestown.org/programs/gta/single/?tx_ttnews[tt_news]=4951&tx_ttnews[backPid]=167&no_cache=1

75. Thomas Ruttig, 'Loya Paktia's Insurgency: (1) The Haqqani Network as an autonomous entity' in A. Giustozzi (ed.), *Decoding the New Taliban*, pp. 64–5.

76. Parallel inspired by a conversation between Dr Alex Marshall and Dr Marc Genest at the conference 'Afghanistan's Next Crossroads: Ten Years of International Intervention', 15–16 March 2010, Glasgow University.

77. Matthew Rosenberg, 'New wave of warlords bedevils U.S.', *Wall Street Journal*, 20 January 2010, available at: http://online.wsj.com/article/SB10001424052748704561004575012703221192966.html

78. Urs Gehringer, 'The new Taliban codex', Sign and Sight website, 28 November 2006, available at: www.signandsight.com/features/1069.html#layeha; Giustozzi, *Koran, Kalashnikov and Laptop*, p. 84.

79. Giustozzi, *Koran, Kalashnikov and Laptop*, pp. 123–6.

80. *ibid.*, p. 101.

81. Joanna Nathan, 'Reading the Taliban' in A. Giustozzi (ed.), *Decoding the New Taliban*, p. 23; Mohammad Tahrir, 'Gulbuddin Hekmatyar's return to the Afghan insurgency'.

82. Vance Serchuk, 'The war we're winning (PRTs in Afghanistan)', *Armed Forces Journal* (November 2005), available at: http://ics.leeds.ac.uk/papers/vp01.cfm?outfit=pmt&folder=607&paper=2533

83. Tim McGurk, 'The Taliban on the run', *Time Magazine*, 28 March 2005, available at: www.time.com/time/magazine/article/0,9171,1042511,00.html; David Rohde, David E. Sanger and Carlotta Gall, 'How a "good war" in Afghanistan went bad', *New York Times*, 12 August 2007.

84. Sean M. Maloney, 'Afghanistan four years on: An assessment', *Parameters* (Autumn 2005), pp. 21, 26.

85. Raymond A. Millen, *Afghanistan: Reconstituting a Collapsed State*, SSI, US Army War College, April 2005, available at: www.strategicstudiesinstitute.army.mil/pubs/display.cfm?pubID=600

86. Jones, *In the Graveyard of Empires.*, p.207; Anthony Cordesman, 'Winning in Afghanistan: Challenges and Response', testimony to the House Committee on Foreign Affairs, 15 February 2007, available at: http://www.internationalrelations.house.gov/110/cor021507.htm; 'Afghanistan: Slow Progress on Security and Rights', Human Rights Watch, 30 January 2007, available at: http://www.hrw.org/en/news/2007/01/29/afghanistan-slow-progress-security-and-rights

87. David W. Barno, 'Fighting "the other war": Counterinsurgency strategy in Afghanistan, 2003–2005', *Military Review* (September–October 2007), p. 43.

88. Neumann, *The Other War*, p. xxi.

89. Mark Landler, 'Petraeus warns of a long and expensive mission in Afghanistan', *New York Times*, 9 December 2009.

90. John McCain, 'Winning the war in Afghanistan', *Small Wars Journal*, 25 February 2009, available at: http://smallwarsjournal.com/blog/2009/02/john-mccain-winning-the-war-in/. Counterinsurgency is in fact better understood as a set of operational-level tactics, rather than as a coherent strategy; but much of that nuance has been lost in recent years. On this, see Gian P. Gentile, 'A strategy of tactics: Population-centric COIN and the army', *Parameters* (Autumn 2009), pp. 5–17.

CHAPTER 5: RETURN TO THE 'FORGOTTEN WAR', 2006–08

1. Christina Lamb, *Small Wars Permitting*, pp. 364–5. In this passage, journalist Christina Lamb witnesses a 2006 Shura, in which an inter-departmental British team engages with tribal leaders in Gereshk, Helmand province. The two women who addressed the Shura were Susan Cronby of the Foreign Office and Wendy Phillips of the Department for International Development. Col. Charlie Knaggs was the British task force commander in Helmand, and Maj. Paul Blair was a company commander in the Parachute Regiment.
2. Craig Smith, 'NATO runs short of troops to expand Afghan peacekeeping', *New York Times*, 18 September 2004.
3. See http://news.bbc.co.uk/1/hi/uk_politics/4935532.stm
4. See Judy Dempsey and David Cloud, 'Europeans balking at new Afghan role', *New York Times*, 14 September 2005.
5. See Eric Schmitt, 'US to cut force in Afghanistan', *New York Times*, 20 September 2005.
6. Neumann, *The Other War*, p. 52.
7. This point was made in an author interview with Col. (Ret.) Philip Wilkinson, August 2010. From September 2004 to July 2006, Col. Wilkinson was director of the UK's support programme to the Office of the National Security Council (ONSC) located next to the president's office in the Arg Palace, Kabul. He was the only permanently based non-Afghan policy adviser in the presidential palace.
8. Other countries that would be present in some capacity included Australia, Denmark, the Czech Republic, Estonia, Jordan and Romania.
9. See Deborah Haynes, 'They went into Helmand with eyes shut and fingers crossed', *The Times*, 9 June 2010.
10. Testimony by General Sir David Richards to the UK House of Commons Defence Committee, 24 April 2007. Transcript of evidence available at www.parliament.uk
11. Haynes, 'They went into Helmand'.
12. James Fergusson, *A Million Bullets*, Bantam Press, London, 2008, p. 172. The title of this book is a deliberately ironic reference to the statement by British Defence Secretary John Reid, noted earlier, that his government would be happy if UK forces left Afghanistan without firing a shot.
13. UNODC, *Afghanistan Opium Survey 2007*, p. 5, available at: www.unodc.org/pdf/research/AFG07_ExSum_web.pdf
14. Maiwand is just over the provincial border in Kandahar, but the battle is part of tribal folklore all over the area, as the British would discover when they deployed.
15. Haynes, 'They went into Helmand'.
16. Woodward, *Plan of Attack*, pp. 88–9.
17. See Rory Stewart 'The irresistible illusion', *London Review of Books*, 31:13 (9 July 2009); and 'Afghan claims "realistic": Brown', BBC News, 4 September 2009, available at: http://news.bbc.co.uk/1/hi/uk_politics/8237207.stm
18. Neumann, *The Other War*, p. 73.
19. Rt Hon. Des Browne MP, testimony given to the UK House of Commons Defence Committee, 20 March 2007. Transcript of evidence available at: www.parliament.uk
20. Deobandi is a sect of Sunni Islam that strongly believes in a very 'active' and confrontational interpretation of the notion of *jihad*.
21. David Kilcullen, *The Accidental Guerrilla*, C. Hurst & Co., London, 2009, p. 81.
22. Thomas Johnson and M. Chris Mason, 'No sign until the burst of fire: Understanding the Pakistan–Afghanistan frontier', *International Security*, 32:4 (Spring 2008), p. 62.

23. See Ian Traynor, 'Netherlands votes on troops for Afghanistan', *Guardian*, 2 February 2006.
24. Declan Walsh, 'Flower power', *Guardian*, 16 August 2008.
25. This point was made in an author interview with Col. Philip Wilkinson, August 2010.
26. The point about the general underestimation of Daoud's local connections was made by Lt. Col. Tom Tugenhat in an author interview, August 2010. Lt. Col. Tugenhat was loaned by the UK Foreign and Commonwealth Office to work in Governor Daoud's office from February 2006 to March 2007.
27. Author interview with Col. Philip Wilkinson, August 2010.
28. The best overview of specifically Helmandi conflict dynamics can be found in Tom Coghlan, 'The Taliban in Helmand: An oral history' in Antonio Giustozzi (ed.), *Decoding the New Taliban*.
29. Damien McElroy, 'Afghan governor turned 3,000 men over to the Taliban', *Daily Telegraph*, 20 November 2009.
30. Coghlan, 'The Taliban in Helmand', p. 124.
31. See Fergusson, *A Million Bullets*, pp. 150–1.
32. Pamela Constable, 'Fighting erupts across Afghanistan', *Washington Post*, 19 May 2006.
33. Fergusson, *A Million Bullets*, p. 154.
34. See Stephen Grey, 'Cracking on in Helmand', *Prospect*, 27 (August 2009).
35. On Tony Blair's disinterest in history, see David Marquand, 'A man without history', *New Statesman*, 7 May 2007.
36. Testimony by General Sir David Richards to the UK House of Commons Defence Committee, 24 April 2007. Transcript of evidence available at: www.parliament.uk.
37. See Barr Bearak, 'Karzai calls coalition "careless" ', *New York Times*, 24 June 2007.
38. On the situation at the time in Musa Qala, see Fergusson, *A Million Bullets*, pp. 266–8.
39. The best account of the Musa Qala Accord can be found in Michael Semple, *Reconciliation in Afghanistan*, United States Institution for Peace, Washington, DC, 2009. pp. 79–88.
40. *ibid.*, pp. 81–2.
41. For a good overview of how the accord polarized opinion, see Carlotta Gall and Abdul Waheed Wafa, 'Peace accord in provincial Afghanistan dividing opinion', *International Herald Tribune*, 1 November 2006.
42. See Arthur Bright, 'Pakistan signs deal with pro-Taliban militants', *Christian Science Monitor*, 6 September 2006.
43. See Neumann, *The Other War*, p. 154.
44. Semple, *Reconciliation in Afghanistan*, p. 83.
45. See Fergusson, *A Million Bullets*, p. 272.
46. For a detailed examination of the events surrounding the battles to retake Musa Qala in December 2007, see Stephen Grey, *Operation Snakebite*, Penguin Books, London, 2009.
47. See Robert Fox, 'Fall of Musa Qala is a huge setback for Britain', *The Week*, 2 February 2007, available at: www.thefirstpost.co.uk/2157
48. Semple, *Reconciliation in Afghanistan*, p. 87.
49. Jones, *In the Graveyard of Empires*, p. 207; Anthony Cordesman, 'Winning in Afghanistan: Challenges and response', Testimony to the House Committee on Foreign Affairs, 15 February 2007, available at: www.internationalrelations.house. gov/110/cor021507.htm; Human Rights Watch, 'Afghanistan: Slow progress on security and rights', Human Rights Watch website, 30 January 2007, available at:

www.hrw.org/en/news/2007/01/29/afghanistan-slow-progress-security-and-rights

50. See Thomas Harding, 'A year in Helmand: 4m bullets fired by the British', RAWA News, available at: www.rawa.org/temp/runews/2008/01/12/a-year-in-helmand-4m-bullets-fired-by-british.html; Ahmed Rashid, 'NATO's top brass accuse Pakistan over Taliban aid', *Daily Telegraph*, 6 October 2006, available at: www.telegraph.co.uk/news/worldnews/1530756/Natos-top-brass-accuse-Pakistan-over-Taliban-aid.html

51. Neumann, *The Other War*, p. 81.

52. *ibid.*, p. 106.

53. See Ted Galen Carpenter, 'How the drug war in Afghanistan undermines America's war on terror', Foreign Policy Briefing 84, Cato Institute, 10 November 2004, available at: www.cato.org/pub_display.php?pub_id=2607

54. See UK House of Commons Defence Committee, 8 May 2007, Ev. 71. Transcript of evidence available at: www.parliament.uk

55. For detailed analysis of how the composition of the 'Taliban' changes across provinces and even districts, see Giustozzi, *Decoding the New Taliban*.

56. Coghlan, 'The Taliban in Helmand', pp. 138–9.

57. Figures drawn from 'Metrics Brief 2007–2008', International Security Assistance Force, January 2009, listed in Steve Bowman and Catherine Dale, 'War in Afghanistan: Strategy, military operations and issues for congress', Congressional Research Service, 8 June 2010, p. 25, available at: http://www.fas.org/sgp/crs/natsec/R40156.pdf

58. See Julian Barnes, 'US calls Iraq the priority', *Los Angeles Times*, 12 December 2007.

59. Christina Lamb, 'Taliban leader killed by SAS was Pakistan officer', *Sunday Times*, 12 October 2008.

60. See Frank Ledwidge, 'Justice and counterinsurgency in Afghanistan: A missing link', *RUSI Journal*, 154:1 (2009), pp. 6–9.

61. See Tom Coghlan and Jeremy Page, 'Afghanistan blames Pakistan for bomb attack outside Indian embassy', *Sunday Times*, 9 July 2008.

62. Admiral Mullen quoted in Kenneth Katzman, 'Afghanistan: Post-Taliban governance, security, and US policy', Congressional Research Service Report for Congress, 29 December 2010 2010, p. 26, available at: http://www.fas.org/sgp/crs/row/RL30588.pdf

63. Bowman and Dale, 'War in Afghanistan', p. 35.

64. *ibid.*

65. Katzman, 'Afghanistan: Post-Taliban governance', p. 26.

CHAPTER 6: THE PAKISTAN PROBLEM

1. 'What does Obama's Afpak policy say', Rediff India Abroad website, 27 March 2009, available at: www.rediff.com/news/2009/mar/27obama-speech-on-new-policy-on-afghanisthan-and-pakistan.htm

2. See, for example, testimony by Dr Stephen Biddle to the US Senate Committee on Foreign Relations, 'Assessing the case for war in Afghanistan', Council on Foreign Relations website, 16 September 2009, available at: www.cfr.org/publication/20220

3. Hilary Synott, *Transforming Pakistan: Ways out of Instability*, Routledge, Abingdon, Oxfordshire, 2009, p. 122.

4. On some of these more recent tensions between India and Pakistan over Afghanistan, see Seth G. Jones, 'Pakistan's dangerous game', *Survival*, 49:1 (Spring

2007), pp. 17, 26–7; and Amin Tarzi, 'Islamabad anxious as Kabul gets chummy with New Delhi', Eurasianet website, 15 April 2006, available at: www.eurasianet.org/departments/insight/articles/pp041606.shtml

5. On the 1999 conflict, see Peter R. Lavoy (ed.), *Asymmetric Warfare in South Asia. The Causes and Consequences of the Kargil Conflict*, Cambridge University Press, Cambridge, 2009.

6. Synott, *Transforming Pakistan*, p. 39.

7. Government Accountability Office, *Combating Terrorism: Increased Oversight and Accountability Needed over Pakistan Reimbursement Claims for Coalition Support Funds*, GAO-08-06, June 2008, p. 7, available at: www.gao.gov/new.items/d08806.pdf

8. Imtiaz Gul, *The Most Dangerous Place: Pakistan's Lawless Frontier*, Penguin Books, London, 2010, pp. 16–18, 90. For background on TNSM, see Hassan Abbas, 'The black turbaned brigade: The rise of TNSM in Pakistan', *Terrorism Monitor*, 4:23 (November 2006), available at: www.jamestown.org/programs/gta/single/?tx_ttnews[tt_news]=986&tx_ttnews[backPid]=181&no_cache=1

9. C. Christine Fair and Seth G. Jones, 'Pakistan's war within', *Survival*, 51:6 (December 2009–January 2010), p. 162.

10. *ibid.*, p. 172; Gul, *The Most Dangerous Place*, p. 19.

11. During this second attempt, Musharraf, who was gripping a Glock semiautomatic pistol as a last-ditch personal defence weapon and was able, from his seat in the back of his 3-tonne Mercedes, to see the first bomber explode, escaped death only by urging his driver to accelerate out of danger; so close did the attackers come that all three cars in the presidential convoy were sprayed with blood, dust, debris and human body parts from the twin explosions, which killed sixteen bystanders.

12. Zaeef, *My Life with the Taliban*, p. 168; Pervez Musharraf, *In the Line of Fire*, Free Press, New York, 2006, p. 237. As a direct consequence of the Bush administration's interrogation procedures (during which KSM was water-boarded at least a hundred times in two weeks), some observers subsequently expressed serious doubts, some four years later, as to whether he remained mentally fit enough to stand trial; Abu Zubaydeh, meanwhile, who was also water-boarded no fewer than eighty-three times during the same time period, soon turned out to be already a hopeless schizophrenic. See Robert Baer, 'Why KSM's confession rings false', *Time Magazine*, 15 March 2007, available at: www.time.com/time/world/article/0,8599,1599861,00.html; Ron Suskind, *The One Percent Doctrine: Deep Inside America's Pursuit of Its Enemies since 9/11*, Simon & Schuster, New York, 2006; 'Top 9/11 suspects to plead guilty', BBC News, 8 December 2008, available at: http://news.bbc.co.uk/1/hi/world/americas/7770856.stm

13. USAID, *Pakistan: Economic Performance Assessment*, September 2007, pp. 24–5, available at: http://pdf.usaid.gov/pdf_docs/PNADK618.pdf. For a text embodying this earlier (temporary) era of relative optimism regarding the Pakistani economy, see Shahid Javed Burki, *Changing Perceptions, Altered Reality: Pakistan's Economy under Musharraf, 1999–2006*, OUP Pakistan, Oxford, 2007.

14. For examples of inadequate accounting of aid schemes, see Government Accountability Office, *Combating Terrorism*, pp. 4, 16, 23.

15. Azeez Ibrahim, 'U.S. aid to Pakistan – U.S. taxpayers have funded Pakistan corruption', Belfer Center Discussion Paper, July 2009, p. 6.

16. David Rohde, Carlotta Gall, Eric Schmitt and David E. Sanger, 'U.S. officials see waste in billions sent to Pakistan', *New York Times*, 24 December 2007; Fair and Jones, 'Pakistan's war within', p. 162; Synott, *Transforming Pakistan'*, p. 188, footnote 3; Ibrahim, 'U.S. aid to Pakistan', pp. 5–6.

17. The official army death toll from operations in the spring of 2004, for example, placed Pakistani army losses at around two hundred, but unofficial estimates suggested a toll closer to eight hundred. Bill Roggio, 'The war in Waziristan', *Long War Journal*, 14 February 2006, available at: www.longwarjournal.org/archives/2006/02/the_war_in_wazirista_1.php
18. Fair and Jones, 'Pakistan's war within', pp. 170–1.
19. Gul, *The Most Dangerous Place*, p. 43.
20. Jones, *In the Graveyard of Empires*, pp. 256–8; Declan Walsh, 'Afghanistan war logs: Secret war along the Pakistan border', *Guardian*, 25 July 2010, available at: www.guardian.co.uk/world/2010/jul/25/afghanistan-war-pakistan-border-taliban; Rashid, *Descent into Chaos*, p. 222. For a typical incident, which occurred in 2007 though the report was only leaked in 2010, see the online Afghan War Diary Wikileaks site at: http://wardiary.wikileaks.org/afg/event/2007/04/AFG20070419n658.html
21. 'Afghan, Pakistani tribal leaders launch "Peace Jirga"', Eurasianet website, 8 August 2007, available at: www.eurasianet.org/departments/insight/articles/pp080907af.shtml; Ron Synovitz, 'Afghanistan: Karzai wants closer ties between Pashtuns on both sides of border', Eurasianet website, 10 November 2006, available at: www.eurasianet.org/departments/insight/articles/pp111106.shtml
22. Johnson and Mason, 'No sign until the burst of fire', p. 57; David Rohde, Carlotta Gall and Ismail Khan, 'Taliban and allies tighten grip in north of Pakistan', *New York Times*, 11 December 2006.
23. Bill Roggio, 'More border wars', *Long War Journal*, 7 February 2006, available at: www.longwarjournal.org/archives/2006/02/more_border_wars.php
24. Tim Albone, 'Terrified villagers flee as bombs strike the Taleban', *The Times*, 9 March 2006, available at: www.timesonline.co.uk/tol/news/world/asia/article739036.ece#cid=OTC-RSS&attr=World
25. Bill Roggio, 'US diplomat murdered by Pakistani Al Qaeda suicide bomber', *Long War Journal*, 2 March 2006, available at: www.longwarjournal.org/archives/2006/03/us_diplomat_murdered.php; Evagoras C. Leventis, 'The Waziristan Accord', *Middle Eastern Review of International Affairs*, 11:4 (December 2007), available at: http://meria.idc.ac.il/journal/2007/issue4/jv11no4a4.asp
26. Stanley Kurtz, 'The Taliban fragments', *National Review Online*, 24 January 2008, available at: www.nationalreview.com/corner/157324/taliban-fragments/stanley-kurtz
27. Ahmed Rashid, 'Pakistan crisis "hits army morale"', BBC News, 13 September 2007, available at: http://news.bbc.co.uk/1/hi/world/south_asia/6978240.stm; Bill Roggio, 'Swat joins Talibanistan', *Long War Journal*, 7 July 2007, available at: www.longwarjournal.org/archives/2007/07/swat_joins_talibanis.php; Bill Roggio, 'Taliban capture over 100 Pakistani soldiers in South Waziristan', *Long War Journal*, 31 August 2007, www.longwarjournal.org/archives/2007/08/taliban_capture_over.php
28. Bill Roggio, 'Taliban, Pakistani army battle in North Waziristan', *Long War Journal*, 9 October 2007, available at: www.longwarjournal.org/archives/2007/10/taliban_pakistani_ar.php; 'Battles rage on Pakistan border', BBC News, 9 October 2007, available at: http://news.bbc.co.uk/1/hi/world/south_asia/7034795.stm
29. Bill Roggio, 'Pakistan army advances in Swat', *Long War Journal*, 2 December 2007, available at: www.longwarjournal.org/archives/2007/12/pakistani_army_advan.php
30. Declan Walsh, 'Video of girl's flogging as Taliban hand out justice', *Guardian*, 2 April 2009 http://www.reuters.com/article/idUSTRE6340HN20100405

31. Phil Stewart, 'Pakistan's Army accused of extra-judicial killings', 5 April 2010, Reuters, available at: http://www.reuters.com/article/idUSTRE6340HN20100405; Jane Perlez and Pir Zubair shah, 'Pakistan Army Said to Be Linked to Swat Killings', 14 September 2009, *The New York Times*, http://www.nytimes.com/2009/09/15/world/asia/15swat.html

32. Declan Walsh, 'Pakistan Taliban chief Hakimullah Mehsud is alive, says spy agency', *Guardian*, 28 April 2010, available at: http://www.guardian.co.uk/world/2010/apr/28/hakimullah-mehsud-survives-cia-drone

33. Interview with former US representative in Kabul, Ambassador James Dobbins, conducted on 7 July 2010.

34. Bill Roggio, 'Taliban advance eastward, threaten Islamabad', The Long War Journal, 23 April 2009, http://www.longwarjournal.org/archives/2009/04/taliban_advance_east.php

35. On these trends, see: Robert Brenner, *The Economics of Global Turbulence: The Advanced Capitalist Economies from Long Boom to Long Downturn, 1945–2005*. London/New York: Verso, 2006, and Loretta Napoleoni, *Terrorism and the Economy: How the War on Terror is Bankrupting the World*. New York: Seven Stories Press, 2010.

36. Synott, *Transforming Pakistan*, pp. 80–2; USAID, *Pakistan: Economic Performance Assessment*, October 2009, pp. 1–14, 44, available at: http://pdf.usaid.gov/pdf_docs/PNADR358.pdf

37. The number of drone strikes is contested, and is inevitably based on the limitations of open source reporting. For one set of statistics, see Bill Roggio and Alexander Mayer, 'Charting the data for US airstrikes in Pakistan, 2004–2010', *Long War Journal*, continuously updated, available at: www.longwarjournal.org/pakistan-strikes.php

38. Daniel Byman, 'Do targeted killings work?' Brookings Institution website, 14 July 2009, available at: www.brookings.edu/opinions/2009/0714_targeted_killings_byman.aspx?p=1

39. Pew Global Attitudes Project, 'America's image remains poor: Concern about extremist threat slips in Pakistan', Pew Research Center, 29 July 2010, available at: http://pewglobal.org/files/pdf/Pew-Global-Attitudes-2010-Pakistan-Report.pdf

40. Masood Haidar, '2.2 million IDPs in Pakistan', Dawn.com, 19 May 2009, available at: www.dawn.com/wps/wcm/connect/dawn-content-library/dawn/news/pakistan/provinces/13+2+million+idps+in+pakistan+un—za-02; Huma Yusuf, 'Estranged from their own land', *Indian Express* website, 12 June 2009, available at: www.indianexpress.com/news/estranged-from-their-own-land/475141/; Ian S. Livingston and Michael O'Hanlon, *Pakistan Index: Tracking Variables of Reconstruction and Security*, Brookings Institution, 30 October 2009, p. 9, available at: www.brookings.edu/~/media/Files/Programs/FP/pakistan%20index/index20091030.pdf

41. IISS, 'Rising extremism in South Asia', International Institute of Strategic Studies, 2010, available at: www.iiss.org/publications/strategic-comments/past-issues/volume-16-2010/january/rising-extremism-in-south-asia/; Yasub Ali Dogar, *The Talibanisation of Pakistan's Western Region*, Institute of South Asian Studies Working Paper No. 98, 24 November 2009, p. 15, available at: www.isas.nus.edu.sg/Attachments/PublisherAttachment/ISAS_Working_Paper_98_-_Email_-_The_Talibanisation_of_Pakistan%27s_Western_Region_18122009122105.pdf

42. Gul, *The Most Dangerous Place*, p. 129.

43. Ann Wilkens, 'Smoke gets in your eyes: Pakistan in 2010', Afghan Analysts Network, March 2010, p. 1, available at: http://aan-afghanistan.com/uploads/20100304-AWilkens-Smoke_Gets_in_Your_Eyes.pdf

44. Syed Saleem Shahzad, 'Al-Qaeda backs massive push in Swat', 7 December 2010, *Asia Times Online*, at: http://www.atimes.com/atimes/South_Asia/LL07Df02.html;

Hamid Hussain, 'Strong military presence necessary in Pakistan's tribal area:analysts', 29 April 2010, available at: http://news.xinhuanet.com/english2010/world/2010-04/29/c_13272912.htm; and, on local militias, Chris Brummitt, 'Pakistan militias both ally, threat', 28 December 2010, at: http://azstarnet.com/news/world/military/article_2302c37c-4c31-5c7b-a11c-bfb6f1d26355.html. On the postponed North Waziristan campaign, whose delay was officially attributed to harsh local weather conditions, see: 'N. Waziristan offensive: Plan put on hold for indefinite period', *The Express Tribune*, 11 January 2011, available online at: http://tribune.com.pk/story/102118/n-waziristan-offensive-plan-put-on-hold-for-indefinite-period/

45. See, for example, the 2010 report for Congress by the Congressional Research Service, 'Security and the Environment in Pakistan' (3 August 2010), which stresses that water resources in Pakistan are being used at an unsustainable rate, and that the combination of high population growth, low economic development, and resource scarcity increase the risk of internal conflict in the immediate future and may also contribute to the further growth and sustenance of Islamist extremism.

46. General James Jones, 'President Obama's Afghanistan–Pakistan (AFPAK) Strategy', US Department of State briefing, 27 March 2009, available at: http://fpc.state.gov/120965.htm

47. Daud Khattak, 'The missing dimension of Pakistan's counterinsurgency policy', Radio Free Europe/Radio Liberty, 10 July 2010, available at: www.jamestown.org/programs/gta/single/?tx_ttnews[tt_news]=36739&cHash=de992b83e4

48. Rahimullah Yusufzai, 'Assessing the progress of Pakistan's South Waziristan offensive', *CTC Sentinel*, 2:12 (December 2009), pp. 8–12. For more upbeat assessments (which actually mostly just note the increased use by the Pakistani military of US drones, airpower and precision guided munitions), see Samir Lalwani, 'The Pakistani military's adaption to counterinsurgency in 2009', *CTC Sentinel*, 3:1 (January 2010), pp. 9–13, and Syed Bukhari, 'New strategies in Pakistan's counter-insurgency operation in South Waziristan', *Terrorism Monitor*, 7:37 (December 2009), available at: www.jamestown.org/single/?no_cache=1&tx_ttnews[tt_news]=35798&tx_ttnews[backPid]=7&cHash=be93771478

49. Tayyab Ali Shah, 'Pakistan's Bajaur agency emerges as new hub for Islamist militancy', *Terrorism Monitor*, 8:32 (August 2010), available at: www.jamestown.org/programs/gta/single/?tx_ttnews[tt_news]=36739&cHash=de992b83e4

50. Bill Roggio, 'Taliban are "patriots" says Pakistani army official', *Long War Journal*, 1 December 2008, available at: www.longwarjournal.org/archives/2008/12/taliban_are_patriots.php

51. Gul, *The Most Dangerous Place*, pp. 206–7, 217–22.

52. Robert Matthews, 'An anvil of clay: Pakistan's military balks at Obama's surge', Norwegian Peacebuilding Centre Noref Report No. 2 (January 2010), pp. 2–4.

53. Matt Waldman, 'The sun in the sky: The relationship between Pakistan's ISI and Afghan insurgents', Development Studies Institute, London School of Economics, Discussion Paper 18 (June 2010), pp. 10–20.

54. Dexter Filkins, 'The long road to chaos in Pakistan', *New York Times*, 27 September 2008, available at: www.nytimes.com/2008/09/28/weekinreview/28filkins.html; 'Afghan bomb strikes India embassy', BBC News, 8 October 2009, available at: http://news.bbc.co.uk/1/hi/world/south_asia/8296137.stm

55. Dexter Filkins, 'Pakistanis tell of motive in Taliban leader's arrest', *New York Times*, 22 August 2010, available at: www.nytimes.com/2010/08/23/world/asia/23taliban.html?_r=2&hp

56. William Dalrymple, 'This is no NATO game but Pakistan's proxy war with its brother in the south', *Guardian*, 1 July 2010, available at: www.guardian.co.uk/commentisfree/2010/jul/01/afghanistan-pakistan-proxy-war-with-india

57. International Crisis Group, 'Pakistan's IDP crisis: Challenges and opportunities', Asia Briefing No. 93, June 2009), available at: www.crisisgroup.org/~/media/Files/asia/south-asia/pakistan/b93_pakistans_idp_crisis___challenges_and_opportunities.ashx; International Crisis Group, 'Pakistan: Countering militancy in FATA', Asia Report No. 178, October 2009, available at: www.crisisgroup.org/~/media/Files/asia/south-asia/pakistan/178_pakistan___countering_militancy_in_fata.ashx

58. Manzoor Ali, 'Forgetting FATA reform', *Foreign Policy* (10 August 2010), available at: www.crisisgroup.org/~/media/Files/asia/south-asia/pakistan/178_pakistan___countering_militancy_in_fata.ashx

CHAPTER 7: SILVER BULLETS AND THE SEARCH FOR AN EXIT, 2009–11

1. Cold War International History Project Virtual Archive, available at: www.wilsoncenter.org/index.cfm?topic_id=1409&fuseaction=va2.document&identifier=5034DF42-96B6-175C-94B37A1064349E42&sort=Collection&item=Soviet%20Invasion%20of%20Afghanistan

2. One Afghan official candidly told his Soviet counterpart at the end of 1987 that statistics on local party membership were routinely exaggerated, so a report that a local Afghan party organization had, say, fifty members would have been grotesquely inflated to 1,000 by the time it reached Moscow. Another insider estimated that the true number of loyal and capable indigenous party personnel in Afghanistan was less than 20,000, rather than the 200,000 spoken of by Sultan Ali Keshtmand, the prime minister at the time. Such assessments at the time painted a bleak picture of the future stability of the Kabul government as it was then configured, not least due to the absence of sufficient cadres of technocrats or trained and literate civil servants. See Vladimir Plastun and Vladimir Andrianov, *Nadzhibulla: Afganistan v tiskakh geopolitiki*, Tipografiia No. 9, Moscow, 1998, pp. 181, 204.

3. 'Troop levels in Afghanistan since 2001', *New York Times*, 1 October 2009, available at: www.nytimes.com/interactive/2009/10/01/world/middleeast/afghanistan-policy.html

4. Ian Traynor, 'NATO Afghan mission in doubt after Dutch withdrawal', *Guardian*, 22 February 2010, available at: www.guardian.co.uk/world/2010/feb/21/dutch-government-falls-over-afghanistan; 'Sarkozy rules out more French troops for Afghanistan', Radio Free Europe/Radio Liberty website, available at: www.rferl.org/content/Sarkozy_Rules_Out_More_French_Troops_For_Afghanistan/1565715.html

5. For a list of countries contributing troops to ISAF, see 'International Security Assistance Force: Key facts and figures', available at: www.isaf.nato.int/images/stories/File/Placemats/100804%20Rev%20Placemat.pdf. As of 6 August 2010, there were forty-seven contributing countries.

6. See Timo Noetzel and Benjamin Schreer, 'Counter-what? Germany and counter-insurgency in Afghanistan', *RUSI Journal*, 153:1 (2008), pp. 42–6.

7. Karen DeYoung, 'Obama sets timetable for Iraq', *Washington Post*, 28 February 2009, available at: www.washingtonpost.com/wp-dyn/content/article/2009/02/27/AR2009022700566.html

8. See http://www.whitehouse.gov/assets/documents/Afghanistan-Pakistan_White_Paper.pdf

9. Elizabeth Rubin, 'Karzai in his labyrinth', *New York Times*, 4 August 2009, available at: www.nytimes.com/2009/08/09/magazine/09Karzai-t.html

10. Author interview with Mr James Dobbins.
11. Author interview with Gerard Russell, 25 August 2010; Susanne Koelbl, 'Corruption in Afghanistan: US cuts aid after millions siphoned off to Dubai', *Der Spiegel*, 7 May 2010, available at: www.spiegel.de/international/world/0,1518,704665,00.html
12. Rubin, 'Karzai in his labyrinth'; Dexter Filkins, Mark Mazzetti and James Risen, 'Karzai's brother is said to be on CIA payroll', *New York Times*, 27 October 2009, available at: www.nytimes.com/2009/10/28/world/asia/28intel.html?hp
13. Material that leaks into the open media regarding these tensions is necessarily speculative, but has been largely corroborated by the authors' personal interviews. For a representative survey of what has leaked into the open-source literature, see Josh Mull, 'McChrystal's revenge: Everyone hates Karl Eikenberry', *Huffington Post*, 24 June 2010, available at: www.huffingtonpost.com/josh-mull/mcchrystals-revenge-every_b_624702.html. On Holbrooke, see Ian Pannell, 'US envoy "in angry Karzai talks"', BBC News, 27 August 2009, available at: http://news.bbc.co.uk/1/hi/8225745.stm
14. Peter W. Galbraith, 'What I saw at the Afghan election', *Washington Post*, 4 October 2009, available at: www.washingtonpost.com/wp-dyn/content/article/2009/10/02/AR2009100202855.html; James Glanz and Richard A. Oppel, 'U.N. officials say American offered plan to replace Karzai', *New York Times*, 16 December 2009, available at: www.nytimes.com/2009/12/17/world/asia/17galbraith.html?_r=1
15. Carlotta Gall, 'Growing accounts of fraud cloud Afghan election', *New York Times*, 30 August 2009, available at: www.nytimes.com/2009/08/31/world/asia/31fraud.html; 'Afghan fraud fear despite UK push', BBC News, 11 September 2009, available at: http://news.bbc.co.uk/1/hi/world/south_asia/8249983.stm
16. See www.icasualties.org/oef/
17. Barnett Rubin and Ahmed Rashid, 'From great game to grand bargain: Ending chaos in Afghanistan and Pakistan', *Foreign Affairs* (November/December 2008), available (by subscription) at: www.foreignaffairs.com/articles/64604/barnett-r-rubin-and-ahmed-rashid/from-great-game-to-grand-bargain
18. Lyse Doucet, 'Pakistan's push for new role in Afghanistan', BBC News, 19 February 2010, available at: http://news.bbc.co.uk/1/hi/8521823.stm
19. Michael Wines, 'Uneasy engagement: China willing to spend big on Afghan commerce', *New York Times*, 29 December 2009, available at: www.nytimes.com/2009/12/30/world/asia/30mine.html?pagewanted=1&_r=1
20. Deidre Tynan, 'Kyrgyzstan: Manas fully operational, but NDN re-supply line still lags', Eurasianet website, 12 April 2010, available at: www.eurasianet.org/departments/insightb/articles/eav041310.shtml; Richard Weitz, 'Russia and NATO clash over Afghan drugs', Central Asia – Caucasus Institute website, 22 July 2010, available at: www.cacianalyst.org/?q=node/5375; 'Russia criticizes US, NATO over Afghan drug trafficking fight', *USA Today*, 12 March 2010, available at: www.usatoday.com/news/world/afghanistan/2010-03-12-russia-us-nato_N.htm
21. Ahmed Rashid, 'If we want peace, we'll have to talk to the Taliban', *London Evening Standard*, 27 September 2009, available at: www.thisislondon.co.uk/standard/article-23724848-if-we-want-peace-well-have-to-talk-to-the-taliban.do
22. Michael O'Hanlon and Hassina Sherjan, *Toughing it out in Afghanistan*, Brookings Institution Press, Washington, DC, 2010, p. 70.
23. Edward Luttwak, 'Take me back to Constantinople: How Byzantium, not Rome, can help preserve Pax Americana', *Foreign Policy* (November/December 2009), available at: www.foreignpolicy.com/articles/2009/10/19/take_me_back_to_constantinople. The reference was, of course, derived from Luttwak's most recent magisterial study, *The Grand Strategy of the Byzantine Empire*, Harvard University Press, Harvard, 2009.

24. Ron Nordland, 'Lacking money and leadership, push for Taliban defectors stalls', *New York Times*, 6 September 2010, available at: www.nytimes.com/2010/09/07/world/asia/07taliban.html?_r=1&src=mv

25. See on this Mark Urban, *Task Force Black: The Explosive True Story of the SAS and the Secret War in Iraq*, Little, Brown and Company, London, 2010.

26. Fred Kaplan, 'It's Obama's war now', 11 May 2009, *Slate Magazine*, available at: www.slate.com/id/2218160/

27. O'Hanlon and Sherjan, *Toughing it out in Afghanistan*, pp. 68–9.

28. Available at: www.cbsnews.com/8301-503544_162-5372306-503544.html

29. Holly Bailey, 'An inconvenient truth teller', *Newsweek*, 10 October 2009, available at: www.newsweek.com/2009/10/09/an-inconvenient-truth-teller.html

30. The full text of Eikenberry's November cables can be found on the *New York Times* website: http://documents.nytimes.com/eikenberry-s-memos-on-the-strategy-in-afghanistan#p=1

31. See the final section of this chapter.

32. Kim Sengupta, ' "We need 30,000 more soldiers to beat Taliban," says general', *Independent*, 17 October 2008; Tom Vanden, 'Commander sees "tough fight" in Afghan war', *USA Today*, 8 December 2008, available at: http://www.usatoday.com/news/military/2008-12-07-afghantroops_N.htm

33. Seth Jones, 'Averting failure in Afghanistan', *Survival*, 48:1 (Spring 2006), p. 119; Seth G. Jones, *Counterinsurgency in Afghanistan*, Santa Monica, RAND, 2008, p. 10.

34. Headquarters Department of the Army, *Counterinsurgency*, FM 3–24, December 2006, p. 1–13, available at: www.fas.org/irp/doddir/army/fm3-24.pdf

35. *ibid.*, pp. 1–23, 6–10.

36. The entire August report can be found at: http://media.washingtonpost.com/wp-srv/politics/documents/Assessment_Redacted_092109.pdf?hpid=topnews

37. For a representative sample of these articles, see Max Boot, 'How to win in Afghanistan', *Wall Street Journal*, 2 September 2009; Frederick W. Kagan, 'We're not the Soviets in Afghanistan', *Weekly Standard*, 21 August 2009, available at: www.weeklystandard.com/Content/Public/Articles/000/000/016/854qadbb.asp; Frederick Kagan, 'Afghanistan is not Vietnam', *Newsweek*, 11 February 2009, available at: www.newsweek.com/2009/02/10/afghanistan-is-not-vietnam.html; and Stephen Biddle, 'Is it worth it? The difficult case for war in Afghanistan', *American Interest Online*, July–August 2009, available at: www.the-american-interest.com/article.cfm?piece=617. On Robert Gates' self-confessed rethink, see his interview with Fred Kaplan: 'Interview: Robert Gates', *Foreign Policy*, 16 August 2010, available at: www.foreignpolicy.com/articles/2010/08/13/robert_gates

38. Sheryl Gay Stolberg and Helene Cooper, 'Obama adds troops, but maps exit plan', *New York Times*, 1 December 2009, available at: www.nytimes.com/2009/12/02/world/asia/02prexy.html

39. House of Commons Foreign Affairs Committee testimony, 8 September 2010, available at: http://www.publications.parliament.uk/pa/cm201011/cmselect/cmfaff/c438-i/c43802.htm. Mr Hague: I do not want anyone to be in any doubt about this: we will be fulfilling the Prime Minister's commitment by 2015. The Prime Minister is very clear that by 2015 British troops will not be in Afghanistan in a combat role, nor in the numbers that are there now.
Mr Baron: Regardless of whether we have achieved the objective?
Mr Hague: Unless we are clear about it, we are not credible about it. We are very clear about it. Of course there could be some troops in a training role and as part of wider diplomatic relations in the longer term, as we have in other countries, but we do not want to be fighting in Afghanistan for a day longer than is necessary.
The authors are grateful to Rory Stewart MP for this reference.

40. See http://english.peopledaily.com.cn/90001/90777/90853/7040136.html and Judy Dempsey and Matthew Saltmarsh, 'Germany will begin Afghan exit next year.' *The New York Times* 16 December 2010, available at: http://www.nytimes.com/2010/12/17/world/europe/17germany.html?_r=1

41. O'Hanlon and Sherjan, *Toughing it out in Afghanistan*, p. 47.

42. Antonio Giustozzi and Christoph Reuter, 'The northern front: The Afghan insurgency spreading beyond the Pashtuns', Afghan Analysts Network, 24 June 2010, available at: http://aan-afghanistan.com/uploads/20100629AGCR-TheNorthernFront1.pdf. The key text arguing for a conscious and centrally controlled Taliban strategy is Gilles Dorronsoro, *The Taliban's Winning Strategy in Afghanistan*, Carnegie Endowment for International Peace, Washington, DC, 2009. Criticism of NATO strategy by Russia has been vociferous over this issue of the increasingly unstable Afghan north: Jonathan Burch, 'Spread of Afghan Insurgency to Russia Worrying', Reuters News Agency, 11 November 2010, available at: http://www.vision.org/visionmedia/article.aspx?id=36997

43. O'Hanlon and Sherjan, *Toughing it out in Afghanistan*, p. 42; Thom Shanker, Peter Baker and Helene Cooper, 'US to protect populous Afghan areas, officials say', *New York Times*, 27 October 2009, available at: www.nytimes.com/2009/10/28/world/asia/28policy.html?_r=1

44. Two new provinces were created in 2004, bringing the previous total of 32 provinces up to 34.

45. UNODC, *Afghan Opium Survey 2009, Summary Findings*, September 2009.

46. Ian Simpson, 'Afghan opium price soars, new planting feared', 12 November 2010, Reuters News Agency, available at: http://in.reuters.com/article/idINIndia-52873220101112. To illustrate how progress was merely relative, there were still more hectares of opium being cultivated in Afghanistan in 2010 than in 2002, 2003, or 2005, or indeed for the entire period 1994–2001. UNODC *Afghanistan Opium Survey 2010*, September 2010, Summary Findings, available at: www.unodc.org/documents/crop-monitoring/Afghanistan/Afg_opium_survey_2010_exsum_web.pdf

47. UNODC, *Corruption in Afghanistan: Bribery as Reported by the Victims*, January 2010, pp. 4–9, available at: www.unodc.org/documents/data-and-analysis/Afghanistan/Afghanistan-corruption-survey2010-Eng.pdf

48. David Montero, 'Kabul bank run may pose more immediate threat than Afghan Taliban', *Christian Science Monitor*, 3 September 2010, available at: www.csmonitor.com/World/terrorism-security/2010/0903/Kabul-Bank-run-may-pose-more-immediate-threat-than-Afghan-Taliban

49. Office of the Special Inspector General for Afghan Reconstruction (SIGAR), *Actions Needed to Improve the Reliability of Afghan Security Force Assessments*, 29 June 2010, pp. 8–21, available at: http://www.sigar.mil/pdf/audits/SIGAR%20Audit-10-11.pdf

50. Martha Raddatz, 'Afghan National Army reaches benchmark, but are they fit for duty?', ABC News,12 August 2010, available at: http://abcnews.go.com/WN/Afghanistan/war-afghanistan-afghan-national-army-meets-134000-trained/story?id=11290464&page=1; 'Afghanistan unable to pay for troops for 15 years', BBC News, 8 December 2009, available at: http://news.bbc.co.uk/1/hi/world/south_asia/8400806.stm

51. O'Hanlon and Sherjan, *Toughing it out in Afghanistan*, p. 74.

52. Dexter Filkins, 'Afghan offensive is new war model', *New York Times*, 12 February 2010, available at: www.nytimes.com/2010/02/13/world/asia/13kabul.html

53. Julius Cavendish, 'Nato's grand experiment leaves Marjah scrambling for a future', *Independent*, 30 June 2010, available at: www.independent.co.uk/news/world/asia/natos-grand-experiment-leaves-marjah-scrabbling-for-a-future-2014043.html;

Abigail Hauslohner, 'As McChrystal stumbles, the U.S. campaign in Marjah struggles', *Time Magazine*, 22 June 2010, available at: www.time.com/time/world/article/0,8599,1998620,00.html

54. 'McChrystal: Kandahar operation will be "slow, rising tide" of security', Eurasianet website, 15 May 2010, available at: www.eurasianet.org/node/61071
55. Robert Haddick, 'This week at war: The foregone conclusion in Kandahar', *Foreign Policy*, 28 May 2010, available at: www.foreignpolicy.com/articles/2010/05/28/this_week_at_war_the_forgone_conclusion_in_kandahar?page=0,1
56. Spencer Ackerman, 'Drones surge, special ops strike in Petraeus campaign plan', *Wired*, 18 August 2010, available at: www.wired.com/dangerroom/2010/08/petraeus-campaign-plan/
57. Carl Forsberg, *Counterinsurgency in Kandahar: Evaluating the 2010 Hamkari Campaign*. December 2010, Institute for the Study of War Afghanistan Report 7, pp. 35, 39–40, 44–45, available at: www.understandingwar.org/files/Afghanistan%20Report%207_16Dec.pdf
58. See for example: Aunohita Mojumdar, 'An inflated claim of health success in Afghanistan exposed', *The Christian Science Monitor*, 8 December 2010 available at: www.csmonitor.com/World/Asia-South-Central/2010/1208/An-inflated-claim-of-health-success-in-Afghanistan-exposed; or Rod Nordland, 'Security in Afghanistan is Deteriorating, Aid Groups Say', *The New York Times*, 11 September 2010, available at: www.nytimes.com/2010/09/12/world/asia/12afghan.html?ref=asia; or Aunohita Mojumdar, 'Afghanistan: Donor Funding Missing Mark', 28 December 2010, available at: http://www.eurasianet.org/node/62640
59. Richard Norton-Taylor, 'Al-Qaida and Taliban threat is exaggerated, says security think tank', *Guardian*, 7 September 2010, available at: www.guardian.co.uk/world/2010/sep/07/al-qaida-taliban-threat-afghanistan
60. Stephen M. Walt, 'A plan B for Afghanistan', *Foreign Policy*, 8 September 2010, available at: http://walt.foreignpolicy.com/posts/2010/09/08/a_plan_b_for_afghanistan
61. Ben Arnoldy, 'Can Afghanistan economy thrive without poppy?', *Christian Science Monitor*, 5 March 2010, available at: www.csmonitor.com/World/Asia-South-Central/2010/0305/Can-Afghanistan-economy-thrive-without-poppy
62. James Risen, 'U.S. identifies vast mineral riches in Afghanistan', *New York Times*, 13 June 2010, available at: www.nytimes.com/2010/06/14/world/asia/14minerals.html?pagewanted=1&_r=1&hp
63. David Robertson, 'Value of Afghanistan's mineral discovery needs to be dealt with cautiously', *The Times*, 14 June 2010, available at: www.timesonline.co.uk/tol/news/world/afghanistan/article7150081.ece

CONCLUSION

1. Walter Lippmann, *US Foreign Policy: Shield of the Republic*, Boston, Little, Brown and Co., 1943.
2. Rory Stewart, former UK diplomat and currently Member of Parliament, in testimony to the Senate Foreign Relations Committee hearing on the future of Afghanistan, 16 September 2009. Testimony available at: http://foreign.senate.gov/imo/media/doc/StewartTestimony090916p1.pdf
3. Robert Kaplan, 'Man versus Afghanistan', *Atlantic*, April 2010.
4. The specific quote comes from O'Hanlon and Sherjan, *Toughing it out in Afghanistan*, p. 12. However, it draws on work by Andrew Enterline and Joseph Magagnoli, 'Is the chance of success in Afghanistan better than a coin toss?', *Foreign Policy*, 27 August 2009.

5. Quarterly report to the US Congress by the Special Inspector General for Afghan Reconstruction (SIGAR), p. 93. Available at: www.sigar.mil/pdf/quarter-lyreports/Jul2010/SIGAR_July2010.pdf
6. Author interview with former Ambassador Sir Sherard Cowper-Coles, June 2010.

BIBLIOGRAPHY

Abbas, Hassan, 'The black turbaned brigade: The rise of TNSM in Pakistan', *Terrorism Monitor*, 4:23 (November 2006), available at: www.jamestown.org/programs/gta/single/?tx_ttnews[tt_news]=986&tx_ttnews[backPid]=181&no_cache=1
——, 'A profile of Tehrik-i-Taliban Pakistan', *CTC Sentinel*, 1:2 (January 2008), pp. 1–4
Adams, Thomas, *The Army after Next*, Stanford University Press, Stanford, 2008
Afghan War Diary Wikileaks website at: http://wardiary.wikileaks.org/afg/event/2007/04/AFG20070419n658.html
Ali, Manzoor, 'Forgetting FATA reform', *Foreign Policy*, 10 August 2010, available at: www.crisisgroup.org/~/media/Files/asia/south-asia/pakistan/178_pakistan___countering_militancy_in_fata.ashx   http://english.aljazeera.net/news/americas/2009/10/20091091814483962.html
Arnoldy, Ben, 'Can Afghanistan economy thrive without poppy?', *Christian Science Monitor*, 5 March 2010, available at: www.csmonitor.com/World/Asia-South-Central/2010/0305/Can-Afghanistan-economy-thrive-without-poppy
Barfield, Thomas, *Afghanistan: A Cultural and Political History*, Princeton University Press, Princeton, 2010
Barno, David W., 'Fighting "the other war": Counterinsurgency strategy in Afghanistan, 2003–2005', *Military Review* (September–October 2007), available at: http://findarticles.com/p/articles/mi_m0PBZ/is_5_87/ai_n27411366/
Belokorenitskii, V.Ia. and A.Z. Egorin (eds), *Musul'manskie strany u granits SNG*, IVRAN-Kraft, Moscow, 2002
Berntsen, Gary, *Jawbreaker: The Attack on bin Laden and Al Qaeda*, Three Rivers Press, New York, 2005
Biddle, Stephen, 'Afghanistan and the future of warfare: Implications for army and defense policy', US Army Strategic Studies Institute, November 2002, available at: www.au.af.mil/au/awc/awcgate/ssi/afghan.pdf

——, 'Is it worth it? The difficult case for war in Afghanistan', *American Interest Online*, July–August 2009, available at: www.newsweek.com/2009/02/10/afghanistan-is-not-vietnam.html

——, 'Assessing the Case for War in Afghanistan', testimony to the US Senate Committee on Foreign Relations, Council on Foreign Relations website, 16 September 2009, available at: www.cfr.org/publication/20220

Blank, Stephen, 'After two wars: Reflections on the American strategic revolution in Central Asia', Conflict Studies Research Centre, Central Asian Series 05/14, April 2005

Bowman, Steve and Catherine Dale, 'War in Afghanistan: Strategy, military operations, and issues for congress', Congressional Research Service Report for Congress, 25 February 2010, available at: http://www.fas.org/sgp/crs/natsec/R40156.pdf

Brenner, Robert, *The Economics of Global Turbulence: The Advanced Capitalist Economies from Long Boom to Long Downturn, 1945–2005*, Verso, London/New York, 2006

Bright, Arthur, 'Pakistan signs deal with pro-Taliban militants', *Christian Science Monitor*, 6 September 2006

Bukhari, Syed, 'New strategies in Pakistan's counter-insurgency operation in South Waziristan', *Terrorism Monitor*, 7:37 (December 2009), available at: www.jamestown.org/single/?no_cache=1&tx_ttnews[tt_news]=35798&tx_ttnews[backPid]=7&cHash=be93771478

Burch, Jonathan, 'Spread of Afghan Insurgency to Russia Worrying', Reuters News Agency, 11 November 2010, available at: http://www.vision.org/visionmedia/article.aspx?id=36997

Burki, Shahid Javed, *Changing Perceptions, Altered Reality: Pakistan's Economy under Musharraf, 1999–2006*, OUP Pakistan, Oxford, 2007

Burton, Paul, 'Developing disorder: Divergent PRT models in Afghanistan', *Jane's Intelligence Review*, 20:10 (October 2008), pp. 31–2

Byman, Daniel, 'Do targeted killings work?' Brookings Institution website, 14 July 2009, available at: www.brookings.edu/opinions/2009/0714_targeted_killings_byman.aspx?p=1

Canfield, Robert, 'Afghanistan: The trajectory of internal alignments', *Middle East Journal*, 43:4 (Autumn 1989), pp. 635–48

Carland, John, 'The campaign against Kandahar', US Army Center of Military History Information Paper, Washington, DC, March 2002

Caroe, Sir Olaf, *The Pathans, With an Epilogue on Russia*, Oxford University Press, Karachi, 1983/2001

Carpenter, Ted Galen, 'How the drug war in Afghanistan undermines America's war on terror', Foreign Policy Briefing 84, Cato Institute, 10 November 2004, available at: www.cato.org/pub_display.php?pub_id=2607

Chandler, David, *Empire in Denial: The Politics of State-building*, Pluto Press, London, 2006

Chang, Ha-Joon, *Kicking Away the Ladder: Development Strategy in Historical Perspective*, Anthem Press, London, 2003

Chayes, Sarah, *The Punishment of Virtue: Inside Afghanistan after the Taliban*, Penguin Books, New York, 2006

Chouvy, Pierre-Arnaud, *Opium: Uncovering the Politics of Poppy*, I.B. Tauris, London, 2009

Clarke, Richard A., *Against All Enemies*, Simon & Schuster, New York, 2004

Coll, Steve, *Ghost Wars: The Secret History of the CIA, Afghanistan and Bin Laden, from the Soviet Invasion to September 10, 2001*, Penguin Books, London, 2005

Cordesman, Anthony, 'Winning in Afghanistan: Challenges and response', testimony to the House Committee on Foreign Affairs, 15 February 2007, available at: www.internationalrelations.house.gov/110/cor021507.htm

BIBLIOGRAPHY

Crews, Robert D. and Amin Tarzi (eds), *The Taliban and the Crisis of Afghanistan*, Harvard University Press, Cambridge, MA, 2008

Davis, Anthony, 'Foreign fighters step up activity in Afghan civil war', *Jane's Intelligence Review*, 13:8 (August 2001), pp. 13–14

——, 'Afghan security deteriorates as Taliban regroup', *Jane's Intelligence Review*, 15:5 (May 2003), pp. 11–12

DeYoung, Karen, 'Obama sets timetable for Iraq', *Washington Post*, 28 February 2009, available at: www.washingtonpost.com/wp-dyn/content/article/2009/02/27/AR2009022700566.html

Dobbins, James, *After the Taliban: Nation-Building in Afghanistan*, Potomac Books, Dulles, VA, 2008

Dogar, Yasub Ali, *The Talibanisation of Pakistan's Western Region*, ISAS Working Paper No. 98, 24 November 2009, available at: www.isas.nus.edu.sg/Attachments/PublisherAttachment/ISAS_Working_Paper_98_-_Email_-_The_Talibanisation_of_Pakistan%27s_Western_Region_18122009122105.pdf

Dorronsoro, Gilles, *Revolution Unending: Afghanistan, 1979 to the Present*, Hurst & Company, London, 2005

——, *The Taliban's Winning Strategy in Afghanistan*, Carnegie Endowment for International Peace, Washington, DC, 2009

Doyle, Michael, 'Kant, liberal legacies, and foreign affairs', *Philosophy and Public Affairs*, 12:3 (Summer 1983), pp. 205–35

—— 'Kant's perpetual peace', *American Political Science Review*, 80:4 (1986), pp. 1115–69.

Duffield, Mark, *Development, Security and Unending War: Governing the World of Peoples*, Polity, Cambridge, 2007

Dunn, David H., 'Innovation and precedent in the Kosovo War: The impact of Operation Allied Force on US foreign policy', *International Affairs*, 85:3 (May 2009), p. 543

Edwards, David B., *Heroes of the Age: Moral Fault Lines on the Afghan Frontier*, University of California Press, California, 1996

Enterline, Andrew and Joseph Magagnoli, 'Is the chance of success in Afghanistan better than a coin toss?', *Foreign Policy*, 27 August 2009

Fair, C. Christine and Seth G. Jones, 'Pakistan's war within', *Survival*, 51:6 (December 2009–January 2010), pp. 161–88

Felbab-Brown, Vanda, 'Kicking the opium habit? Afghanistan's drug economy and politics since the 1980s', *Conflict, Security & Development*, 6:2 (June 2006), pp. 127–49

——, 'Peacekeepers among poppies: Afghanistan, illicit economies, and intervention', *International Peacekeeping*, 16:1 (February 2009), pp. 100–14

Fergusson, James, *A Million Bullets*, Bantam Press, London, 2008

Forsberg, Carl, *Counterinsurgency in Kandahar: Evaluating the 2010 Hamkari Campaign*. December 2010, Institute for the Study of War Afghanistan Report 7, available at: www.understandingwar.org/files/Afghanistan%20Report%207_16Dec.pdf

Franks, General Tommy, *American Soldier*, HarperCollins, New York, 2004

'Fury, Dalton' [pseudonym], *Kill bin Laden: A Delta Force Commander's Account of the Hunt for the World's Most Wanted Man*, St Martin's Press, New York, 2008

Gareev, M.A., *Afganskaia Strada (s Sovetskimi voiskami i bez nikh)*, 'INSAN', Moscow, 1999

Geller, Armando and Scott Moss, 'The Afghan nexus: Anomie, neo-patrimonialism and the emergence of small-world networks', Centre for Policy Modelling Report 07-179, July 2007, available at: http://cfpm.org/pub/papers/Geller&Moss_TheAfghanNexus.pdf

Gibbs, David N., 'Reassessing Soviet motives for invading Afghanistan', *Critical Asian Studies*, 38:2 (2006), pp. 239–63

Giustozzi, Antonio, *War, Politics and Society in Afghanistan, 1978–1992*, Hurst & Company, London, 2000

——, 'Afghanistan: The Soviet invasion in retrospect', *International Politics*, 37:2 (June 2000), pp. 233–45

——, ' "Good" state vs "bad" warlords? A critique of state-building strategies in Afghanistan', London School of Economics Crisis States Programme Working Paper No. 51, October 2004

——, *Koran, Kalashnikov and Laptop: The Neo-Taliban Insurgency in Afghanistan*, Hurst & Company, London, 2007

——, 'Auxiliary force or national army? Afghanistan's "ANA" and the Counter-Insurgency Effort, 2002–2006', *Small Wars and Insurgencies*, 18:1 (March 2007), pp. 48–56

——, 'Bureaucratic façade and political realities of disarmament and demobilisation in Afghanistan', *Conflict, Security and Development*, 8:2 (June 2008), pp. 169–92

—— (ed.), *Decoding the New Taliban: Insights from the Afghan Field*, Hurst & Company, London, 2009

—— (ed.), *Empires of Mud: War and Warlords in Afghanistan*, Hurst & Company, London, 2009

Giustozzi, Antonio and Christoph Reuter, 'The Northern Front: The Afghan insurgency spreading beyond the Pashtuns', Afghan Analysts Network, 24 June 2010, available at: http://aan-afghanistan.com/uploads/20100629AGCR-TheNorthernFront1.pdf

Goodhand, Jonathan, 'From war economy to peace economy? Reconstruction and state building in Afghanistan', *Journal of International Affairs*, 58:1 (Fall 2004), pp 155–74

——, 'Corrupting or consolidating the peace? The drugs economy and post-conflict peacebuilding in Afghanistan', *International Peacekeeping* 15:3 (June 2008), pp. 405–23

Gordon, Michael and Bernard Trainor, *Cobra II*, Atlantic Books, London, 2006

Gordon, Philip and Jeremy Shapiro, *Allies at War: America, Europe and the Crisis over Iraq*, McGraw-Hill, New York, 2004

Grau, Lester W., 'Breaking contact without leaving chaos: The Soviet withdrawal from Afghanistan', *Journal of Slavic Military Studies*, 20:2 (April–June 2007), pp. 235–61

Grey, Stephen, *Operation Snakebite*, Penguin Books, London, 2009

——, 'Cracking on in Helmand', *Prospect*, 27 August 2009

Gul, Imtiaz, *The Most Dangerous Place: Pakistan's Lawless Frontier*, Penguin Books, London, 2010

Haddick, Robert, 'This week at war: The foregone conclusion in Kandahar', *Foreign Policy*, 28 May 2010, available at: www.foreignpolicy.com/articles/2010/05/28/this_week_at_war_the_forgone_conclusion_in_kandahar?page=0,1

Haq, Ikramul, 'Pak-Afghan drug trade in historical perspective', *Asian Affairs*, XXXVI:10 (October 1996), pp. 945–63

Haqqani, Hussein, *Pakistan: Between Mosque and Military*, Carnegie Endowment for International Peace, Washington, DC, 2005

Hartman, Andrew, ' "The Red Template": US policy in Soviet-occupied Afghanistan', *Third World Quarterly*, 23:3 (2002), pp. 467–89

Hastert, Paul, 'Operation Anaconda: Perception meets reality in the hills of Afghanistan', *Studies in Conflict and Terrorism*, 28:1 (January/February 2005), pp. 11–20

Headquarters Department of the Army, *Counterinsurgency*, FM 3-24, December 2006, available at: www.fas.org/irp/doddir/army/fm3-24.pdf

Herold, Marc W., 'Pulling the rug out: Pseudo-development in Karzai's Afghanistan', 7 March 2006, available at: http://cursor.org/stories/emptyspace2.html

Hersh, Seymour, 'The getaway', *New Yorker*, 28 January 2002

BIBLIOGRAPHY

Holt, Frank L., *Into the Land of Bones: Alexander the Great in Afghanistan*, University of California Press, London, 2005

Human Rights Watch, 'Afghanistan: Slow progress on security and rights', Human Rights Watch website, 30 January 2007, available at: www.hrw.org/en/news/2007/01/29/afghanistan-slow-progress-security-and-rights

Hussein, Rizwan, *Pakistan and the Emergence of Islamic Militancy in Afghanistan*, Ashgate Publishing Limited, Aldershot, 2005

Ibrahim, Azeem, 'U.S. Aid to Pakistan – U.S. Taxpayers have funded Pakistan corruption', Belfer Center Discussion Paper, July 2009 available at: http://belfercenter.ksg.harvard.edu/files/Final_DP_2009_06_08092009.pdf

Ibrahimi, Sayed Yaqub, 'Afghan disarmament a never-ending process', Institute for War & Peace Reporting *ARR*, 215, 12 May 2006

International Crisis Group, 'Pakistan's IDP crisis: Challenges and opportunities', Asia Briefing No. 3, June 2009, available at: www.crisisgroup.org/~/media/Files/asia/south-asia/pakistan/b93_pakistans_idp_crisis___challenges_and_opportunities.ashx

———, 'Pakistan: Countering militancy in FATA', Asia Report No. 178, 21 October 2009, available at: www.crisisgroup.org/~/media/Files/asia/south-asia/pakistan/178_pakistan___countering_militancy_in_fata.ashx

International Institute of Strategic Studies (IISS), 'Rising extremism in South Asia', International Institute of Strategic Studies website, 2010, available at: www.iiss.org/publications/strategic-comments/past-issues/volume-16-2010/january/rising-extremism-in-south-asia/

ISAF, 'International Security Assistance Force: Key facts and figures', available at: www.isaf.nato.int/images/stories/File/Placemats/100804%20Rev%20Placemat.pdf

Ispahani, Mahnaz Z., *Roads and Rivals: The Politics of Access in the Borderlands of Asia*, I.B. Tauris, London, 1989

Jalali, Ali A., 'Afghanistan: The anatomy of an ongoing crisis', *Parameters* (Spring 2001), pp. 85–98

———, 'Afghanistan: Regaining momentum', *Parameters* (Winter 2007–08), pp. 5–19

Johnson, Chris and Jolyon Leslie, *Afghanistan: The Mirage of Peace*, Zed Books, London, 2004

Johnson, Thomas H. and Chris M. Mason, 'Understanding the Taliban insurgency in Afghanistan', *Orbis* (Winter 2007), pp. 71–89

———, 'No sign until the burst of fire: Understanding the Pakistan–Afghanistan frontier', *International Security*, 32:4 (Spring 2008), pp. 41–77

Jones, Seth 'Averting failure in Afghanistan', *Survival*, 48:1 (Spring 2006), pp. 111–28

———, 'Pakistan's dangerous game', *Survival*, 49:1 (Spring 2007), pp. 15–32

———, *Counterinsurgency in Afghanistan*, RAND, Santa Monica, CA, 2008

———, 'The rise of Afghanistan's insurgency: State failure and jihad', *International Security*, 32:4 (2008), pp. 7–40

———, *In the Graveyard of Empires: America's War in Afghanistan*, W.W. Norton & Company, London/New York, 2009

Kaplan, Robert D., 'Saving Afghanistan', *The Atlantic*, 24 March 2009, available at: www.theatlantic.com/doc/200903u/saving-afghanistan

———, 'Man versus Afghanistan', *The Atlantic*, April 2010, available at: www.theatlantic.com/magazine/archive/2010/04/man-versus-afghanistan/7983/

Katzman, Kenneth, 'Afghanistan: Post-Taliban governance, security, and US policy', Congressional Research Service Report for Congress, 11 May 2010, available at: http://www.fas.org/sgp/crs/row/RL30588.pdf

Khattak, Daud, 'The missing dimension of Pakistan's counterinsurgency policy', Radio Free Europe/Radio Liberty, 10 July 2010, available at: www.jamestown.org/programs/gta/single/?tx_ttnews[tt_news]=36739&cHash=de992b83e4

Kilcullen, David, *The Accidental Guerrilla*, C. Hurst & Company, London, 2009

Kolhatkar, Sonali and James Ingalls, *Bleeding Afghanistan: Washington, Warlords, and the Propaganda of Silence*, Seven Stories Press, New York, 2006

Krause, Peter, 'The last good chance: A reassessment of US operations at Tora Bora', *Security Studies*, 17:4 (2008), pp. 644–84

Lamb, Christina, *Small Wars Permitting: Dispatches from Foreign Lands*, HarperPress, London, 2008

Lavoy, Peter R. (ed.), *Asymmetric Warfare in South Asia: The Causes and Consequences of the Kargil Conflict*, CUP, Cambridge, 2009

Leventis, Evagoras C., 'The Waziristan Accord', *Middle Eastern Review of International Affairs*, 11:4 (December 2007), available at: http://meria.idc.ac.il/journal/2007/issue4/jv11no4a4.asp

Lippmann, Walter, *US Foreign Policy: Shield of the Republic*, Little, Brown and Co., Boston, 1943

Livingston, Ian S. and Michael O'Hanlon, *Pakistan Index: Tracking Variables of Reconstruction and Security*, Brookings Institution, 30 October 2009, available at: www.brookings.edu/~/media/Files/Programs/FP/pakistan%20index/index20091030.pdf

Luttwak, Edward, *The Grand Strategy of the Byzantine Empire*, Harvard University Press, Harvard, 2009

——, 'Take me back to Constantinople: How Byzantium, not Rome, can help preserve Pax Americana', *Foreign Policy* (November/December 2009), available at: www.foreignpolicy.com/articles/2009/10/19/take_me_back_to_constantinople

McCoy, William, *The Politics of Heroin: CIA Complicity in the Global Drug Trade, Afghanistan, Southeast Asia, Central America, Columbia*, revised edition, Lawrence Hill Books, Chicago, 2003

McNerney, Michael J., 'Stabilization and reconstruction in Afghanistan: Are PRTs a model or a muddle?', *Parameters* (Winter 2005–06), pp. 32–46

Maley, William (ed.), *Fundamentalism Reborn? Afghanistan and the Taliban*, Hurst & Company, London, 1998/2001

——, *Rescuing Afghanistan*, Hurst & Company, London, 2006

Maloney, Sean M., 'Afghanistan four years on: An assessment', *Parameters* (Autumn 2005), pp. 21–32

Mann, James, *Rise of the Vulcans: The History of Bush's War Cabinet*, Penguin Books, New York, 2004

Margolis, Eric S., *War at the Top of the World: The Struggle for Afghanistan, Kashmir, and Tibet*, Routledge, New York, 2000

Markey, Daniel, 'Don't waste the Afghan election crisis', *Foreign Policy*, 15 September 2009

Marsden, Peter, *Afghanistan: Aid, Armies and Empires*, I.B. Tauris & Co. Ltd., London, 2009

Marshall, Alex, 'Managing withdrawal: Afghanistan as the forgotten example in attempting conflict resolution and state reconstruction', *Small Wars & Insurgencies*, 18:1 (March 2007), pp. 68–89

Matinuddin, Kamal, *The Taliban Phenomenon: Afghanistan 1994–1997, With an Afterword covering Major Events since 1997*, OUP, Oxford, 1999

Matlock, Jack, *Superpower Illusions*, Yale University Press, New Haven, 2010

Matthews, Robert, 'An anvil of clay: Pakistan's military balks at Obama's Surge', Norwegian Peacebuilding Centre, Noref Report No. 2 (January 2010)

Medvedev, R.A., 'Pod kontrolem naroda', *Voenno-Istoricheskii Zhurnal*, 2 (1999), pp. 62–73

Metz, Steven, *Iraq and the Evolution of American Strategy*, Potomac Books, Dulles, VA, 2008

Meyer, Christopher, *DC Confidential*, Phoenix, London, 2006

Millen, Raymond A., *Afghanistan: Reconstituting a Collapsed State*, SSI, US Army War College, April 2005, available at: www.strategicstudiesinstitute.army.mil/pubs/display.cfm?pubID=600

Minkov, Dr Anton and Dr Gregory Smolynec, *3D Soviet Style: A Presentation on Lessons Learned from the Soviet Experience in Afghanistan*, Defence R&D Canada, October 2007

Misdaq, Nabi, *Afghanistan: Political Frailty and Foreign Interference*, Routledge, London, 2006

Murray, Tonita, 'Police-building in Afghanistan: A case study of civil security reform', *International Peacekeeping*, 12:1 (January 2007), pp. 108–26

Musharraf, Pervez, *In the Line of Fire*, Free Press, New York, 2006

Napoleoni, Loretta, *Terrorism and the Economy: How the War on Terror is Bankrupting the World*, Seven Stories Press, New York, 2010

Nasr, Seyyed Vali Reza, *The Vanguard of the Islamic Revolution. The Jama'at-i Islami of Pakistan*, University of California Press, Berkeley/Los Angeles, 1994

National Commission on Terrorist Attacks upon the United States, *The 9/11 Commission Report* (Final Report), 22 July 2004, available at: http://govinfo.library.unt.edu/911/report/911Report.pdf

Naylor, Sean, *Not a Good Day to Die: The Untold Story of Operation Anaconda*, Penguin Books, London, 2006

Neumann, Ronald E., *The Other War: Winning and Losing in Afghanistan*, Potomac Books Inc., Washington, DC, 2009

Nikitenko, Evgenii, *Afganistan: Ot voiny 80-kh do prognoza novykh voin*, AST, Moscow, 2004

Noetzel, Timo and Benjamin Schreer, 'Counter-what? Germany and counter-insurgency in Afghanistan', *RUSI Journal*, 153:1 (2008), pp. 42–6

Nojumi, Neamatollah, *The Rise of the Taliban in Afghanistan. Mass Mobilization, Civil War, and the Future of the Region*, Palgrave, New York, 2002

Office of the Special Inspector General for Afghan Reconstruction (SIGAR), *Actions Needed to Improve the Reliability of Afghan Security Force Assessments*, 29 June 2010, available at: www.sigar.mil/pdf/audits/SIGAR%20Audit-10-11.pdf

—— Quarterly report to the US Congress, available at: www.sigar.mil/pdf/quarterlyreports/Jul2010/SIGAR_July2010.pdf

O'Hanlon, Michael, 'A flawed masterpiece', *Foreign Affairs*, 81:3 (May/June 2002), pp. 47–63

O'Hanlon, Michael and Hassina Sherjan, *Toughing it out in Afghanistan*, Brookings Institution Press, Washington, DC, 2010

Paris, Roland, 'Peacebuilding and the limits of liberal internationalism', *International Security*, 22:2 (Fall 1997), pp. 54–89

——, *At War's End: Building Peace After Civil Conflict*, Cambridge University Press, Cambridge, 2004

Pew Global Attitudes Project, 'America's image remains poor: Concern about extremist threat slips in Pakistan', Pew Research Center, 29 July 2010, available at: http://pewglobal.org/files/pdf/Pew-Global-Attitudes-2010-Pakistan-Report.pdf

Piiparinen, Touko, 'A clash of mindsets? An insider's account of provincial reconstruction teams', *International Peacekeeping*, 14:1 (January 2007)

Plastun, Vladimir and Vladimir Andrianov, *Nadzhibulla. Afganistan v tiskakh geopolitiki*, Tipografiia No. 9, Moscow, 1998

Pond, Elizabeth, *Friendly Fire: The Near Death of the Transatlantic Alliance*, Brookings/EUSA, Washington, DC, 2003

Powell, Colin, *My American Journey*, Ballantine Books, New York, 1995

Rasanayagam, A., *Afghanistan: A Modern History*. I.B. Tauris, London, 2005

Rashid, Ahmed, *Taliban: Islam, Oil and the New Great Game in Central Asia*, I.B. Tauris, London, 2000

——, 'Afghanistan and its future', Eurasianet website, 26 June 2006, available at: www.eurasianet.org/departments/insight/articles/eav062606.shtml

——, *Descent into Chaos: How the War against Islamic Extremism is Being Lost in Pakistan, Afghanistan and Central Asia*, Allen Lane, London, 2008.

Rediff India Abroad, 'What does Obama's Afpak policy say', 27 March 2009, available at: www.rediff.com/news/2009/mar/27obama-speech-on-new-policy-on-afghanisthan-and-pakistan.htm

Richards, General Sir David, testimony to the UK House of Commons Defence Committee, 24 April 2007. Transcript of evidence available at: www.parliament.uk

Richmond, Oliver P., 'A post-liberal peace: Eirenism and the everyday', *Review of International Studies*, 35 (2009), pp. 557–80

Roberts, Jeffrey J., *The Origins of Conflict in Afghanistan*, Praeger Publishers, Westport, CT, 2003

Robichaud, Carl, 'Remember Afghanistan? A glass half full, on the Titanic', *World Policy Journal*, 23:1 (Spring 2006), pp. 17–24

Roy, Olivier, *Islam and Resistance in Afghanistan*, second edition, Cambridge University Press, Cambridge, 1990

Rubin, Barnett R., *The Fragmentation of Afghanistan: State Formation and Collapse in the International System*, Yale University Press, New Haven, 2002

——, '(Re)Building Afghanistan: The folly of stateless democracy', *Current History* (April 2004), pp. 165–70

——, *Road to Ruin: Afghanistan's Booming Opium Industry*, Center on International Cooperation, New York, 7 October 2004, available at: www.cic.nyu.edu/archive/pdf/RoadtoRuin.pdf

——, 'Making aid to Afghanistan effective', testimony before the House Committee on International Relations, Subcommittee on Oversight, 9 March 2006

——, 'Afghan dilemmas: Defining commitments', *American Interest Online* (May–June 2008), available at: www.the-american-interest.com/ai2/article-bd.cfm?Id=423&MId=19

Rubin, Barnett and Ahmed Rashid, 'From great game to grand bargain. Ending chaos in Afghanistan and Pakistan', *Foreign Affairs*, 87:6 (November/December 2008), available at: www.foreignaffairs.com/articles/64604/barnett-r-rubin-and-ahmed-rashid/from-great-game-to-grand-bargain

Rumsfeld, Donald, 'Transforming the military', *Foreign Affairs*, 81:3 (May/June 2002), pp. 20–32

Runge, Peter, 'The provisional reconstruction teams in Afghanistan: Role model for civil–military relations?' Bonn International Center for Conversion (BICC) Occasional Paper IV, October 2009, pp. 21–4, available at: www.bicc.de/uploads/pdf/publications/papers/occ_paper_04/occasional_paper_IV_11_09.pdf

Ruttig, Thomas, 'The other side: Dimensions of the Afghan insurgency: Causes, actors, and approaches to "talks" ', Afghan Analysts Network, July 2009, available at: http://aan-afghanistan.com/uploads/200907%20AAN%20Report%20Ruttig%20-%20The%20Other%20Side.pdf

Save the Children Fund, 'Provincial reconstruction teams and humanitarian-military relations in Afghanistan', 2004, available at: www.rusi.org/downloads/assets/Save_the_Children_UK_-_PRTs_and_Humanitarian-Military_Relations_in_Afghanistan_2004_09.pdf

Schroen, Gary, *First In: An Insider's Account of How the CIA Spearheaded the War on Terror in Afghanistan*, Presidio Press, New York, 2007

Sedra, Mark (ed.), *Confronting Afghanistan's Security Dilemma: Reforming the Security Sector*, Brief 28, BICC, Bonn, September 2003

Sedra, Mark and Peter Middlebrook, 'Beyond Bonn. Revisioning the international compact for Afghanistan', Foreign Policy in Focus brief, November 2005

Semple, Michael, *Reconciliation in Afghanistan*, United States Institution for Peace, Washington, DC, 2009

Serchuk, Vance, 'The war we're winning (PRTs in Afghanistan)', *Armed Forces Journal* (November 2005), available at: http://ics.leeds.ac.uk/papers/vp01.cfm?outfit=pmt&folder=607&paper=2533

Shah, Tayyab Ali, 'Pakistan's Bajaur agency emerges as new hub for Islamist militancy', *Terrorism Monitor*, 8:32 (August 2010), available at: www.jamestown.org/programs/gta/single/?tx_ttnews[tt_news]=36739&cHash=de992b83e4

Sherry, Michael, *The Course of Operation Enduring Freedom in Southern and Eastern Afghanistan*, US Army Center of Military History Information Paper, Washington, DC, 15 March 2002

Sinno, Abdulkader H., *Organizations at War in Afghanistan and Beyond*, Cornell University Press, Ithaca and London, 2008

Sky, Emma, 'The lead nation approach: The case of Afghanistan', *RUSI Journal*, 151:6 (December 2006), pp. 22–6

Smucker, Philip, *Al Qaeda's Great Escape: The Military and the Media on Terror's Trail*, Brassey's, Washington, DC, 2004

Sorley, Lewis, *A Better War: The Unexamined Victories and Final Tragedy of America's Last Years in Vietnam*, Mariner Books, New York, 2007

Stewart, Rory, 'The irresistible illusion', *London Review of Books*, 31:13 (9 July 2009), pp. 3–6

——, testimony to the Senate Foreign Relations Committee hearing on the future of Afghanistan, 16 September 2009, available at: http://foreign.senate.gov/imo/media/doc/StewartTestimony090916p1.pdf

Suskind, Ron, *The One Percent Doctrine: Deep Inside America's Pursuit of Its Enemies Since 9/11*, Simon & Schuster, New York, 2006

Synott, Hilary, *Transforming Pakistan: Ways out of Instability*, Routledge, Abingdon, Oxfordshire, 2009

Tadjbakhsh, Shahrbanou and Michael Schoiswohl, 'Playing with fire? The international community's democratization experiment in Afghanistan', *International Peacekeeping*, 1:2 (April 2008), pp. 252–67

Tahir, Muhammad, 'Gulbuddin Hekmatyar's return to the Afghan insurgency', *Terrorism Monitor*, 6:11 (May 2008), available at: www.jamestown.org/programs/gta/single/?tx_ttnews[tt_news]=4951&tx_ttnews[backPid]=167&no_cache=1

Tapper, Richard, 'Ethnicity, order, and meaning in the anthropology of Iran and Afghanistan', in J.P. Digard (ed.), *Le Fait Ethnique en Iran et en Afghanistan*, Editions du CNRS, Paris, 1988

Tenet, George, *At the Center of the Storm: My Years at the CIA*, HarperCollins, New York, 2007

Terriff, Terry, 'Fear and loathing in NATO: The Atlantic Alliance after the crisis over Iraq', *Perspectives on European Politics and Society*, 5:3 (September 2004), pp. 419–46

United States Congressional Research Service, 'Security and the environment in Pakistan', CRS Report for Congress, 3 August 2010

United States Government Accountability Office, *Afghanistan Security. Efforts to Establish Army and Police Have Made Progress, but Future Plans Need to be Better Defined*, GAO-05-575, June 2005, available at: www.gao.gov/new.items/d05575.pdf

——, *Combating Terrorism: Increased Oversight and Accountability Needed over Pakistan Reimbursement Claims for Coalition Support Funds*, GAO-08-06, June 2008, available at: www.gao.gov/new.items/d08806.pdf

United States Senate Committee on Foreign Relations, *Tora Bora Revisited: How We Failed to Get bin Laden and Why it Matters Today*, Washington, DC, 30 November 2009

UNODC, *Afghanistan: Opium Survey 2005*, available at: www.unodc.org/pdf/afg/afg_survey_2005.pdf
——, *Afghanistan: Opium Survey 2007*, available at: www.unodc.org/pdf/research/AFG07_ExSum_web.pdf
——, *Afghan Opium Survey 2009*, Summary Findings, September 2009
——, *Afghan Opium Survey 2010*, Summary Findings, September 2010
——, *Corruption in Afghanistan. Bribery as Reported by the Victims*, January 2010
Urban, Mark, *Task Force Black: The Explosive True Story of the SAS and the Secret War in Iraq*, Little, Brown and Company, London, 2010
USAID, *Pakistan: Economic Performance Assessment*, September 2007, available at: http://pdf.usaid.gov/pdf_docs/PNADK618.pdf
——, *Pakistan: Economic Performance Assessment*, October 2009, available at: http://pdf.usaid.gov/pdf_docs/PNADR358.pdf
Waldman, Matt, *Falling Short: Aid Effectiveness in Afghanistan*, Kabul, ACBAR, March 2008, available at: www.oxfam.org.uk/resources/policy/debt_aid/downloads/aid_effectiveness_afghanistan.pdf
——, 'The sun in the sky: The relationship between Pakistan's ISI and Afghan insurgents', Development Studies Institute, London School of Economics, Discussion Paper 18 (June 2010)
Walt, Stephen M., 'A plan B for Afghanistan', *Foreign Policy*, 8 September 2010, available at: http://walt.foreignpolicy.com/posts/2010/09/08/a_plan_b_for_afghanistan
Westad, Odd Arne, *The Global Cold War*, CUP, Cambridge, 2005
Wilkens, Ann, 'Smoke gets in your eyes: Pakistan in 2010', Afghan Analysts Network, March 2010
Wilton Park Conference, 'Winning "Hearts and Minds" in Afghanistan: Assessing the Effectiveness of Development Aid in COIN Operations', 2010, available at: http://kingsofwar.org.uk/wp-content/uploads/2010/04/WP1022-Final-Report.pdf
Woodward, Bob, *Bush at War*, Pocket Books, London, 2003
——, *Plan of Attack*, Pocket Books, London, 2004
Wright, Donald P., James R. Bird, Steven E. Clay, Peter W. Connors, Lt. Col. Scott C. Farquhar, Lynn Chandler Garcia and Dennis Van Wey, 'A different kind of war. The United States Army in Operation Enduring Freedom (OEF) October 2001–September 2005', Combat Studies Institute, Ft Leavenworth, KA, 2010, available at: http://documents.nytimes.com/a-different-kind-of-war#p=1
Wright, Joanna, 'Afghanistan's opiate economy and terrorist financing', *Jane's Intelligence Review*, 18:3 (March 2006), pp. 36–7
Yousaf, Mohammad and Mark Adkin, *Afghanistan – The Bear Trap: The Defeat of a Superpower*, Leo Cooper, Barnsley, 1992
Yusufzai, Rahimullah, 'Assessing the progress of Pakistan's South Waziristan offensive', *CTC Sentinel*, 2:12 (December 2009), pp. 8–12
Zaeef, Abdul Salam, *My Life with the Taliban*, Hurst & Company, London, 2010

INDEX

Abdullah, Abdullah, 74, 97, 99, 136,
    223, 225, 270 n.50
Afghan National Army (ANA)
    formation of, 114, 119–21
    performance of, 240–1, 243
    troop numbers, 114, 235, 240
Afghan National Police (ANP)
    formation of, 119, 122
    performance of, 122–3, 240
    police numbers, 235, 240
Afghanistan
    US relations with, *see* United States
    constitution of, 101, 111, 140–1
    corruption, 222–3, 232, 239–40,
        244, 261
    counter-narcotics in, 119, 124–8, 159,
        178–9, 227, 238–9
    economy, 19–20, 23, 34–7, 44, 113,
        126–8, 132–3, 229, 241, 244–8,
        250–1, 257–8
    elections, 112, 126, 136, 139–41,
        221–6
    ethnic balance of, 18
    foundation of, 12–16
    Indian relations with, *see* India

map vi
Pakistani relations with, *see* Pakistan
Soviet intervention in, *see* Soviet
    Union
Ahmad, Mahmood (head of ISI), 62–3,
    76, 80, 192
Akhundzada, Sher Mohammed, 166–9,
    171, 174–5
Al Qaeda, 1, 4, 7, 10, 45, 54–62, 72,
    74–5, 78, 93, 108
    escapes Tora Bora 90, 92–3
    Operation Anaconda, 105
    and Pakistan, 174, 194–5, 199, 201,
        207, 209
    and Taliban, 60–1, 63–4, 66, 79,
        81–3, 101, 110, 143–5,
        148, 156
    and 'war on terror', 108–9, 154,
        185, 220–1, 230–1, 245, 251–3,
        255, 259
Alexander the Great, 24, 264 n.21
Ali, Hazrat, 88–90, 269 n.33
Amin, Hafizullah, 21–2
Andropov, Yurii, 24
Anglo–Afghan wars, 10–11

Armitage, Richard, 63, 65, 68
Australia, 8, 105, 219, 276 n.8

Balochistan (Pakistan), 84, 189
Barno, David, 138, 149–50, 275 n.87
Berntsen, Gary 89–91, 268 nn.2 & 5,
    269 nn.17, 21, 25, 33 & 35, 270
    nn.39 & 51
Bhutto, Benazir, 30, 34, 37, 190–1, 203–4
Biden, Joe, 230–1, 245
bin Laden, Osama, 1, 45, 54–61, 66,
    76–8, 185, 207
  escapes Tora Bora, 89–93, 100, 251
Black, Cofer, 73–4
Blair, Tony, 4, 172, 277 n.35
Bonn Conference, 95–8, 100, 103, 107,
    112, 129, 131–3, 139, 222, 247
Brahimi, Lakhdar, 95, 98, 103, 112
Brezhnev, Leonid, 22
Brown, Gordon, 161
Browne, Des, 162–3, 165
Brzezinski, Zbigniew, 22
Bush, George W.
  Afghan intervention and, 78, 91–3,
    94–5, 103, 106–8, 113–14, 118,
    252
  'axis of evil', 99, 113
  on Iraq, see Iraq
  reaction to 9/11, 53–5, 63–4
  and 'war on terror', 47–8, 57, 61,
    65–6, 67, 182, 194
  see also United States
Butler, Ed, 170–1, 173

Canada, 8, 105, 157–8, 170, 218–9
Cheney, Dick, 49, 51, 56, 68–70, 91–2,
    117, 267 nn.28 & 36
China, 7, 14, 22, 226–7, 284 n.19
CIA
  assassination attempt on Hikmatyar,
    144
  as mujahidin arms suppliers, 29,
    31–2, 35
  pursuit of bin Laden, 54–5, 56, 58,
    62, 89, 91, 98, 207
  see also 'Jawbreaker'
Clarke, Richard, 55, 57, 61, 267
    nn.11 & 12
Clinton, Bill, 49, 51, 55, 58–9, 61, 67
COIN (counter-insurgency)

  in Afghanistan see McChrystal
  vs. counter-terrorism, 230–1, 245,
    253
Cowper-Coles, Sherard, 228, 258,
    288 n.6
Crumpton, Henry, 91, 268 n.3

'Dado, Amir' see Khan, Dad
    Mohammad
Daoud, Mohammed (Afghan prime
    minister and later president), 17,
    20–1, 145, 264 n.4, 277 n.6
Daoud, Mohammed (governor of
    Helmand Province), 166–7,
    169, 171
Denmark, 8, 105, 219, 276 n.8
Dobbins, James, 95, 97–100, 102, 222
Dostum, Rashid, 27, 32, 34, 42, 44–5,
    75, 79–82, 88, 96, 107
Durrani (dynasty), 12, 17–18, 83

Eide, Kai, 224
Eikenberry, Karl
  as military commander, 150
  as US ambassador to Afghanistan,
    223–4, 232, 284 n.13, 285 n.30

Fahim, Mohammed Qasim, 74–5, 81–2,
    88, 99, 107, 114, 131
FATA (Federally Administered Tribal
    Areas, Pakistan)
  formation of, 15
  haven for mujahidin/Taliban, 1, 7, 38,
    90, 110, 142, 167–8, 182, 185,
    188, 192, 237
  map 184
  military operations in, 143, 174, 193,
    196–208, 210–11
  need for land and legal reform, 214
Fazlullah, Maulana, 193, 201–2, 212
Finland, 138
France, 105, 115–16, 218, 225, 234
Franks, Tommy, 65, 91–2, 94, 101,
    268 n.46, 269 n.16, 270
    nn.42 & 45

Galbraith, Peter, 224, 284 n.14
Gates, Robert, 230, 235, 285 n.37
Germany, 95, 105, 115–16, 119, 122,
    135, 219, 236

Ghani, Ashraf, 126, 131, 223, 224
Gorbachev, Mikhail, 23, 217
Gul, Hamid, 213
Gul, Imtiaz, 212, 279 n.8

Haq, Abdul, 87–8
Haqqani, Jalaluddin, 145, 214
Helmand Province
    British operations in, 151, 153,
        158–9, 166–8, 171–3, 176, 181,
        211, 225
    US operations in (Marjah), 241–2
Herat, 21, 40, 42–3, 75, 81, 126, 143
Hikmatyar, Gulbuddin, 30, 32–4, 36–8,
    40, 42, 144–5, 265 n.29
Holbrooke, Richard, 224, 226–7, 229,
    284 n.13

India
    and Pakistan, see Pakistan
    role in Afghanistan, 96–7, 99, 189
    terrorist attacks upon, 146, 182,
        187, 212
Iran, 7, 28, 30–1, 34–7, 45, 56, 113,
    126, 144, 189, 255
    as political mediator, 25, 96–9, 226–7
Iraq
    distraction from Afghanistan, 104,
        109, 111, 181
    US invasion of, 114–17, 148
ISAF (International Security and
    Assistance Force), 103–4, 111,
    113, 117–18, 137–8, 155, 162,
    167, 170, 172–3, 175–6
ISI (Inter-Services Intelligence agency,
    Pakistan)
    alleged support for Taliban see
        Pakistan
    role in Pakistan, 28–9, 35, 37, 60
Italy, 119

Jalali, Ali Ahmad, 123, 131, 224, 265 n.38
'Jawbreaker', Operation
    and CIA in Afghanistan, 66–7, 71,
        74–5, 78, 83–5, 109, 268 nn.2 &
        5, 269 nn.17, 21, 25, 26, 33 &
        35, 270 nn.39 & 51

Kabul, 3, 7, 9, 11, 16, 19–21, 22, 25–6,
    27, 34, 44, 106

damage to, 32–3
military fortunes, 42–3, 81–2, 89, 113
reconstruction, 95, 101, 103, 120,
    126, 128, 239–40
transport hub, 40, 44, 108
Kandahar (city), 20, 38–44, 83, 85–6,
    91, 97, 135, 146, 158–9, 170–1,
    176, 187, 225
    battle for (2010), 238, 242–3
Kandahar Province, 143
Karimov, Islam, 71–2
Karzai, Hamid
    appointed interim president, 97, 100
    assassination attempt on, 182
    background to appointment, 83–6,
        96–8, 101, 106–8, 126
    elected president 2004 and 2009, 112,
        139–41, 221–26
    and ISAF, 117–8, 130, 162, 166–7,
        173, 181
    and peace talks, 144, 145, 175,
        198, 214
    personality, 223–4, 232, 239
Kashmir, 15, 29, 60–1, 63, 187–8, 190,
    192, 213, 227
Kayani, Ashfaq (head of ISI and later
    Pakistani Chief of the Army
    Staff), 192
Khalilzad, Zalmay, 51, 106, 113, 140, 150
Khan, Dad Mohammad, 168–9, 171
Khan, Ismail, 42, 75, 81, 96, 126
Kilcullen, David, 164, 276 n.21

Lamb, Christina, 77, 269 n.11, 276 n.1,
    278 n.59
Lashkar-e-Jhangvi, 192
Lashkar-e-Taiba (LeT), 187, 192, 212
London Conference, 112, 133

McChrystal, Stanley, 223–4, 229–32
    and COIN, 233–8, 241–2
McColl, John, 103–4, 156, 270 n.59
McKiernan, David, 183, 230, 232–3
McNeill, Dan, 113, 175–6, 183
madrasas (religious schools), 38, 142,
    164, 167–8, 179, 190
Marjah, 241–2
Marlowe, Ann, 142, 271 n.1
Massoud, Ahmed Shah, 27, 31–4, 36,
    42–4, 66, 74–5

Mehsud, Baitullah, 144, 197, 200–4, 212
Mehsud, Hakimullah, 203, 212
Meyer, Christopher, 55, 267 n.14
Mohammad, Khalid Sheikh (KSM), 194
Mohammad, Nek (TTP leader), 143, 197, 200
Mohammad, Sufi, 193
Mullen, Michael, 181–2, 278 n.62
Musa Qala, 173–6
Musharraf, Pervez
  assassination attempt on, 194, 279 n.11
  attitude to terrorism, 190, 192–3, 198, 201
  government, see Pakistan
  relationship with Washington, 61, 63–4, 76, 80, 82, 174, 190, 192, 194–5
  resignation, 192, 203–4

Najibullah, Muhammad, 23, 25–7, 32–3, 39, 41, 187, 217–18
NATO
  policy towards Afghanistan, 25, 117–18, 138, 145, 149, 154–6, 165, 167, 170, 227
  splits within, 114–16, 157–8, 182, 218–19, 235–6
Netherlands, 8, 158, 165, 219, 277 n.23
Neumann, Ronald E., 150, 162, 178, 273 n.51, 275 n.88, 276 nn.6 & 18, 277 n.43, 278 n.51
Northern Alliance (NA), 1, 34, 60, 66, 73–4, 96, 126, 187
Norway, 135, 138
NWFP (North West Frontier Province, Pakistan) 188, 192–3, 196–7, 200, 204, 208, 210
  map 184

Obama, Barack
  Afghan strategy review, 183, 215, 220–1, 226–9, 231–2
  drawdown of US forces in 2011, 236, 244
  election of, 209, 220
  recall of McChrystal, 242
Omar, Mullah Muhammad, 18, 39, 43, 60, 76–8, 85–6, 142, 190, 200, 213; see also Taliban

Pakistan
  Afghan insurgency supported by, 31–2, 38, 43, 213–14
  Afghan insurgent bases in, 143
  Afghan relations with, 60, 82–4, 167–8, 182, 198
  borders of, 188–9, 192
  economy of, 194–6, 205–6
  government of, 190–1, 200, 203–4
  India's relations with, 14–16, 29, 59, 60, 63, 186–90
  Islamic fundamentalism in, 186, 192, 201
  military forces of, 195–6
  terrorist attacks in, 198–200, 209
  US relations with, 62, 64, 76, 80, 192, 194–6
Pashtuns
  culture, 6, 17, 198
  'Pashtunistan Question', 15, 60
  rule of law, 163–5
  tribal structure, 16–17, 31, 41, 45, 168, 250
PDPA (People's Democratic Party of Afghanistan), 10, 20–1, 24, 27, 32, 264 n.14
Petraeus, David, 235, 242–3, 246, 254–5
Powell, Colin, 56, 63, 68–9, 95, 100, 267 nn.28 & 36, 268 n.44
Project for a New American Century, 51
PRTs (Provincial Reconstruction Teams), 118, 136–9, 170, 237

Qanooni, Younis, 96, 98–9, 106

Rabbani, Burhannudin, 31–3, 36, 43, 84, 97–8, 265 n.29
Rahman, Amir Abdur, 11–14, 18–19, 25
RAND Corp., 233–4
Rashid, Ahmed, 85, 265 n.32, 266 n.48, 49 & 64, 267 n.34, 268 n.6, 269 n.18
Reid, John, 155, 276 n.12
Rice, Condoleeza, 49, 61, 69, 267 nn.28 & 36
Richards, David, 157–9, 172–3, 175–7, 233, 276 n.10, 277 n.36
Rumsfeld, Donald, 68–9, 92, 115, 156, 267 nn.28 & 36, 270 nn.66 & 67

'mission accomplished' regarding
    Afghanistan, 148
on 9/11, 54
role in Afghan planning, 56–8, 65,
    67, 70, 72, 78, 91, 94, 99, 101,
    108–9, 113–14, 117
transformation agenda for US
    military, 49–51
Russell, Gerard, 222
Russia
    criticism of US policy in
        Afghanistan, 227
    role in Afghanistan, 25, 96–9, 226–7
    Soviet intervention in Afghanistan,
        see Soviet Union

Saudi Arabia
    backer of mujahidin/Taliban 23, 29,
        32, 38, 41
    mediator of peace talks, 229
Scheffer, Jaap de Hoop, 118, 182
Sherzai, Gul Agha, 86–7
Shevardnadze, Eduard, 217
Soviet Union
    intervention in Afghanistan, 10, 20–4,
        30, 137
    withdrawal strategy and National
        Reconciliation Policy, 25–7,
        217–18
State Department, US, see United
    States
Stewart, Rory, 253, 276 n.17, 281 n.31,
    285 n.39, 287 n.2
Swat district, Pakistan, 197, 200–2, 205,
    209, 280 n.27

Taliban
    adaptability of, 38, 41, 43, 45–6,
        147, 151
    in Afghan insurgency, 39
    Afghan regime of, 43–4, 60, 76–7
    relationship with Al Qaeda see Al
        Qaeda
    structure of, 142–6
    talks with Western powers, 144, 145,
        175, 198, 214, 229
Taraki, Nur Mohammad, 17, 20–2
Tenet, George, 54, 56, 61, 66, 85, 100,
    267 nn.11, 23, 25, 28, 32 & 36,
    269 nn.23, 24 & 31, 270 n.54

TNSM (Tehreek-e-Nifaze Shariate
    Mohammadi), 192–3, 201–2,
    279 n.8
Tokyo Conference, 102, 113, 119, 133
TTP (Tehrik-i-Taliban Pakistan),
    143–4, 200, 202–4, 209, 212, 214

United Kingdom, 103, 119, 124–5, 132,
    135–6, 138, 155–7, 159, 163, 230
    credibility of, 4, 157, 169, 172–3
    political role, 225, 228–9
    withdrawal date, 236
    see also Anglo-Afghan wars; Blair,
        Tony; Helmand Province; Reid,
        John; London Conference
United Nations, 97, 103, 224
United States of America
    Afghan relations with, 2–4, 19–20,
        22–5, 33, 41, 56–7, 59–60,
        113–14, 140, 150, 223–4, 226; see
        also Bush; CIA; 'Jawbreaker';
        Rumsfeld
    Bush administration's internal
        politics, 4, 49–50, 68–70, 100,
        139, 160–1, 221
    and Iraq, 254–6; see also Iraq
    Obama's Afghan strategy review, 183,
        215, 220–1, 226–9, 231–2
    Pakistan relations with, 62, 64, 76,
        80, 192, 194–6
    State Department, 25, 32–3, 63, 95,
        100, 122
    and State Department conflict with
        Pentagon, 4, 51, 68, 70
    and 'War on Terror', 251–4;
        see also Bush
Uzbekistan, 71–2, 91, 268 n.48

Wilkinson, Philip, 168, 276 n.7, 277
    nn.25 & 27
Wolfowitz, Paul, 51, 57, 65, 68,
    268 n.36

Zaeef, Abdul Salam, 76–7, 194, 266
    n.52, 268 nn.7 & 9, 279 n.12
Zahir, Haji, 88, 90, 269 n.33
Zahir Shah, King Muhammad, 17, 96
Zaman, Haji, 88–90, 269 n.33
Zardari, Asif Ali, 204
Zawahiri, Ayman al-, 185, 194, 199, 201